WHO IS THIS KRASSNER GUY?

Paul's own writing, in particular, seemed daring and adventurous to me; it took big chances and made important arguments in relentlessly funny ways. I felt, down deep, that maybe I had some of that in me, too; that maybe I could be using my skills to better express my beliefs. *The Realist* was the inspiration that kept pushing me to the next level; there was no way I could continue reading it and remain the same.

— *George Carlin*

Paul Krassner — confidant of Lenny Bruce, co-founder of the Yippies, defiler of Disney characters, publisher of *The Realist*, and investigative satirist extraordinaire. As soon as we decided to create *The Huffington Post*, I knew I wanted him involved. His irreverence was just what the blog doctor ordered.

— *Arianna Huffington*

Krassner loves ironies, especially stinging ironies that nettle public figures. He would rather savor a piquant irony about a public figure than eat a bowl of fresh strawberries and ice cream.

— *Ken Kesey*

I told Krassner one time that his writings made me hopeful. He found this an odd compliment to offer a satirist. I explained that he made supposedly serious matters seem ridiculous, and that this inspired many of his readers to decide for themselves what was ridiculous and what was not. Knowing that there were people doing that, better late than never, made me optimistic.

— *Kurt Vonnegut*

I have been a fan of his since I was a snot-nosed kid, and his words have been a driving force and influence on my life. If you have read his work before, you know the joys that you are in for. If you haven't, start reading, and consider this your lucky day. For Paul Krassner is an activist, a philosopher, a lunatic, and a saint, but most of all he is funny.

— *Lewis Black*

Paul taught me that extreme stylistic accuracy could make even the most bizarre comedic concept credible. He is a unique character on the American landscape. A self-described 'investigative satirist,' he straddles the lines between politics, culture, pornography, and drugs — in other words, the land where all of us, were we really honest with ourselves, would choose to dwell.

—— *Harry Shearer*

Mr. Krassner is an expert at ferreting out hypocrisy and absurdism from the more solemn crannies of American culture.

—— *The New York Times*

Krassner has the uncanny ability to alter your perceptions permanently.

—— *Los Angeles Times*

He has lived on the edge so long, he gets his mailed delivered there.

—— *San Francisco Chronicle*

Krassner lives in a world where Truth and Satire are swingers, changing partners so often you never know who belongs with whom.

—— *Playboy*

Perhaps the satire magazine that most closely resembles *Charlie Hebdo* in terms of inflammatory imagery was *The Realist*, created by Paul Krassner...

—— *Time*

ZAPPED BY THE GOD OF ABSURDITY
The Best of Paul Krassner

OTHER BOOKS BY PAUL KRASSNER

*How a Satirical Editor Became a Yippie Conspirator
in Ten Easy Years*

Best of The Realist (Editor)

The Winner of the Slow Bicycle Race

Impolite Interviews

Psychedelic Trips for the Mind (Editor)

*Magic Mushrooms and Other Highs:
From Toad Slime to Ecstasy* (Editor)

*Murder at the Conspiracy Convention
and Other American Absurdities*

One Hand Jerking

Tales of Tongue Fu

*In Praise of Indecency:
Dispatches from the Valley of Porn*

*Who's to Say What's Obscene:
Politics, Culture, and Comedy in America Today*

*Pot Stories for the Soul:
An Updated Edition for a Stoned America* (Editor)

*Confessions of a Raving, Unconfined Nut:
Misadventures in the Counterculture*

*Patty Hearst and the Twinkie Murders:
A Tale of Two Trials*

The Realist Cartoons (Editor)

THE
BEST
of
PAUL
KRASSNER

FANTAGRAPHICS BOOKS | SEATTLE

Many of the pieces in this collection originally appeared in *The Realist*, *High Times*, AVN, *New York Press*, *National Lampoon*, *The Nation*, *Los Angeles Times*, *Whole Earth Review*, *HuffPost* (*The Huffington Post*), *Alternet*, *CounterPunch*, *Truthdig*, *Reason*, and *Variety*. Several pieces appear here for the first time.

Publisher: GARY GROTH
Editor: J. MICHAEL CATRON
Designer: JUSTIN ALLAN-SPENCER
Associate Publisher: ERIC REYNOLDS

 Fantagraphics Books, Inc.
7563 Lake City Way NE
Seattle WA 98115

(800) 657-1100 · Fantagraphics.com
Twitter: @fantagraphics · facebook.com/fantagraphics

Special thanks to Ethan Persoff, Linda Grossman, and Bill Griffith.

First Fantagraphics Books edition: October 2019
ISBN 978-1-68396-184-0
Library of Congress Control Number: 2018949719
Printed in The Republic of Korea

For George Carlin, who continues to
serve as a satirical touchstone.

❄ ❄ ❄

"Hypocrisy is better than having no values at all."

—— William Bennett, former education czar,
drug czar, morality czar, and gambling czar

"MTV actually told us, 'You can make fun of God because he doesn't
exist, but you can't make fun of Jesus because he's God's son.'"

—— Vernon Chatman and John Lee, quoted in *Satiristas!*

Introduction
by Andy Borowitz

IS SATIRE DEAD?

When the President of the United States is a former game-show host with the self-control of an incontinent hamster, that's a reasonable question.

With satire under daily assault from an increasingly absurd reality, satirists can't be blamed if they sink into a slough of despond, or consider driving for Uber. How can you satirize a world this moronic? But maybe that's the wrong question to ask. Maybe, instead, satirists should ask themselves, "What would Paul Krassner do?"

This collection of Krassner's work couldn't have come at a better time. It serves as a welcome reminder that satire has been under threat from reality before — almost continuously, it seems — and as a bracing demonstration of how an indefatigable satirist faced down that threat and won, again and again.

It's undeniable that the current leader of the free world, through his uniquely demented brand of infantile performance art, has raised the bar for satire to an almost unreachable height. But over the past sixty years, Paul Krassner faced similar challenges from such daunting surrealists as Richard Nixon, O.J. Simpson, and Charles Manson — and never blinked.

At this point, you couldn't be blamed for thinking, "Wait. Things have been fucked up before — but never *this* fucked up. Things are so fucked up now that readers can't tell the difference between a fake

OPPOSITE: Paul Krassner. Photo illustration by Justin Allan-Spencer and Ethan Persoff. Original photo by Linda Grossman.

news story and a real one." It might be reassuring to know that this supposedly new problem is not, in fact, new at all. In 1967, when the historian William Manchester was preparing to publish a book about JFK's assassination, *The Death of a President*, members of the Kennedy family succeeded in having sections of the manuscript removed before publication.

Always trying to be helpful, Krassner published a satire, "The Parts That Were Left Out of the Kennedy Book," which was outlandish, ridiculous, pornographic and, naturally, widely believed to be true. There are at least two lessons in this episode: first, that a satirist cannot be held responsible for others' reading comprehension skills; and second, if satire has become indistinguishable from reality, it's probably reality's fault.

It's impossible to overstate Paul Krassner's impact on American comedy. He has influenced everyone from George Carlin to Harry Shearer to Lewis Black and will continue to inspire the satirists of the future — assuming, of course, that there is a future. But as tempting as it is to enshrine Krassner as a comic legend, worthy of our reverence and genuflection, let's not. That would mean saddling him with the kind of respectability that, in his work, he reflexively mocks. Given the choice between respect and laughter, Krassner always goes for the laugh.

And, finally, that's the most important reason why this book couldn't have come at a better time. It's full of laughs when we need them most, the kind of laughs that lift us out of despair and help us see the world more clearly. Somehow, through the alchemy of his genius, Paul Krassner, the pot-smoking Yippie provocateur, emerges from these pages sounding like the sanest man in the world.

If only there were some way to give him control of the nuclear codes. We'd all sleep better at night.

New York City, November 2017

The Early Years

From Carnegie Hall to *Mad* Magazine

I FIRST WOKE UP at the age of 6.

It began with an itch in my leg. My left leg. But somehow, I knew I wasn't supposed to scratch it. Although my eyes were closed, I was standing up. In fact, I was standing on a huge stage. And I was playing the violin. I was in the middle of playing the "Vivaldi Concerto in A Minor." I was wearing a Little Lord Fauntleroy suit — ruffled white silk shirt with puffy sleeves, black velvet short pants with ivory buttons and matching vest, white socks, and black patent-leather shoes. My hair was platinum blond and wavy. On this particular Saturday evening — January 14, 1939 — I was in the process of becoming the youngest concert artist in any field ever to perform at Carnegie Hall. But all I knew was that I was being taunted by an itch. An itch that had become my adversary.

I was tempted to stop playing the violin, just for a second, and scratch my leg with the bow, yet I was vaguely aware that this would not be appropriate. I had been well trained. I was a true professional. But that itch kept getting fiercer and fiercer. Then, suddenly, an impulse surfaced from my hidden laboratory of alternative possibilities, and I surrendered to it. Balancing on my left foot, I scratched my left leg with my right foot, without missing a note of the "Vivaldi Concerto."

Between the impulse and the surrender, there was a choice — I had *decided* to balance on one foot — and it was that simple act of choosing that triggered the precise moment of my awakening to the mystery of consciousness. *This is me!* The relief of scratching my leg was overshadowed by a surge of energy throughout my body. I was being engulfed by some kind of spiritual orgasm. By a wave of born-again ecstasy with no ideological context. No doctrine to explain the shock of my own existence. No dogma to function as a metaphor for the mystery. Instead, I woke up to the sound of laughter.

I had heard that sound before, sweet and comforting, but never like this. Now I could hear a whole *symphony* of delight and reassurance, like clarinets and guitars harmonizing with saxophones and drums. It was the audience laughing. I opened my eyes. There were rows upon rows of people sitting out there in the dark, and they were all laughing together.

They had understood my plight. It was easier for them to identify with the urge to scratch than with a little freak playing the violin. And I could identify with *them* identifying with me. I knew that laughter felt good, and I was pleased that it made the audience feel good — but I hadn't *intended* to make them laugh. I was merely trying to solve a personal dilemma. So the lesson I woke up to — this totally nonverbal, internal *buzz* — would serve as my lifetime filter for perceiving reality and its rules. If you could somehow translate that buzz into words, it would spell out: *One person's logic is another person's humor.*

I finished playing "Vivaldi" by rote. Then I bowed to the audience and walked off stage. The applause continued, and I was pushed back on stage by my violin teacher to play an encore, "Orientale." I had previously asked him — while rehearsing the encore — why it wasn't listed on the program since we already knew that I would play it at the concert. But instead of answering my question, he poked me in the chest, verbalizing each poke: "Violin *up!* Violin *up!*" Now, while playing "Orientale," I heard the echo of his voice, and I automatically raised my violin higher.

Then my ears popped, and suddenly the music sounded clearer. I wondered if it sounded clearer to the audience, too. They had no idea that their laughter had woken me up. I was overwhelmed by the notion that everybody in the audience had their own individual *This-is-me*, but maybe some of *them* were still asleep and didn't know it. How could you tell who was awake and who was asleep? After all, I hadn't known that I was asleep, and look what I had accomplished *before* I woke up. If it hadn't been for that itch, I might *still* be asleep.

There is, of course, an objective, scientific explanation for what happened on the stage of Carnegie Hall. According to a textbook, *Physiological Psychology,* "It is now rather well accepted that 'itch' is a variant of the pain experience and employs the same sensory mechanisms." But for me, something beyond an ordinary itch had occurred that night.

It was as though I had been zapped by the God of Absurdity. I didn't even know there was such a concept as absurdity. I simply experienced an overpowering awareness of *something* when the audience applauded me for doing what I had learned while I was asleep. But it was only when they laughed that we had really connected, and I imprinted on that sound. I wanted to hear it again. I was hooked. And the first laugh was free.

A couple of decades later, as if it was inevitable, I sold a few freelance pieces to *Mad* magazine. But when I suggested a satire on the pros and cons of unions, the editor wasn't interested in even seeing it because the subject was "too adult." Since *Mad*'s circulation had already gone over the million mark, publisher Bill Gaines intended to keep aiming the magazine at teenagers.

"I guess you don't wanna change horses in midstream," I said.

"Not when the horse has a rocket up its ass," Gaines replied.

And that moment served as the conception of an irreverent magazine for grown-ups, *The Realist* ...

PAUL KRASSNER

Sex Education for the Modern Catholic Child

THIS IS A DIAPHRAGM. Women use it when they don't want to have a baby. That is very immoral. Why, you ask? Because it is artificial, that's why. But never fear. There are other methods to prevent conception. They are very moral. Why, you ask? Because they are natural, that's why.

This is big brother's pajama bottoms. He had a nocturnal emission last night. What a shame. It woke him up. But see the semen stain. It has millions of dead sperms. They were killed the natural way.

This is his sister's sanitary napkin. It doesn't look very sanitary anymore, does it? There is an ovum somewhere in that bloody mess. But it will never be fertilized. It will be flushed down the toilet bowl. That's the natural way, too.

This is a baby. It was born dead. Every day in the U.S.A., 136,000 infants are stillborn or die within a month. Now suppose their mommies and daddies had interfered artificially with the process of procreation. God's purpose would never have been achieved. Just think what a tragedy that would've been. But at least some of the dead babies were baptized. That's the natural way.

This is a special calendar. It marks off menstrual periods. That's for the rhythm system of not having babies. A husband and his wife are in bed. They start to make love. Then they get out of bed. Because they have to look at the calendar. That's the natural way.

This is a husband and wife who don't want to have a baby yet. But the calendar says that the time is fertile. So they stop making love. Because one thing would lead to another. Ask [advice columnist] Dorothy Dix. She should know. She tried it once with [advice columnist] Dr. Crane. Just to prove her theory. Later she had to write to his Worry

Clinic. She was worried because she missed her period. She missed it very much.

This is a husband and wife who *do* want to have a baby. But the calendar says that the time is sterile. Lucky for them they have a calendar. It saves them from having unnecessary intercourse. Unless they like to gamble on having unwanted babies. That's the natural way.

This is a confessional booth. There is a screen in the middle. The person on one side is a priest. The person on the other side is a confessor. He is confessing that he has had evil thoughts. The priest tells him that to have an evil thought is evil. It is just as evil as committing the evil act that the evil thought is about. Priests never have evil thoughts themselves. They don't have to. They have an ample supply of other people's evil thoughts to draw upon.

This is the husband and his wife again. The ones who don't want to have a baby yet. Now the calendar says that the time is sterile. How convenient. Now they can make love without stopping. And without worrying. But they're good, consistent Catholics. And so they *are* worrying. Because they know that evil thoughts are evil. Their evil thought is to have intercourse but to avoid having a baby. They can't be *sure* they won't have a baby — that's why the rhythm system is moral — but the *intention* is there. Tomorrow they will go to confession.

POSTSCRIPT

I WROTE the above piece in 1958 (before the Pill), and it turned out to be theologically correct in 1984, when Pope John Paul II warned that the rhythm method of birth control can be "an abuse if the couple is seeking in this way to avoid children for unworthy reasons."

A Child's Primer on
Fighting Communism

NOW WE ARE GOING TO have some fun fighting Communism. Let us play a game of Make Believe. Close your eyes and concentrate. We are going to pretend that Red China doesn't exist. They are the Bad Guys. Because they make people slaves.

Nationalist China is different. They are the Good Guys. There, hundreds of thousands of little unwanted children are sold. They work in coal mines. Then they are wanted. The older girls work in brothels. How nice to be so wanted. Open your eyes now. Anyone around our base is *it*.

Fidel Castro says Cuba is a socialist state. That proves they are Communists. But we knew it before. You could tell by the way Castro and Khrushchev hugged each other. So we stopped buying sugar from Cuba. Now other countries buy sugar from Cuba.

Iran has bought 10,000 tons of sugar from Cuba. Iran gets a lot of economic and military aid from us. So we are helping Cuba anyway. Maybe we should trade tractors for prisoners then. But we will fool them. We will put treads on all the old Edsels that didn't sell.

There are Communists in the United States, too. They are dangerous. So the Supreme Court says they have to register as foreign agents. Otherwise they have to go to jail. So they register as foreign agents. Then they have to go to jail under the Smith Act.

So the Communist Party isn't very much fun to belong to anymore. But there's a way to belong without going to jail. You have to join the FBI first. Most of the members do it that way. J. Edgar Hoover is the head of the Communist Party.

Why are Communists such a threat to us? Because they advocate the violent overthrow of the government. That is why Governor Rockefeller wrote his name on the bottom of a new law. Now anyone who gets convicted in Federal Court for advocating the violent overthrow of the government will lose his driver's license.

That law was passed in April 1961. But on the 4th of July holiday, the United States broke all previous traffic accident records. More people got killed in cars than ever before. The roads are still full of dangerous Communist spies.

How can we defeat Communism all over the world? By foreign aid. That turns Neutral Guys into Good Guys. Meanwhile there is a great big famine in Red China. So Canada will ship wheat to them. But special machinery is needed for this. It is made in America. And the U.S. Justice Department doesn't allow such sales. Because Bad Guys deserve to starve. Everybody knows that. Especially the Neutral Guys.

So Canada shouldn't be mad at us. Didn't President Kennedy plant a tree there? That's personal diplomacy. It has nothing to do with hungry human beings in Red China. The way to avoid feeling guilty about suffering people is just don't recognize them.

A Child's Primer on Telethons

SEE THE TIRED MAN. He has been up all night. He is running a telethon. He wants the people to send money. It is for leukemia. That is a disease. Little children like you can catch it. Evil.

See the sexy girl. She is a singer. She doesn't know whether the telethon is for leukemia or dystrophy or gonorrhea. Her agent got her the booking. She needs the exposure. Notice her cleavage.

See the handsome man. He *does* know that it's for leukemia. You can tell. He is singing a calypso melody. Listen to the lyrics. "Give-your-money," he sings, "to-leukemia. Give-your-money, to-leukemia." Listen to the audience applaud. He is very talented.

See the sincere politician. He is running for reelection in November. He is against leukemia. He is willing to take an oath against it. That proves he is against it.

See the wealthy businessman. He is making a donation. He wants his company's name mentioned. Then we can buy his product. Then he will make profits. Then he can make another donation next year. Splendid.

See the little boy. He has leukemia. Too bad for him. The nice lady is holding him up to the TV camera. Aren't you glad it's not you? But wouldn't you like to be on television? Maybe you can fall down a well.

See the pretty scoreboard. It tells how much money they get. They want a million dollars. Uncle Sam has many millions of dollars. He cuts medical research funds by more than seven million dollars. Why? He needs the money for more important things.

See the mushroom cloud. That costs lots of money. It has loads of particles. They cause leukemia. Money might help to find a cure. That is why we have telethons.

See the tired man...

PAUL KRASSNER

A Child's Primer on Divorce

OH, LOOK. Mommy and Daddy are having another fight. Is it just an attention-getting device this time? Listen. They are having an adult discussion. They are agreeing on a separation. That means you will come from a broken home. What a shame. Even if they fight all the time, they should stay together for your sake. Now you will be insecure.

Mommy and Daddy are modern people. They drink Pepsi-Cola. They also have a modern marriage. They left the word "obey" out of their wedding ceremony. Wasn't that modern? But they didn't leave out the words "love" and "honor." Mommy and Daddy are only modern, not avant-garde. They left "till death do us part" in the ceremony, too. But they are going to get a divorce anyway. They don't have to *obey* their marriage vows. Lucky thing they left out that word.

What is to be done to keep Mommy and Daddy together? *The Ladies' Home Journal* will help. They have a regular feature in their magazine. It is called "Can This Marriage Be Saved?" Readers send in Betty Crocker box tops and try to guess the correct answer.

Maybe Mommy and Daddy will go on television. There is a program all about *Divorce Court.* Dr. Paul Popenoe is the master of ceremonies. He wears glasses. Sometimes while the commercial is on, the actors have reconciliation. It is a real fun show.

Mommy and Daddy live in New York State. To get a divorce there, one of them has to commit adultery. Daddy has a tryst with a girl. Mommy raids the joint. She brings along a photographer. Mommy has secretly been having an affair with the photographer. What Daddy doesn't know won't hurt him. He always wanted to be on Page 3 of the *Daily News* anyhow. Mommy made sure that his undershorts were ironed.

Benjamin Brenner lives in Brooklyn. He is a Supreme Court Justice there. He makes decisions. He decided that raiding the joint is illegal from now on. Unless you have a search warrant. Then it's legal, but you have to knock first and say, "Benny sent me." This new rule doesn't count for hotel rooms. Then it's okay to raid the joint. So Daddy better get his own apartment. Judge Brenner is really under the thumb of real-estate agents.

There is another way. Mommy can go to Reno. She lives there for six weeks. That is called "establishing residence." Reno is Keno but Alabama is Clamor. Same-day service. The Chamber of Commerce invites lawyers to practice there. They are promised the run of the divorce mill. More people are traveling to Alabama than ever before. They are called Freedom Riders.

Here comes the governor of New York. See him eat the potato knish. He wants to get a divorce. He will establish residence in another state. But then he can't be governor. Instead he will get a divorce in New York. But you know what that means. Dirty, dirty. Some deserving Young Republican girl will get the assignment. This is known as political patronage. The governor has a horny dilemma, though. Either he commits scandal, or he commits perjury. Maybe he will propose a new law.

Religion for Dummies

Pope Endorses Condoms

WHEN I WAS A KID, condoms were called prophylactics, prophylactics were called rubbers, and rubbers were called scumbags. My friends and I would find used scumbags in a vacant lot or in the alley between buildings. Once, while snooping, I found a large package of unused prophylactics in my father's sock drawer. It must have held a dozen. Now there were nine left. Each was tightly rolled, bound by a miniature cigar-like band. I selected one, took the band off, and carefully unrolled it.

There was a legend imprinted on the prophylactic: "Sold in Drug Stores Only For the Prevention of Disease." What hypocrisy! They were sold for the prevention of *pregnancy*, which is a condition, not a disease. The irony is that now condoms *don't* carry that message, but they *are* used for the prevention of disease. Anyway, I tried to re-roll my father's prophylactic and stuff it back into the band, but it was a losing battle, so I decided not to put it back in the package, figuring that my dad wasn't counting his condoms and would never know.

As an adolescent, I found that purchasing condoms was a traumatic experience. I would buy other stuff to avoid being embarrassed. "I'd like a Batman comic book, and this Snickers candy bar, and [*whispering*] a pack of Trojans, and a tube of Crest toothpaste, please." But four decades later there were huge billboards, warning: "If you can't say no, use condoms." However, an executive of the Gannett Outdoor Advertising Company confirmed that they held off putting up those signs until after a visit by the Pope.

Members of the Roman Catholic Church hierarchy have been faced with an interesting dilemma. On the one hand, they are opposed to condoms as an artificial method of birth control. On the other hand, they are aware that condoms can serve as a protection against AIDS. But a group of bishops issued a statement that educational programs which include information about condoms should also stress that they are morally incorrect.

That's sort of like in the Watergate scandal when Richard Nixon said, "We could get the million dollars — but that would be *wrong*."

Coincidentally, in November 2010, while the porn industry in California was being pressured to require all male actors to wear condoms to prevent AIDS, in the Vatican it was revealed that, for the exact same reason, Pope Benedict — in his official capacity as the Church's chief spin doctor — went on record proclaiming that under some circumstances it might be acceptable for a (male) prostitute to use a condom.

"There can be single justified cases," he rationalized, "for example, when a prostitute uses a condom, and this can be a first step toward a moralization, a first act of responsibility in developing anew an awareness of the fact that not everything is permissible and that we cannot do everything we want. However, this is not the best way to overcome the infection of HIV. It is really necessary to humanize sexuality."

Daniel Maguire, author of *Sacred Rights: The Case for Contraception and Abortion in World Religions*, observed that the pope's change in policy represents a significant "crack in the dike" of Catholic opposition to condom use. The opposition stems from Catholic dogma that sex is for reproduction, and nothing should interfere with that.

An issue of *The Realist* reprinted an article from the *London Observer*, which began: "Three Roman Catholic theologians have expressed the opinion that, in times of revolution and violence, it is lawful for women, particularly for nuns, to take contraceptive pills and precautions against the danger of becoming pregnant through rape."

On that same page was our *Rumor of the Month*: "So-called 'flying saucers' are actually diaphragms being dropped by nuns on their way to Heaven."

I Ran an Underground Abortion Referral Service

WHEN ABORTION WAS ILLEGAL, women had no choice but to seek out back-alley butchers for what should have been a medical procedure in a sterile environment. If there was a botched surgery and the victim went to a hospital, the police were called, and they wouldn't allow the doctor to provide a painkiller until the patient gave them the information they sought.

In 1962, there was an article in *Look* magazine that stated, "There is no such thing as a 'good' abortionist. All of them are in business strictly for money." But in an issue of *The Realist*, I published an anonymous interview with Dr. Robert Spencer, a truly humane abortionist, promising that I would go to prison sooner than reveal his identity.

He had served as an Army doctor in World War I, then became a pathologist at a hospital in Ashland, Pennsylvania. He went down into the shafts after a mine accident, and aided miners to obtain Workmen's Compensation for lung disease. At a time when 5,000 women were killed each year by criminal abortionists who charged as much as $1,500, his reputation had spread by word of mouth, and he was known as "The Saint." Patients came to his clinic in Ashland from around the country.

I took the five-hour bus trip from New York to Ashland with my gigantic Webcor tape recorder. Dr. Spencer was the cheerful personification of an old-fashioned physician. He wore a red beret and used folksy expressions like "by golly." He had been performing abortions for 40 years. He started out charging $5, and never more than $100. He rarely used the word *pregnant*. Rather, he would say, "She was *that way*, and she came to me for help."

Ashland was a small town, and Dr. Spencer's work was not merely tolerated; the community *depended* on it — the hotel, the restaurant, the dress shop — all thrived on the extra business that came from his out-of-town patients. However, he built facilities at his clinic for African-American patients who weren't allowed to obtain overnight lodgings elsewhere. The walls of his office were decorated with those little wooden signs that tourists like to buy. A sign on the ceiling over his operating table said *Keep Calm*.

Here's an excerpt from our dialogue:

Q. *Do you have any idea about how many actual abortions you've performed during all these years?*

A. To be accurate, it's 27,006.

Q. *Have medical people come to you who would otherwise shun you?*

A. Oh, yes. I've had medical people who bring me their wives, and I've had quite a few medical people send me patients.

Q. *But they wouldn't perform the operation themselves?*

A. No, they'd never perform it, and just exactly what their attitude would be, I don't really know. Some of them, I presume, were absolutely against it, because I've had ministers, and they'd bring me their daughters or their nieces.

Q. *Have police come to you for professional services?*

A. Oh, yes, I've had police in here, too. I've helped them out. I've helped a hell of a lot of police out. I've helped a lot of FBI men out. They would be here, and they had me a little bit scared — I didn't know whether they were just in to get me or not.

Q. *What would you say is the most significant lesson you've learned in all your years as a practicing abortionist?*

A. You've got to be careful. That's the most important thing. And you've got to be cocksure that everything's removed. And even the uterus speaks to you and tells you. I could be blind. You see, this is an operation no eye sees. You go by the sense of feel and touch. The voice of the uterus. But the only thing I can see is hypocrisy, hypocrisy. Everywhere I look is hypocrisy, because the politicians — and I've had politicians in here — they still keep those laws in existence, but yet, if some friend of theirs is in trouble ...

Even priests came to his clinic with the housekeepers they had impregnated. As if to retroactively approve of such hypocrisy, the

Colorado Independent reported in 2013, "A chain of Catholic hospitals has beaten a malpractice lawsuit by saying that fetuses are not equivalent to human lives." Their attorneys argued that in cases of wrongful death, the term "person" only applies to individuals born alive, and not those who die in utero.

After the issue of *The Realist* featuring that interview with Dr. Spencer was published, I began to get phone calls from scared female voices. They were all in desperate search of a safe abortionist. It was preposterous that they should have to seek out the editor of a satirical magazine, but their quest so far had been futile, and they simply didn't know where else to turn.

With Dr. Spencer's permission, I referred them to him. At first there were only a few calls each week, then several every day. I had never intended to become an underground abortion referral service, but it wasn't going to stop just because in the next issue of *The Realist* I would publish an interview with somebody else.

A few years later, state police raided Dr. Spencer's clinic and arrested him. He remained out of jail only by the grace of political pressure from those he'd helped. He was finally forced to retire from his practice, but I continued mine, referring callers to other physicians that he had recommended. Occasionally I would be offered money by a patient, but I never accepted it. And whenever a doctor offered me a kickback, I refused, but I also insisted that he give a discount for the same amount to those patients referred by me.

Eventually, I was subpoenaed by district attorneys in two cities to appear before grand juries investigating criminal charges against abortionists. On both occasions I refused to testify, and each time the D.A. tried to frighten me into cooperating with the threat of arrest.

In Liberty, New York, my name had been extorted from a patient by threatening her with arrest. The D.A. told me that the doctor had confessed everything, and they got it all on tape. He gave me until 2:00 that afternoon to change my mind about testifying, or else the police would come to take me away.

"I'd better call my lawyer," I told him.

I went outside to a public phone booth and called, not a lawyer, but the doctor.

"That never happened," he said.

I returned to the D.A.'s office and told him that my lawyer said to continue being uncooperative. Then I just sat there waiting for the cops.

"They're on their way," the D.A. kept warning me.

But at 2:00, he simply said, "Okay, you can go home now."

Bronx District Attorney (later Judge) Burton Roberts took a different approach. In September 1969, he told me that his staff had found an abortionist's financial records, which showed all the money that I had received, but he would grant me immunity from prosecution if I cooperated with the grand jury. He extended his hand as a gesture of trust.

"That's not true," I said, refusing to shake hands with him.

If I *had* ever accepted any money, I'd have no way of knowing that he was bluffing. The D.A. was angry, but he finally had to let me go.

Attorney Gerald Lefcourt (later president of the National Association of Criminal Defense Lawyers) filed a suit on my behalf, challenging the constitutionality of the abortion law. He pointed out that the district attorney had no power to investigate the violation of an unconstitutional law, and therefore he could not force me to testify.

In 1970, I became the only plaintiff in the first lawsuit to declare the abortion laws unconstitutional in New York State. "Later, various women's groups joined the suit," Lefcourt recalls, "and ultimately the New York legislature repealed the criminal sanctions against abortion, prior to the Supreme Court decision in *Roe v. Wade.*"

Dr. Spencer never knew about that. He had died in 1969. The obituary in *The New York Times* acknowledged the existence of his abortion clinic. The obituary in the local paper in Ashland did not.

I continued to carry on my underground abortion referral service. Each time, though, I would flash on the notion that this was my own mother asking for help, and that she was pregnant with *me*. I would try to identify with the fetus that was going to be aborted even while I was serving as a conduit to the performance of that very abortion. Every day I would think about the possibility of never having existed, and I would only appreciate being alive all the more.

Of course, I couldn't possibly have known the difference if my fetus had been aborted. Pretending to be the fetus was just a way of focusing on my role as a referral service. I didn't want it to become so casual that I would grow unaware of the implications. By personalizing it, I had to accept my own responsibility for each fetus whose potential I was helping to disappear. That was about as mystical as I got. Maybe I was simply projecting my own ego.

In any case, by the time these women came to me for help, they had *already* searched their souls and made up their minds. This was not some abstract cause far away — these were real people in real distress — and I just couldn't say no. For nearly a decade, that became my fetal yoga. And, in the process, I had evolved from a satirist into an activist.

PAUL KRASSNER

There Are No Atheists
in the White House

IT WAS GOD who instructed Bill O'Reilly to consider every utterance of "Happy Holidays" to be a verbalization of "the war on Christmas." Whenever anybody claims that God talks directly to them, I think they're totally delusional. George W. Bush is no exception. Not only was he told by his senior adviser, Karen Hughes, not to refer to terrorists as "folks," but Bush was also being prompted by God Him-Her-or-Itself: "God would tell me, 'George, go and end the tyranny in Iraq.' And I did." As if he were merely following divine orders.

In July 2003, during a meeting with Palestinian Prime Minister Mahmoud Abbas, Bush told the newly elected leader, "God told me to strike at Al-Qaeda, and I struck them, and then He instructed me to strike at Saddam, which I did. And now I am determined to solve the problem in the Middle East. If you help me, I will act, and if not, the elections will come, and I will have to focus on them."

Abu Bakar Bashir, an Islamic cleric and accused terrorist leader, has said, "America's aim in attacking Iraq is to attack Islam, so it is justified for Muslims to target America to defend themselves." That's exactly interchangeable with this description of Bush by an unidentified family member, quoted in the *Los Angeles Times*: "George sees [the war on terror] as a religious war. His view is that they are trying to kill the Christians. And the Christians will strike back with more force and more ferocity than they will ever know."

Indeed, General William Boykin, Deputy Undersecretary of Defense for Intelligence, said, "George Bush was not elected by a majority of the voters in the United States, he was appointed by God." Discussing the battle against a Muslim warlord in Somalia, Boykin explained,

"I knew my God was bigger than his. I knew that my God was a real God and his was an idol."

Apparently, religious bigotry runs in the family. Bush's father, the former president: "I don't know that atheists should be considered citizens, nor should they be considered patriots. This is one nation under God." And before him, there was Ronald Reagan: "For the first time ever, everything is in place for the Battle of Armageddon and the Second Coming of Christ." Not to mention Reagan's Secretary of the Interior, James Watt, responsible for national policy on the environment: "We don't have to protect the environment — the Second Coming is at hand."

In 1966, Lyndon Johnson told the Austrian ambassador that the deity "comes and speaks to me about 2:00 in the morning when I have to give the word to the boys, and I get the word from God whether to bomb or not." So maybe there's some kind of bipartisan theological tradition going on in the White House.

But if these leaders are *not* delusional, then they're deceptive. And in order to deceive others, one must first deceive oneself until self-deception morphs into virtual reality. In any case, we have *our* religious fanatics, and they have *theirs*. In September 2007, on the eve of the sixth anniversary of 9/11, Osama bin Laden warned the American people that they should reject their capitalist way of life and embrace Islam to end the Iraq war, or else his followers would "escalate the killing and fighting against you."

George Bush once proclaimed, "God is not neutral," which is the antithesis of my own spiritual path, my own peculiar relationship with the universe — based on the notion that God is *totally* neutral — though I've learned that whatever people believe in, works for them.

My own belief in a deity disappeared when I was 13. I was working early mornings in a candy store across the street from our apartment building. My job was to insert different sections of the newspaper into the main section. On the day after the United States dropped the first atomic bomb on Hiroshima, I read that headline over and over and over again while I was working. That afternoon, I told God I couldn't believe in him anymore because — even though he was supposed to be a loving and all-powerful being — he had allowed such devastation to happen. And then I heard the voice of God:

"ALLOWED? WHY DO YOU THINK I GAVE HUMANS FREE WILL?"

"Okay, well, I'm exercising my free will to believe that you don't exist."

"ALL RIGHT, PAL, IT'S YOUR LOSS!"

At least we would remain on speaking terms. But I knew it was a game. I enjoyed the paradox of developing a dialogue with a being whose reality now ranked with that of Santa Claus. Our previous relationship had instilled in me a touchstone of objectivity that could still serve to help keep me honest. I realized, though, that whenever I prayed, I was only talking to myself.

The only thing I can remember from my entire college education is a definition of philosophy as "the rationalization of life." For my term paper, I decided to write a dialogue between Plato and an atheist. On a whim, I looked up Atheism in the Manhattan phone book, and there it was: "Atheism, American Association for the Advancement of." I went to their office for background material.

The AAAA sponsored the Ism Forum, where anybody could speak about any "ism" of their choice. I invited a few friends to meet me there. The event was held in a dingy hotel ballroom. There was a small platform with a podium at one end of the room and heavy wooden folding chairs lined around the perimeter. My favorite speaker declared the Eleventh Commandment: "Thou shalt not take thyself too goddamned seriously." Taking that as my unspoken theme, I got up and parodied the previous speakers. The folks there were mostly middle-aged and elderly. They seemed to relish the notion of fresh young blood in their movement.

However, my companions weren't interested in staying. If I had left with them that evening in 1953, the rest of my life could have taken a totally different path. Instead, I went along with a group to a nearby cafeteria, where I learned about the New York Rationalist Society. A whole new world of disbelief was opening up to me. That Saturday night, I went to their meeting. The emcee was a former circus performer who entertained his fellow rationalists by putting four golf balls into his mouth. He also recommended an anti-censorship paper, *The Independent*.

The next week, I went to *The Independent*'s office to subscribe and get back issues. I ended up with a part-time job, stuffing envelopes for a dollar an hour. My apprenticeship had begun. The editor, Lyle Stuart, was the most dynamic individual I'd ever met. His integrity was such that if he possessed information that he had a vested interest in keeping quiet — say, corruption involving a corporation in which he owned stock — it would become top priority for him to publish. Lyle became my media mentor, my unrelenting guru, and my closest friend. He was responsible for launching *The Realist*. The masthead announced, "Freethought Criticism and Satire."

IN THE WORDS of the late Jerry Falwell — who once said that God is pro-war — "If you're not a born-again Christian, you're a failure as a human being." We salute, then, a few *successful* human beings:

- The individual who placed the winning bid of $1,800 on eBay for a slab of concrete with a smudge of driveway sealant resembling the face of Jesus.

- The man who tried to crucify himself after seeing "pictures of God on the computer." He took two pieces of wood, nailed them together in the form of a cross, and placed it on his living-room floor. He proceeded to hammer one of his hands to the crucifix, using a 14-penny nail. According to a county sheriff spokesperson, "When he realized that he was unable to nail his other hand to the board, he called 911." It was unclear whether he was seeking assistance for his injury or help in nailing his other hand.

- The Sunday School teacher who advised one of his students to write on his penis, "What would Jesus do?" Presumably, "Masturbate" was not considered to be the correct answer.

- And, of course, the anonymous authors of the following quotes from various state constitutions. Arkansas: "No person who denies the being of a God shall hold any office." Mississippi: "No person who denies the existence of a Supreme Being shall hold any office in this state." North Carolina: "The following persons shall be disqualified for office: First, any person who shall deny the being of Almighty God." South Carolina: "No person shall be eligible to the office of Governor who denies the existence of the Supreme Being." Tennessee: "No person who denies the being of God, or a future state of rewards and punishments, shall hold any office in the civil department of this state." Texas: "Nor shall anyone be excluded from holding office on account of his religious sentiments, provided he acknowledge the existence of a Supreme Being."

Rick Warren, pastor of America's fourth-largest church, told his congregation, "I could not vote for an atheist because an atheist says, 'I don't need God.'"

In 2006, the Secular Coalition of America offered a $1,000 prize to anyone who identified the highest-ranking non-theist public official in the country. Almost 60 members of Congress were nominated, out of which 22 confided that they didn't believe in a Supreme Being, but they wanted their disbelief kept secret. Only Pete Stark admitted that he was a nonbeliever, and, in 2007, he became the first member of Congress ever to identify himself publicly as a nonbeliever.

In the week following that announcement, he received over 5,000 emails from around the globe, almost all congratulating him for his courage. "Like our nation's founders," he stated, "I strongly support the separation of church and state. I look forward to working with the Secular Coalition to stop the promotion of narrow religious beliefs in science, marriage contracts, the military, and the provision of social services." In 2008, he was elected to his 19th term with 76.5% of the votes.

In the 2008 primaries, three presidential wannabes raised their hands during a Republican "debate" to signify that they didn't believe in evolution, although one of them, Mike Huckabee, admitted, "I don't know if the world was created in six days. I wasn't there." He has also said, "If there was ever an occasion for someone to have argued against the death penalty, I think Jesus could have done so on the cross and said, 'This is an unjust punishment, and I deserve clemency.'"

Such Western fundamentalists have been waging a battle against the teaching of meditation in publicly funded schools, as though slow, deep breathing is inextricably connected with the practice of Eastern religious disciplines. What's next, forbidding the teaching of empathy because that's what Christians and Jews are supposed to practice?

It was a pleasant surprise when Barack Obama acknowledged "unbelievers" among others in his inauguration speech. However, I don't exempt unbelievers from criticism.

I ridicule officially atheist China's leaders for banning Tibet's living Buddhas from reincarnation without permission. According to the order, issued by the State Administration for Religious Affairs, "The so-called reincarnated living Buddha without government approval is illegal and invalid." That regulation is aimed at limiting the influence of the Dalai Lama, even though China officially *denies* the possibility of reincarnation. (I used to believe in reincarnation, but that was in a previous lifetime.)

The United States borrows trillions from China — a Big-Brother, slave-labor-driven, human-rights-violating, Maoist dictatorship — then proceeds to purchase their poisoned food, leaded Christmas toys, and "Made in China" American flags.

America remains a living paradox, where our citizens are force-fed misinformation and disinformation, so that we can continue to fund incompetent and illegal activities in the U.S. — even though our revolution was fought because of taxation without representation. And yet I live in this country where at least I still have complete freedom to openly condemn the government, the corporations, and the organized religions that continue enabling each other to reek with greed, corruption, and inhumanity.

The Sex Lives of Presidents

The Parts That Were Left Out
of the Kennedy Book

AN EXECUTIVE IN THE PUBLISHING INDUSTRY, who obviously must remain anonymous, has made available to The Realist *a photostat copy of the original manuscript of William Manchester's book,* The Death of a President. *Those passages which are printed here were marked for deletion months before Harper & Row sold the serialization rights to* Look *magazine; hence they do not appear even in the so-called "complete" version published by the German magazine* Stern.

AT THE DEMOCRATIC NATIONAL CONVENTION in the summer of 1960, Los Angeles was the scene of a political visitation of the alleged sins of the father upon the son. Lyndon Johnson found himself battling for the presidential nomination with a young, handsome, charming, and witty adversary, John F. Kennedy.

The Texan in his understandable anxiety degenerated to a strange campaign tactic. He attacked his opponent on the grounds that his father, Joseph P. Kennedy, was a Nazi sympathizer during the time he was United States Ambassador to Great Britain, from 1938 to 1940. The senior Kennedy had predicted that Germany would defeat England and he therefore urged President Franklin D. Roosevelt to withhold aid. Now Johnson found himself fighting pragmatism with pragmatism. It did not work; he lost the nomination.

Ironically, the vicissitudes of regional bloc voting forced Kennedy into selecting Johnson as his running mate. Jack rationalized the practicality of the situation, but Jackie was constitutionally unable to forgive Johnson. Her attitude toward him always remained one of controlled paroxysm.

It was common knowledge in Washington social circles that the Chief Executive was something of a ladies' man. His staff included a Secret Service agent, referred to by the code name *Dentist*, whose duties virtually centered around escorting to and from a rendezvous site — either in the District of Columbia or while traveling — the models, actresses, and other strikingly attractive females chosen by the president for his not-at-all infrequent trysts. "Get me that," he had said of a certain former Dallas beauty contest winner when plans for the tour were first being discussed. That particular aspect of the itinerary was changed, of course, when Mrs. Kennedy decided to accompany her husband.

She was aware of his philandering but would cover up her dismay by joking, "It runs in the family." The story had gotten back to her about the late Marilyn Monroe using the telephone in her Hollywood bathroom to make a long-distance call to *New York Post* film-gossip columnist Sidney Skolsky.

"Sid, you won't believe this," she had whispered, "but the Attorney General of our country is waiting for me in my bed this very minute — I just had to tell you."

❊ ❊ ❊

IT IS DIFFICULT to ascertain where on the continuum of Lyndon Johnson's personality innocent boorishness ends and deliberate sadism begins. To have summoned then-Secretary of the Treasury Douglas Dillon for a conference wherein he, the new president, sat defecating as he spoke, might charitably be an example of the former; but to challenge under the same circumstances Senator J. William Fulbright for his opposition to Administration policy in Vietnam is considered by insiders to be a frightening instance of the latter. The more Jacqueline Kennedy has tried to erase the crudeness of her husband's successor from consciousness, the more it has impinged upon her memories and reinforced her resentment. "It's beyond style," she would confide to friends. "Jack had style, but this is beyond style."

When Arthur Schlesinger, Jr. related to her an incident that he had witnessed firsthand — Mr. Johnson had actually placed his penis over the railing of the yacht, bragging to onlookers, "Watch it touch bottom!" — Mrs. Kennedy could not help but shiver with disgust. Capitol

Hill reporters have observed the logical extension of Mr. Johnson boasting about his 6:00-in-the-morning forays with Lady Bird, to his bursts of phallic exhibitionism, whether it be on a boat or at the swimming pool or in the lavatory. Apropos of this tendency, Drew Pearson's assistant, Jack Anderson, has remarked: "When Lyndon announces there's going to be a joint session of Congress, everybody cringes."

It is true that Mrs. Kennedy withstood the pressures of publicized scandal, ranging from the woman who picketed the White House carrying a blown-up photograph supposedly of Jack Kennedy sneaking away from the home of Jackie's press secretary, Pamela Turnure, to the *Blauvelt Family Genealogy* which claimed on page 884, under Eleventh Generation, that one Durie Malcolm had "married, third, John F. Kennedy, son of Joseph P. Kennedy, one time Ambassador to England." But it was the personal infidelities that gnawed away at her — as indeed they would gnaw away at *any* wife who has been shaped by this culture — until finally Jackie left in exasperation. Her father-in-law offered her one million dollars to reconcile. She came back, not for the money, but because she sincerely believed that the nation needed Jack Kennedy, and she didn't want to bear the burden of losing enough public favor to forestall his winning the presidency.

Consequently, she was destined to bear a quite different burden — with great ambivalence — the paradox of fame. She enjoyed playing her role to the hilt, but complained, "Can't they get it into their heads that there's a difference between being the First Lady and being Elizabeth Taylor?" Even after she became First Widow, the movie magazines would not — or could not — leave her alone.

Probably the most bizarre invasion of her privacy occurred in *Photoplay*, which asked the question, "Too Soon for Love?" — then proceeded to print a coupon that readers were requested to answer and send in. They had a multiple choice: "Should Jackie (1) Devote her life exclusively to her children and the memory of her husband? (2) Begin to date — privately or publicly — and eventually remarry? (3) "Marry right away?" Mrs. Kennedy fumed. "Why don't they give them some more decisions to make for me? Some *real* ones. Should I live in occasional sin? Should I use a diaphragm or the pill? Should I keep it in the medicine cabinet or the bureau drawer?" But she would never lose her dignity in public; she had too deep a faith in her own image.

❋ ❋ ❋

AMERICAN LEADERS SEEM to have a schizophrenic approach toward each other. They *want* to expose their human frailties at the same time that they do *not* want to remove them from their pedestals. Bobby Kennedy privately abhors Lyndon Johnson, but publicly calls him "great, and I mean that in every sense of the word." Johnson has referred to Bobby as "that little shit" in private but continues to laud him for the media. Gore Vidal has no such restraint. On a television program in London, he explained why Jacqueline Kennedy would never relate to Lyndon Johnson. During that tense flight from Dallas to Washington after the assassination, she inadvertently walked in on him as he was standing over the casket of his predecessor and chuckling. This disclosure was the talk of London but did not reach these shores.

Of course, President Johnson is often given to inappropriate response — witness the puzzled timing of his smiles when he speaks of grave matters — but we must also assume that Mrs. Kennedy had been traumatized that day and her perception was likely to have been tainted by the tragedy. This state of shock must have underlain an incident on Air Force One which this writer conceives to be delirium, but which Mrs. Kennedy insists she actually saw. "I'm telling you this for the historical record," she said, "so that people a hundred years from now will know what I had to go through."

She corroborated Gore Vidal's story, continuing: "That man [Johnson] was crouching over the corpse, no longer chuckling but breathing hard and moving his body rhythmically. At first, I thought he must be performing some mysterious symbolic rite he'd learned from Mexicans or Indians as a boy. And then I realized — there is only one way to say this — he was literally fucking my husband in the throat. In the bullet wound in the front of his throat. He reached a climax and dismounted. I froze. The next thing I remember, he was being sworn in as the new president."

[Handwritten marginal notes: *1. Check with Rankin — did secret autopsy show semen in throat wound? 2. Is this simply necrophilia, or was LBJ trying to change entry wound from grassy knoll into exit wound from Book Depository by enlarging it?*]

The glaze lifted from Jacqueline Kennedy's eyes.

"I don't believe that Lyndon Johnson had anything to do with a conspiracy, but I do know this — Jack taught me about the nuances of power — if he were miraculously to come back to life and suddenly appear in front of him, the first thing Johnson would do now is kill him."

She smiled sardonically, adding, "Unless Bobby beat him to it."

POSTSCRIPT

THE MOST SIGNIFICANT thing about "The Parts That Were Left Out of the Kennedy Book" was its widespread *acceptance* — if only for a moment — by intelligent, literate people, from an ACLU official to a Peabody Award-winning journalist to members of the intelligence community who knew that sort of thing actually *does* go on. Daniel Ellsberg said, "Maybe it was just because I *wanted* to believe it so badly."

One caller claimed that he could determine, by feeding the article into a computer, whether Manchester had written the portions I published. Several individuals queried that final arbiter of truth, the *Playboy* Adviser. One reader "went out and bought the original *Death of a President* just to see if your parts would fit into the book — they did. Amazing!"

I also received a call from Ray Marcus, a critic of the *Warren Commission Report*, who had discovered a chronological flaw in my article. How could William Manchester leave something out of his book that was itself a report of something that he'd left out of his book? Marcus deduced that The Realist must have been given the excerpts by a CIA operative in order to discredit *valid* dissent on the assassination.

My favorite response came from Merriman Smith, the syndicated UPI correspondent who always ended White House press conferences with the traditional "Thank you, Mr. President." He wrote:

> One of the filthiest printed attacks ever made on a President of the United States is now for sale on Washington newsstands. The target: President Johnson. This is the May edition of a so-called magazine which says it is entered as second-class mail. One newsstand owner says sales of this particular issue have been "quite active." This reporter is not embarked here on any defense of Johnson politically or personally, nor, for that matter, is this to suggest the need for greater respect for the presidency.

These are matters that have been dealt with extensively in other forums. Certain unadorned facts, however, do stand out in the open circulation, mailing and other forms of distribution of this sort of slime: If a magazine of major national standing tries to use the same sort of language, federal action to stop it would be almost certain. The language referred to is not conventional hell or damn profanity — it is filth attributed to someone of national stature supposedly describing something Johnson allegedly did. The incident, of course, never took place ...

A Sneak Preview of
Richard Nixon's Memoir

AN OLD FRIEND APPROACHED us with a thick sheaf of what was purported to be a photocopy of the autobiographical manuscript on which former President Richard M. Nixon was still at work. Our first reaction was skepticism. While most of the contents dealt predictably with contemporary history as it has already been recorded, there were enough surprises to shock even our own jaded psyche.

Just to be sure, we employed the services of a reputable private investigative firm. Their report verified that our source did indeed know an individual inside the San Clemente hideaway. The next step was to hire a professional graphologist, who determined the authenticity of Mr. Nixon's handwritten notes on the typed transcript. Finally, our attorneys assured us that there was no violation of copyright laws involved, because it was unlikely that Nixon had submitted such unfinished material for copyright protection.

The book, as yet untitled, is dedicated "To Patricia Ryan Nixon, who has been named the most admired woman in the country, and deservedly so, for your loyalty has been a continuing inspiration, not only to your husband and family, but to Americans everywhere." Here, then, are several excerpts from this preliminary draft of the memoir of the only United States president ever to resign from office.

ALTHOUGH PRESIDENT DWIGHT DAVID EISENHOWER encouraged me to call him Ike during the years I served as Vice President, it was a superficial form of intimacy. I regretted his failure to share decision-making responsibility with me at the White House. That privilege he reserved for his special assistant, Sherman Adams.

When media coverage of a minor scandal in 1958 involving a rug and a vicuna coat pressured him into letting Adams go, Ike at last revealed a facet of his humanity to me. "By sheer force of habit," he remarked, "I was ready to seek out Sherman's advice on whether or not I should fire him."

It was not until 1961, after Ike's farewell address, that he confided in me again, this time about a more momentous occasion. "I suppose," he began, "my reference to the dangers of the military-industrial complex in my speech came as something of a surprise to you, eh?"

"Well, sir, it did strike me as a rather incongruous position for a renowned Army general to take —"

"I had a visitation," he interrupted, "while I was in the process of composing my farewell address — now this is utterly impossible to describe — but I do believe it was some kind of extraterrestrial communication."

"In English or what?" I was dumbfounded.

"It was in English but also beyond all language. They told me that their associates had been to see Harry Truman when he was president. Now remember, Dick, he's the one who ordered the atomic bomb to be dropped on Hiroshima and Nagasaki. And yet these creatures convinced him not to turn Korea into another nuclear holocaust. That's really why he brought back General Douglas MacArthur."

Ike stared ahead with a blank expression in his eyes.

"Sir, are you all right?"

"Yes. Yes. I just don't know if I can articulate this extraterrestrial experience. It was as though my body remained in the chair and my spirit was taken on a journey. All I know is that when I returned, I just had to tell the truth. There was no other choice —"

Ike stopped in mid-sentence. He never mentioned that incident again. Nor did I feel it would be proper for me to broach the subject. I dismissed it from my mind. It would not be until nearly fourteen years later that my *visceral* understanding of his experience would occur.

The year 1974 was so rough on me that for a while I thought I could actually be going insane. I wondered if I was being drugged without my knowledge. I found myself wallowing in paranoid fantasies, and I gave voice to these at press conferences. I expressed the fear that my plane might crash. I resorted to using expressions like "They can point a gun at your head." I was practically begging for mercy.

When I entered Memorial Hospital Medical Center in Long Beach on October 23 for my phlebitis condition, I brought my own jar of wheat germ, because I was afraid that poison would be put in my food.

On October 29, the doctors placed a clamp on a vein in my pelvis in order to prevent the blood clot from moving to my lungs where it could have killed me. It was then that I went into cardiovascular failure.

On October 30, Ron Ziegler announced, "We almost lost President Nixon yesterday afternoon." This was almost three months after my resignation, and he was still referring to me as President.

"Poor Ron," I thought to myself. "He thinks he's still in Disneyland."

For a few hours I was considered to be clinically dead. It was an incredibly ecstatic feeling. I was conscious, but on some other plane of existence, and there was an overwhelming temptation to remain in that blissful limbo. Yet there was also something in me that kept saying "Don't give up!" It was my survival instinct speaking.

But why not give up? What was there left for me? The answer came to me by the same extraterrestrial path it had come to Ike: *Tell the truth!* That was the turning point of my life. And these memoirs are the tangible result of my transformation. No one shall be spared, least of all myself.

Those hairless creatures told me that President John F. Kennedy had also been visited by their kind. His father, old Joe Kennedy, had gotten rich off illegal booze during Prohibition, and you can be certain that the underworld bootleggers he was tied up with were not about to dissolve their silent partnership in this huge liquor industry they had built up simply because Prohibition had been repealed. Yet there was Joe Kennedy's own son, Jack — not to mention his brother Bobby — refusing to cooperate any longer in allowing organized crime to have a comeback in Cuba, and furthermore, going after organized crime in *this* country. At best this was ingratitude; at worst it was treason.

But I finally understood the extraterrestrial force that had motivated young Kennedy. And so now I am ready to peel away the final layers of my poker-face mask.

For example, I occasionally went too far while wearing my anti-Communist mask. When former Attorney General Nicholas Katzenbach exposed the DuBois Clubs as a Communist front organization, poison-pen letters and threatening telephone calls were received by many of the Boys Clubs from patriotic Americans who were understandably confused by the ostensibly coincidental pronunciations. But in my function as National Board Chairman of the Boys Clubs of America, I charged that the name choice was "an almost classic example of Communist deception and duplicity" and that the W.E.B. DuBois Clubs "are not unaware of the confusion they are causing among our supporters and among many other good citizens."

In retrospect, however, I admit that this was a slightly foolish position to espouse.

IN AUGUST OF 1945, while I was still serving in the Navy, stationed in Maryland, there was a Committee of 100 seeking — according to an advertisement they placed in several California newspapers — a candidate for Congress "with no previous political experience, to defeat a man who has represented the district in the House for ten years." This was a reference to Jerry Voorhis.

I did not see the ad, but destiny acted as though I had answered it when I was contacted by Murray Chotiner for Herman Perry, vice president of the Bank of America. Perry later became vice president of the Western Tube Corporation, a CIA front located in the Whittier Bank of America building. But now he wanted to know only if I was a Republican and if I was available.

My responses were both affirmative.

It was Perry who brought me out for an extremely brief meeting with Howard Hughes. Hughes was handsome, dynamic, self-assured. Somehow he had seen the FBI dossier on me, which had apparently been compiled when I applied for a position with the Bureau after graduating law school. Oddly enough, I had never heard back from the FBI directly.

"Nixon," he addressed me, "you have a magnificent political future ahead. You will be able to steer your ship independently. But always keep it in a tiny compartment of your mind that you do not own the ocean. I do."

I never saw Howard Hughes face to face again.

THE SEEDS OF MY DISTRUST of the Justice Department were sown in 1948 during the Alger Hiss case. Those people just sat on each other's hands. If not for the work of our House Un-American Activities Committee, the prosecution would never have been so successful.

I refused to turn over to those bunglers the microfilms we had in evidence. When there was a possibility I might be cited for contempt, I raised the point of what a dangerous precedent could be set, since here I was, a U.S. Congressman, appearing voluntarily before a grand jury.

But the truth of the matter was that those microfilms were copies of documents forged on an old Woodstock typewriter that had been specially constructed to resemble — to have the same peculiarities as — the typewriter that had actually belonged to Alger Hiss's wife, Priscilla.

Then Whittaker Chambers hid these "old" 1938 microfilms inside a pumpkin on his pumpkin farm. The trouble was, the Eastman Kodak people stated that the type of film we used was not manufactured by their company until 1945.

To this day, whenever the comic strip *Peanuts* mentions that bird named Woodstock or the mysterious "pumpkin papers," I suspect Charles Schulz is trying to remind me of something.

THERE SEEMS TO BE a tradition of accusing those who fight Communism of being homosexual. This smear tactic was used against Whittaker Chambers, against Senator Joseph McCarthy, and against J. Edgar Hoover. In that vein, gossips used to rant about Hoover and Clyde Tolson double-dating with Charles "Bebe" Rebozo and myself.

Neither Rebozo nor I are "gay." We have been very close friends since 1950. What we enjoy most about each other's company is the fact that small talk becomes unnecessary. We are not afraid of silence. But we have never had any kind of sexual relationship.

We were introduced by Senator George Smathers, who was infamous for supplying female companions to his fellow legislators. It was Smathers who eventually sent Mary Jo Kopechne to be with Senator Edward Kennedy.

Whenever I was in Florida, I would stay with Bebe, and he would occasionally get a couple of beautiful $200-a-night girls. Or as they would be called nowadays, $200-a-night women. But when I bought my own home in Key Biscayne, then his yacht became our rendezvous site.

I was certainly not promiscuous, but I had been a virgin until marriage. I proposed to Pat Ryan the very same night I met her. She refused, but I was a determined son-of-a-gun. I even drove her to Los Angeles when she dated other men while I waited in the wings. I finally charmed her with my perseverance and self-effacement.

Once I express concern to Bebe that word might get out about my "affairs" in Key Biscayne. "These girls," I pointed out, "are likely to brag about going to bed with a United States senator."

"They're professionals," Bebe reassured me. "It's just like your lawyer-client privilege. Stop worrying."

ONE EVENING IN 1949, while I was still serving in Congress, I received an anonymous call at my home. A male voice said three words, "Watch Jeane Dixon," and hung up the telephone.

A week later, the psychic Jeane Dixon held a press conference. One of the reporters asked her to predict my future. She drew a blank, however, explaining that she needed time to meditate. I believe that in show business parlance this is known as "milking the audience." Finally, she said it: "I predict that one day, Richard Nixon will become president of the United States."

I could only conclude that the higher source from which she had received her intelligence was not necessarily supernatural. When I lost the presidential election to John F. Kennedy in 1960, Jeane Dixon *continued* to predict that I would be president. "Destiny," she said, "cannot be denied."

Even after I was defeated in the 1962 California gubernatorial election and announced that I was through with politics, she said, "Richard Nixon has not even begun his rise in politics." And then she predicted the assassination of President Kennedy in 1963.

After the Watergate affair, she stated: "God gave us Richard Nixon to divide us, to test us where our faith is concerned, to see if we could come together." A local paper published her statement ("God gave us Nixon to divide us. — Jeane Dixon") as the caption for a cartoon showing a cloud with the voice of God saying, "Don't blame me — I voted for McGovern." I had to admit it was funny, even though she had been quoted out of context.

HARRY ROBBINS "BOB" HALDEMAN came into my life when I was a senator in 1951. He volunteered to work on my vice-presidential campaign the next year, but that campaign was not to be for him, so he tried again in 1956, and this time we took him on. He rose to be my chief advance man for the presidential race in 1960.

After my defeat, Haldeman remained loyal. He volunteered to help me with my book, *Six Crises*. I wrote the chapter on the 1960 campaign myself because it was so fresh in my mind. Al Moscow drafted four other chapters with Haldeman — this was not ghostwritten material because I rewrote what they presented — and Haldeman worked mostly on the Alger Hiss chapter.

He was apparently so eager to please, though, that he screwed up on his research. He had it that the FBI found the old Woodstock typewriter. And the book was published that way. Then the facts came out, the trial records and all, and we had to change it for the paperback edition. So now it reads that the FBI was *unable* to find the typewriter.

The truth is, Alger Hiss found it himself. But the FBI had *planted* this fake Woodstock typewriter. And then the *defense* presented it in the trial as what they *assumed* was evidence in their favor. So at least Hiss was found guilty of perjury.

That verdict added immeasurably to my political strength. I had the courage of Alger Hiss's conviction, and it served as the magic carpet that transported me from the Congress to the Senate to the vice presidency. I would have had the presidency in my pocket if not for Kennedy's performance in the Great Debates — but only on television; I fared better on radio. Kennedy's charisma was the variable that none of us had counted on.

HOW STRANGE that the incident from the entire eight years I spent as Vice President that stands out most prominently in my memory occurred not in the White House but in Peru. There was a rioter who spat on me, and it was with great pleasure that I kicked him in the shins.

Back in the safety of our hotel that night, I recalled an early formal debate at Whittier College — "Resolved: that insects are more beneficial than harmful" — because I had been so intrigued as to how insects did not think, they just acted. Now, having myself acted totally without hesitation, I was able to identify with those insects.

As Vice President, I labored diligently behind the scenes to establish Operation 40, by which our CIA covertly trained Cuban intelligence officers in exile. Operation 40 was to serve as our link between the White House and the CIA in April of 1961. My plan was to invade Cuba.

Ironically, during the 1960 presidential campaign, Kennedy began advocating *my* plan. I could not reveal that it was *already* in effect because Operation 40 was a *secret* project. Further, I found myself in the schizophrenic position of attacking my own idea whenever Kennedy articulated it, because it violated our treaty commitments.

OF ALL THE PROFESSIONAL NEWSCASTERS I have met, Walter Cronkite of CBS was the most charming. He treated me with respect and dignity. After the broadcast interview, we sat in his anteroom and talked informally.

"I've always wanted to thank you," he said, "for inadvertently bringing me back to sanity that horrible weekend John Kennedy was killed."

"Oh, really — how so?"

"This followed on the heels of the televised shooting of Lee Harvey Oswald by Jack Ruby. A journalist asked for your reaction, and you replied with a slip of the tongue, 'Two rights don't make a wrong.' Before you could correct yourself, I was finally able to break through my depression with a bit of laughter."

"Yes, those were muddled times. Do you know I *forgot* where I was the day the assassination took place? I had to tell the FBI I couldn't remember, and it was not until later that I remembered I had been in Dallas, of all places. There was a convention of the American Bottlers of Carbonated Beverages, and I was there representing Pepsi-Cola. But

I flew out of there at 11:00 that morning. Kennedy was shot around 1:00, as I recall. Where were *you* that day?"

"In my office," Cronkite said. "When we got the word from Bethesda that he had passed, I cried openly."

"And you're supposed to be objective," I teased him. "I didn't realize you were that much of a Kennedy supporter."

"Well, by that time I was crying because it had also come over the wires that Lyndon Johnson was already preparing to be sworn in as the new president."

It was encouraging to find that in person this superstar really was just like your favorite uncle.

WHEN ROBERT KENNEDY was attorney general in 1962, he was busy checking out the Hiss case for some reason. Of course, he discovered that the FBI never had the Woodstock typewriter.

Then, in 1968, when he was running for president, he approached New Orleans District Attorney Jim Garrison to be *his* attorney general. Garrison had gotten a lot of publicity due to his investigation of the assassination of Bobby's brother.

During that campaign, Howard Hughes dispatched Robert Maheu to visit me. Hughes felt strongly that the Vietnam War should continue — he had a huge defense contract for helicopters — yet at the same time he wanted a halt to underground nuclear testing, presumably because it upset the roulette wheels in his Las Vegas casinos.

I mentioned the Bobby Kennedy information to Maheu, and he said, "Uh-oh, the boss will have to keep a sharper eye on *him*."

It was poetic irony that while Bobby Kennedy was giving official permission to J. Edgar Hoover to spy on Martin Luther King, I was giving unofficial permission to Hoover to spy on *Kennedy*. That is to say, Robert Maheu may have been working for Howard Hughes, but he had also continued working for the FBI. So when he referred to "the boss," I asked, "Which one?"

Maheu smiled and held up his arms, two fingers from each hand extending up into the air. "Both," he said. This was the exact moment I decided to use that gesture for the crowds.

Winston Churchill had used the V-sign to signify Victory. Then the antiwar protesters perverted its meaning to signify Defeat. Now I was restoring its original victorious symbolism by co-opting the co-opters. Or so I believed.

❊ ❊ ❊

THE PROBLEM WAS that Lyndon Johnson desperately wanted to have the Vietnam War settled before he left office. Whereas, I am ashamed to admit, we were trying to prolong it.

Anna Chennault — the Dragon Lady, as we called her — was our liaison to South Vietnamese government officials. Her task was to dissuade their ambassador to the U.S, Bui Diem, from attending the Paris peace talks.

But LBJ got wise to this. I had to call and cajole him personally. He was absolutely furious. He complained bitterly at how "shit-kickin' pissed off" he was. "Thieu is *our* boy," he shouted, "and don't you fuckin' forget that!"

On November 1, 1968, only four days before the American election, President Nguyen Van Thieu announced that Saigon was pulling out of the peace talks. The Dragon Lady had obviously convinced his associates that they would obtain a juicier deal under our new administration than under Johnson or his chosen successor, Hubert Humphrey, who would surely have won if the Democrats had ended the war.

And so, because it was in the mutual interest of the South Vietnamese and the Republicans to extend the war for several more years, we became the recipients of kickbacks from our own government's aid to the Saigon government.

I do not ask for forgiveness. No, rather I must live with the memory of myself as an idealistic adolescent first reading about the Teapot Dome scandal and saying to my mother, while helping her to mash the potatoes, "I would like to become an honest lawyer who can't be bought by crooks." But my character had already been set. When I was only 5 years old, my mother intended to buy me a copy of *The Prince and the Pauper*, but she asked a bookstore clerk for *The Prince*, and so, of course, he gave her Machiavelli's book. My mother was a saint. Her little mistake changed my life, and I will always be grateful for what I feel must have been a touch of divine intervention.

✳ ✳ ✳

WE CREATED A COUPLE of Frankenstein monsters, and when I say we, I mean the administration and the media in an unintentional collaboration.

One such monster was Martha Mitchell. The first time she made one of her famous telephone calls and we saw how the press ate it up, we realized we had a political gold mine. The wife of the attorney general could serve as our mouthpiece for floating various trial balloons.

John Mitchell would get thoroughly briefed on whatever the issue was — Haiphong Harbor or Senator Fulbright or the need for increased spending — and then, without ever letting Martha know that he *expected* her to give a scoop to some lucky reporter that evening, John would simply smoke his pipe and just happen to engage her in casual conversation about the matter.

Martha was much too strong-willed to be *instructed* to make a call, but she could be counted on to make the call, even if it was 3:00 in the morning when the urge hit her. This was a great joke among the reporters. One little news item quoted her latest pronouncement, and after the quote that sentence was completed with, "Martha Mitchell confided to the Washington Star yesterday ..." Confided, indeed — to a *newspaper.*

But in the process of becoming a public character, she developed many contacts in the media. By the time her husband became my campaign manager, Martha Mitchell was already a household word. We thought she would prove to be a wonderful asset until she started blabbing about Watergate.

Another Frankenstein monster we created was Henry Kissinger. I never really wanted him in the first place. He had insulted me publicly when I received the nomination in '68. But I made an agreement with Nelson Rockefeller that if he would actively support me, I would take Kissinger onto the team, and, of course, I had to keep my word.

We all felt somewhat uncomfortable about his German accent. H.R. Haldeman decided that whenever Kissinger made any statement, his picture could be shown on TV, but there would be no audio. And the electronic media cooperated.

Meanwhile, we built up his image, got him dates with glamorous movie stars — Jill St. John, Marlo Thomas, Liv Ullmann — until he became known as a harmless, pudgy playboy. Then it was acceptable for his voice to be heard.

"Henry," I once remarked to him, "there's a rumor going around Washington that you're lousy in bed."

"Mr. President" — speaking very slowly and distinctly — "I can only say that ... *power* ... is the ultimate aphrodisiac."

And he just kept glaring at me with those worried-looking eyebrows frowning over his spectacles. This was just three days after our destabilization of the Chilean government. Kissinger wanted all the credit, but it was really a team effort.

We could not have succeeded, for example, without the invaluable aid of Teamsters Union President Frank Fitzsimmons and his Bob Hope-like timing in manipulating the truckers' strike in Chile. It is possible to bring about the collapse of an entire economy by shutting down one integral aspect, especially communications or transportation.

Moreover, the Soviet Union was trying to cut off the United States' supply of a metal vital to jet engine production, by their support of the Allende government in Chile and also by backing guerrilla actions in Angola. In order to maintain the war in Vietnam, we needed Chilean copper as well as the trace metal. At any rate, we were a smooth, well-oiled team, on the way to winning the whole, beautiful, global game.

IN 1968, GEORGE WALLACE ran for president as the candidate of the American Independent Party. This almost lost me the election to Hubert Humphrey. In 1972, Wallace ran for president again. This almost cost him his life. I honestly have no knowledge as to how long Arthur Bremer was in our employ, but I do know that the cover story of his having stalked me before he went after Wallace was fabricated simply to defuse any suspicion that might have pointed to our role in the tragic event.

After all, my supposed public mandate that November came from a majority that included twenty million votes that would otherwise have gone to George Wallace. We had not expected him to pose so much of a threat. In fact, we had already taken certain steps to preclude any such possibility. In 1970, immediately after he became governor of Alabama again, the IRS and the Justice Department launched an investigation of Wallace and his brother Gerald for tax evasion and other forms of financial corruption.

I don't fault Wallace for family loyalty, by the way. I have carried out similar filial responsibility to my own brother, Donald. This is only natural.

In any event, John Mitchell, still attorney general at the time, came to me early in 1971 and said, "We've got to stop George Wallace. He could force the election into the House of Representatives if he runs on a third-party ticket again."

In May of that year, I was in Mobile and invited Wallace to fly with me on the presidential plane to Birmingham. En route, we shook hands on an agreement. I promised that Mitchell would call off the investigation of Wallace and his brother — although their underlings would still be subject to prosecution — and the governor in turn promised me that if he ran in '72 it would only be as a Democrat.

In August 1971, we discovered that CBS correspondent Daniel Schorr had been asking around about the possibility of such a deal. Haldeman commented, "We'd better get on his ass — fast."

Two years later, when Schorr reported that John Dean was afraid of going to prison because he might get raped there, we were able to find out immediately from the FBI that his source was Dean's own attorney, but there was nothing constructive we could do with that information.

However, it must be noted for posterity that John Dean was a closet queen supreme. His lovely wife, Maureen, is merely window dressing. Oh, how neatly she rolled up her blonde tresses into a perfect bun and sat behind him at the Watergate hearings every day, blatantly projecting a modern-day American Gothic image. I recall how it came out that Dean had taken almost $5,000 from a White House safe for a hurried honeymoon right smack in the middle of the cover-up, he was already disguising his tracks. Their marriage was purely protective coloration.

The case of John Dean does raise the question: when is a so-called leak actually convenient propaganda?

Maureen Dean was on an airplane flight when she "accidentally" dropped her purse and spilled a vial of amyl nitrate capsules on the floor. She explained to the man sitting next to her how wonderful these were for enhancing her sex life with John. Is it not possible that this lady was protesting just a mite too much, particularly to someone who would just happen to let the media in on her secret?

No wonder G. Gordon Liddy said that John Dean was qualified to sing the title role in *Der Rosenkavalier* — because it is sung by a woman. Liddy once made a remark in German that I asked him to translate for me. He said, "John Dean's priorities are all screwed up. He doesn't know whether he wants to go down in history or down on a historian."

YOUNG PEOPLE MIGHT USE the expression "karma returning" to describe a deal we made with Jack Anderson, who had himself exposed the corruption of so many others in his syndicated column for *The Washington Post*.

We were tipped off that Anderson was researching the Dragon Lady connection. He had learned that her late husband, General Claire Chennault, who had commanded the Flying Tigers in World War II, had in 1946 formed a private commercial airline that later merged with the CIA's Air America.

He also learned that our Dragon Lady was currently profiting from a Pepsi-Cola factory I had established in Laos, but which had never spewed forth a single drop of Pepsi. Air America had been shuttling out its *actual* product: heroin.

However, Anderson agreed not to publish this material. In return, we agreed not to publicize the fact that he knew about the Watergate break-in weeks before it occurred. He had warned Lawrence O'Brien at Democratic National Committee headquarters, but O'Brien remained silent because he assumed that such a scandal would provide ammunition for a Democrat coup in the '72 election. He overestimated public outrage.

Anderson held back because he did not wish to endanger his source, one of the "burglars," Frank Sturgis, whom he had known for some twenty years. Shortly after my resignation in 1974, I received a long letter from Sturgis. I shall quote here a portion of that correspondence:

> Now, I'm telling you this because I still consider you my Commander in
> Chief. I realize that the same faction of the CIA that masterminded the
> assassination of Kennedy was also behind your downfall. They thought JFK

was soft on Communism in Cuba, and that you were soft on Communism in China, but that they didn't necessarily have to kill you to get rid of you.

While I participated in Operation 40, our job was primarily to infiltrate foreign countries. I was a member of the Assassination Section. Orders would filter down, and our job would be to kill, say, a military official or a politician. Even in those days, unstated policy included domestic as well as foreign enemies.

But I had nothing to do with the Kennedy assassination myself. The FBI came to interview me the day after it happened, and I didn't have a thing to tell them, except that I could agree with their speculation that the motive was revenge for the Bay of Pigs failure. There's no doubt in my mind that if you had been elected in 1960, the invasion would have been completely successful.

For a while I believed that Bernard Barker was the double agent in Watergate, but I have since come to the conclusion that our leader, James McCord, was guided to do the things he did by certain officials in the CIA. We were definitely set up. They used us to eventually destroy the office of the presidency. You were just as expendable as Kennedy.

I shouldn't have been surprised Mr. McCord was our Security Chief. I myself, as an infiltrator of Castro's inner circle, rose to Director of Security for the Cuban Air Force and Director of Intelligence. Who can you trust?

Whereas I agree with Frank Sturgis that the Watergate burglars were "set up," I question the reason he gives. The CIA was fully aware that relations with the People's Republic of China were bound to open up sooner or later. And, of course, I wanted to earn credit for that in history.

Rather, I am convinced that there was a power struggle *within* the Agency. The "faction" to which Sturgis alludes — most likely led by CIA's Richard Helms — was jealous of the Special Intelligence Unit we had developed inside the White House.

NOT ONLY WAS the Watergate break-in deliberately bungled in order to discredit me, but the White House taping system was never part of my domain. I knew it had been installed by the Secret Service, but I lacked access to the tapes and, more important, to any switch that would shut off a recording device.

I was a prisoner in the Oval Office. A mobile prisoner, to be sure — I could go to the Cabinet Room or the Lincoln Room — but it didn't make any difference; there were bugs everywhere. They even bugged my cabin at Camp David. I was under more surveillance than Larry O'Brien could ever imagine.

If I had the tapes in my possession, don't you think I would have gotten rid of them? Just the way I did with those microfilms in the Hiss case. Everybody was recommending this — from John Connally to Chuck Colson — but I simply did not have access to the system.

I should explain that "Bay of Pigs" was our code word for the assassination of President Kennedy. When we were attempting to put the brakes on the FBI investigation of Watergate, I told Haldeman to get word to Helms that otherwise, because of E. Howard Hunt's involvement, the whole Bay of Pigs thing would open up.

Hunt was the CIA station chief in Mexico when agent Lee Harvey Oswald made contact there in 1963. The whole world already knows what a fiasco the Bay of Pigs operation turned out to be — that is, the invasion of Cuba — but because Kennedy didn't keep his campaign promise to support the exiles, he then became the prime "Bay of Pigs" target.

Had the Watergate mission not been aborted, Hunt would have continued to simulate documents blaming Kennedy and Ted Sorensen for the murder of Che Guevara, just as he forged those cables blaming Kennedy for the murder of Ngo Dinh Diem.

I hasten to add that Hunt was merely *clarifying* the issues. The Kennedy Administration was responsible. But what we were trying to do was hurt Ted Kennedy's chances if he decided to run. However, that is guilt by relationship, which is wrong and irrelevant.

I WAS CONVINCED that Nelson Rockefeller was behind it all. He had never forgiven me for defeating him for the Republican nomination in 1968. What with that whole 25th Amendment arrangement, I figured their chronological plan was to:

1. Get Spiro Agnew out of office.
2. Replace him with Gerald Ford.
3. Get me out of office.
4. Replace me with Ford.
5. Replace Ford (as vice president) with Rockefeller.
6. Knock off Ford before the election by Squeaky Fromme, Sara Jane Moore, whoever.
7. Replace Ford again with Rockefeller, declare martial law, and cancel the election.

Alternatively, this could be done by killing Jimmy Carter before the inauguration.

Now I realize how naïve I was. Granted, Carter is more progressive than I am — after all, politics is the art of finding a balance between the status quo and the force of evolution — but it became crystal clear to me that he had made some kind of deal. The intelligence-gathering system knew about G. Harrold Carswell's tragic gay problem. Now, *he* would have been a fine prospect for blackmail: "We have this photo of you and a friend in the men's room, Justice Carswell, but don't worry, we won't leak it." I wonder, if I had been successful in appointing him to the Supreme Court, how would he have voted on the constitutionality of entrapping homosexuals? Anyway, my suspicions were aroused when it did not come out in the media until *after* the election — immediately before Carter's inauguration when it was too late to do us any good — that his son Jack had been discharged from the Navy because of marijuana.

Our hammer over George McGovern's head in 1972 was that his daughter had been hospitalized for an LSD freakout. We never had to resort to using that particular bit of intelligence, however, despite the fact that it was *we* who had arranged for her to be "dosed" in the first place.

WOODWARD AND BERNSTEIN WERE NOT the only ones with reliable sources. According to one of my contacts in the intelligence community, the Democrats' first choice for a presidential candidate in the 1976 elections was a Southern governor — Askew of Florida — but their analysts calculated that Jimmy Carter's resemblance to Howdy Doody would provide a subconscious association in the minds of voters who were weaned on that folksy puppet.

What the American public does not realize is the impact of the long-range planning that goes on in think tanks such as Stanford Research, the Rand Corporation, and the Hudson Institute. They are already beginning to orchestrate the Bimillennium, the 2,000th birthday of Christ. The function of Jimmy Carter — with all his religiosity and his talk about not living in sin — is to provide an opening wedge for the Christianization of the United States. The arms manufacturers would be well pleased by a repeat performance of the Crusades. After those Korean bribes via Reverend Moon's Unification Church and the brainwashing of the Moonies, they'll finally figure it's time to make Christ an *American* again.

Incidentally, Billy Graham recently tried to convert me, the same way he did with that professional gangster, Mickey Cohen. "Think what it would be like," he said, "if you were to go on an evangelistic tour with Eldridge Cleaver and Colonel Sanders."

"You mean the Kentucky Fried Chicken guy?"

"Yes, he has been born again, too."

"No, thank you, Billy, I seem to have found serenity in my own way."

I truly have been able to gain real humility now that Chuck Colson and Susan Atkins are saying the same things about Jesus Christ that they were once saying about myself and Charles Manson, respectively.

HISTORY IS AN UNENDING CONVEYOR BELT that either perpetuates or corrects the inaccuracies of the past.

Therefore, the first thing I wish to point out, concerning that infamous 18-and-a-half-minute gap in the White House tape of June 20, 1972, is that it actually lasted only 18-and-a-quarter minutes. At 10:30 that morning, John Ehrlichman was in my office. We did not discuss Watergate. Before leaving, however, he handed me two sealed envelopes. One contained a gram of cocaine; the other contained a preliminary report on the surveillance of Woodward and Bernstein. This task had been assigned to Tony Ulasewicz immediately after their first story on the break-in was published in *The Washington Post*.

It was strange. Ehrlichman's own first assignment had been to spy on the Nelson Rockefeller people for us during the 1960 campaign, and now he had his own chain of command. I have noticed that Ehrlichman's brow has become more knitted as he has advanced in his career. When he left, I opened the sealed envelope and read the report. It was brief:

Bernstein, Carl: Heavy pot smoker. Living apart from his wife. Began affair with Nora Ephron, *Esquire* columnist, in New York while her husband, Dan Greenburg, book author, was at EST, Erhard Seminar Training.

Woodward, Bob: A loner. Clean as a hound's tooth. So far.

Then I began to "chop the coke," as they say, with a razor blade. When Bob Haldeman entered, we each took a couple of snorts. Haldeman was my Sherman Adams. I had always felt I could depend on him. We were discussing whether my itinerary for an upcoming trip to the West Coast might include Ely, Nevada, which was the birthplace of Mrs. Nixon.

"That's perfect," Haldeman said. "We need anything we can get, PR-wise."

"But you know something, Bob? It's all image."

"Well, that is precisely the *purpose* of public relations."

"No, I mean my so-called marriage is all image. Pat and I have not, you know, slept together for many years. My God, I was the President of the United States, and I couldn't even get laid by my own wife."

"Sir, you don't really want to talk about this —"

"And I'll tell you where it started. During the Cuban Crisis in October '62. Boy, Kennedy sure won a helluva lot of points on that one. And it could've been *me* confronting Khrushchev. I mean a real international shootdown, not just waving my finger at him in Safire's goddamn make-shift kitchen."

"That would have been the logical extension of your Russian trip."

"I tell you, the unspeakable frustration of not being in a position to negotiate that missile thing. I just couldn't get it up for Pat, plus the pressure of the California campaign was going on then, too. And after we lost that election, she started talking about a divorce. We compromised with separate bedrooms."

Suddenly I stood up, walked around my desk to where Haldeman was sitting, and I ran my hand back and forth across the top of his crewcut. I am not very physically demonstrative, but I had always wanted to do that. Still, this was almost a spontaneous gesture.

"You stuck by me, Bob," I said while rubbing his hair. "Finch dropped out, but you ..."

And I began weeping uncontrollably.

"Sir, is there anything I can do?"

Between sobs I blurted out, "Oh, sure" — I certainly did not intend for this to be taken literally — "Why don't you try sucking my cock? Maybe *that'll* help."

To my utter astonishment, Haldeman unzipped my fly and proceeded with what can only be described as extreme efficiency. The whole thing could not have taken more than five minutes from beginning to end. He must have had some practice during his old prep-school days. Neither of us said a word — before, during, or after.

This misunderstanding was comparable to the time that Jeb Magruder remarked how convenient it would be if we could get rid of Jack Anderson, and G. Gordon Liddy assumed that was a direct order and rushed out to accomplish the act. If Liddy had not blabbed his "assignment" to an aide in the corridor, Anderson might not be alive today.

As for my own motivation, here was an experience not of homosexuality but of power. I realized that if I could order the Pentagon to bomb Cambodia, it was of no great consequence that I was now merely permitting my chief of staff to perform fellatio on me. In fact, I was fully cognizant of what an honor it must have been for him.

When the incident was over, I simply returned to my desk, and although the tension of vulnerability was still in the air, we resumed our discussion as if nothing had occurred.

"Now," I said in a normal tone of voice, "what's on the agenda?"

"Sir," Haldeman began, "on this Watergate problem, it would be advantageous to us if any similar activity on the part of the Democrats could be leaked to the media."

"Well, Hoover once told me — this was right after we won in '68 — he said that within the previous month, LBJ had the FBI put the bug on Agnew and me. Ramsey Clark was attorney general then, but he never authorized it, so that was an *illegal* wiretap."

"Perfect. We start with Lyndon Johnson and work our way back."

"But no, on second thought, the LBJ tap would open up the whole Dragon Lady can of beans. I mean that was the goddamn *excuse* they had for spying on us."

Then Haldeman delivered a resounding pep talk — when he lets loose, he can be an emotional marvel — about the importance of launching a counterattack against our enemies.

I must say at this point that Rose Mary Woods deserves a Medal of Honor for the way she was willing to humiliate herself by taking full blame for accidentally erasing those first five minutes rather than stand by while my public image was being destroyed.

Moreover, when General Alexander Haig learned from Haldeman's notes that during those additional thirteen-and-a-quarter-minutes there was a discussion of how to deal with Watergate, thereby proving that I was involved in the cover-up only three days after the break-in, Haig attributed the erasure to "sinister forces." He said this under oath in Judge John Sirica's courtroom.

Now *that* is loyalty above and beyond the call of duty.

IN RETROSPECT, I realize that H.R. Haldeman was part of the plot against me all along, always trying to ingratiate himself — anything to impress me — when actually he was trying to hurt my political career. Not that he was against me personally; I was just his particular assignment as part of an overall plan "to destroy," in the words of Frank Sturgis, "the office of the presidency."

Haldeman was a saboteur in the guise of a sycophant. In 1967, when he was a vice president at the J. Walter Thompson advertising agency, he sent me a long memo on how I could use the media in my '68 campaign. I have since learned that during World War II, various corporations — Standard Oil, Wrigley Chewing Gum, Paramount Pictures — lent their services to the Office of Strategic Services, which later became the CIA. The Thompson Agency supplied Kenneth Hinks to be chief of the OSS planning staff. One of Haldeman's predecessors, Richard de Rochemont, a vice president of J. Walter Thompson, was offered a position with the Secret Intelligence Branch of the OSS. Another

Thompson official, Donald Coster, stayed on with the CIA in South Vietnam from 1959 to 1962.

That's when Haldeman really latched on to me, in the '62 campaign. And when we lost, it was Haldeman who persuaded me to make a public fool of myself with that godawful "You won't have Nixon to kick around anymore" press conference. It was Haldeman in 1972 who acted as a double agent and conspired with Dick Tuck to have all those Chinese fortune cookies contain the same message: "What about the Howard Hughes loan?" And it was Haldeman who consciously sabotaged the research on the Hiss chapter in *Six Crises*.

On one occasion, I was meeting with a group of blind veterans in the Oval Office. I wanted to display my empathy with them, so I began describing the Presidential Seal, which was woven into the carpet we happened to be standing on. A blind veteran got down on his knees and started feeling that design with his hands. I closed my eyes and proceeded to do the same. It was perhaps the most spontaneous gesture of my life, although I must admit I was grateful to hear the sound of cameras whirring. I was pleased that this scene of my true humanity was being recorded for posterity. But Haldeman ordered an embargo on that photograph, ostensibly to protect the dignity of my image, because the president should never be seen in a kneeling position.

Even a year after he resigned, there he was, old faithful Bob Haldeman, backstage with me at the Grand Ole Opry in Nashville. He chided Johnny Cash for that time he refused to sing "Welfare Cadillac" at the White House, and Cash now replied, "Should I do it tonight and dedicate the song to you now that *you're* on welfare?"

Haldeman did not appreciate the humor in that. He was too preoccupied with the betrayal of me that he had in mind. He handed me a yellow yo-yo and said, "This will really please the crowd. It's an official Roy Acuff model." I put the yo-yo in my pocket. Haldeman did not mention that the string had been loosened at the bottom, so when I was onstage and flung that yo-yo down, it just *stayed* there. Once again, Haldeman had transformed the president into an asshole.

It was Haldeman who had urged me to install the White House taping system. It was Haldeman who hired Alexander Butterfield, who testified to the whole world about the tapes and told the FBI about E. Howard Hunt. Butterfield brought in Al Wong to set up the system and check it every day. And it was Wong who brought James McCord onto the team. It all seems so obvious now.

One thing about Gerald Ford, though: He keeps his promises — not only to pardon me, but also his promise to fire Alexander Butterfield, even though Ford was actually grateful to him. As for me, I should have listened to L. Patrick Gray when he warned me, "People on your staff are trying to mortally wound you."

My wife, Pat, has sworn to me that she never told anyone about our marital difficulties, and, of course, I believe her, so the leak to Woodward and Bernstein could *only* have come from Haldeman. On top of all his other betrayals, he must have been Deep Throat, too.

THERE WAS ONE PLAN of the White House Plumbers that never came to fruition. It involved the theft of Patricia Ellsberg's dental records. This was my own idea — not Haldeman's, not Hunt's, not Liddy's — *they* were satisfied with obtaining the records of Daniel Ellsberg's psychiatrist.

But I remembered that the first time Alger Hiss confronted Whittaker Chambers, he requested to see his *teeth*. Hiss explained to me that he suspected Chambers might be someone he had known years before, and he wanted to see his teeth to make sure.

Well, that recollection inspired me. We were able to obtain the dental records of Ellsberg's wife, all right, but did not have the opportunity to use them in helping to prove that she was guilty of espionage. I could not imagine exactly how we were going to achieve this, but I did know that, *whatever*, it would be accepted by the public simply because the charge itself was so "off the wall."

How odd that Whittaker Chambers, the dignified translator of *Bambi*, had been asked to publicly show his teeth as if he were some kind of stud at a horse show. I have never been able to forget that moment.

THE PARADOX OF OUR NATION is that we turn our vices into virtues. As the truth about political assassinations — from Malcolm X to Mrs. Dorothy Hunt — finally begins to emerge, we may truthfully say, "Only in America does there exist the freedom to reveal how insidious we have been, and then to continue in our insidious way with an even more determined spirit."

I still believe that the United States is the greatest country in the world. It is also the greatest show on Earth.

I once had a vision of myself leaving Washington the way Jimmy Durante used to end his TV program, standing in a spotlight and bowing gracefully to the audience, then walking back a few steps into another spotlight, bowing again, and so on. Instead, I ended up sounding as helpless as Hal the Computer in the movie *2001*, unable to control my own memory banks.

My consolation for this personal tragedy is summed up in Jeane Dixon's prediction: "Historians yet unborn are going to take the facts, and Richard Nixon will go down as a great President. They're going to find that the price the world is paying for trying to discredit Nixon is going to be that we'll practically lose our freedom."

In the meantime, I am, at long last, completely at peace with myself. It has been worth all the struggle.

POSTSCRIPT

AFTER "A SNEAK PREVIEW OF RICHARD NIXON'S MEMOIR" was published, syndicated columnist Liz Smith — who hadn't seen that piece — wrote that H.R. Haldeman had been in the Oval Office with Nixon, and that Nixon's trousers were down to his ankles. Hoping to smoke out the truth, I retyped one page of the manuscript, inserting a phrase (shown in italics) in this sentence: "When the incident was over, I simply returned to my desk, and although the tension of vulnerability was still in the air *and my trousers were still around my ankles*, we resumed our discussion as if nothing had occurred." I then photocopied the manuscript and sent it to Liz Smith. I had assumed she would check with her source. Instead, she wrote in her column that she had been fooled by *me*, implying that her source had based that revelation on my article. Somehow my hoax on Liz Smith backfired. I had become a victim of my own satirical prophecy.

Additionally, in 1978, Haldeman in his book, *The Ends of Power*, revealed that Nixon used code words when talking about the murder of President

Kennedy. Haldeman said that Nixon always referred to the assassination as "the Bay of Pigs."

And, on May 5, 1977, the *Houston Post* published a UPI dispatch that stated:

> Watergate burglar Frank Sturgis said Wednesday that the CIA planned the break-in because high officials felt Richard Nixon was becoming too powerful and was overly interested in the assassination of John Kennedy ... "Several times the President asked CIA director Richard Helms for the files on the Kennedy assassination, but Helms refused to give them to him, refused a direct order from the President," Sturgis said. "I believe Nixon would have uncovered the true facts in the assassination of President Kennedy and that would have taken off the heat in Watergate. Because Nixon wanted files, the CIA felt they had to get rid of him." Asked if Nixon ever was in danger, Sturgis replied, "Yes, absolutely. Nixon was lucky he wasn't killed — assassinated like President Kennedy."

One other thing. In "A Sneak Preview of Richard Nixon's Memoir," originally published in 1976, I had Nixon insisting that Watergate was a setup to get rid of him as president. About a decade later, Tricky Dick made that exact same claim on a network television interview.

Satirical prophecy in action.

PAUL KRASSNER

Why I Leaked the Anita Hill Affidavit

I SHALL IDENTIFY MYSELF only as a female aide to a Republican senator. It is also relevant that I have long nurtured a keen interest in psycho-history, the process by which a nation's direction is interpreted as an extension of the psychological makeup of those individuals who govern it.

Without going into specific detail, let me simply state that on October 5, 1991, I happened to hear part of a conversation among Judge — now Supreme Court Justice — Clarence Thomas, Senator Orrin Hatch, and Senator Alan Simpson. The three were meeting informally one week after the Judiciary Committee voted, first 7–7, then 13–1, to recommend the confirmation of Judge Thomas, and one day after the full Senate indicated that he *would* be confirmed.

The conversation I happened to hear had to do with those charges brought by Anita Hill and ignored by the members of the committee, both Democratic and Republican. At that point in time I still thought this was an appropriate response, because the alternative would have been to hold an executive session, and Judge Thomas would then have had no practical choice but to resort to heavy denial. Now, however, these men were, in a jocular fashion, acknowledging the truth of what would turn out to be Professor Hill's allegations.

Senator Simpson was saying, "Y'know, Clarence, I've seen some pretty raunchy porno movies in my time, but I never did see one where a lady was having sex with an *animal*."

"I'll never forget it," Judge Thomas replied in his riveting sonorous tone. "They were in a barn. Except that the inside of the barn was like a theater."

Senator Hatch interjected, "Summer stock, eh? No pun intended."

"There was a stage at one end," Judge Thomas continued his description, "and the stage was facing rows and rows of wooden folding chairs. There were haystacks piled up on the stage, and in front of the haystacks there was a beautiful, buxom, blonde woman — and a donkey. Well, the woman began disrobing, and she started stroking the donkey to arousal."

"Doesn't sound at all sleazy to me," Senator Simpson said.

"Actually, it had Beethoven piano sonatas playing in the background," Judge Thomas said. "Well, when the woman was fully disrobed and the donkey was fully aroused, they began copulating, right there in front of those haystacks on the stage of that barn. Slow and sensual. Then bumping and grinding away, accompanied by passionate moans and wild braying. You've never seen a sight like this, I promise. And then the camera panned slowly toward the audience ... and the audience consisted entirely of *donkeys*."

The Senate office shook with raucous laughter, especially that of Judge Thomas. His booming guffaws rang like huge gongs in a church belfry. And, I must admit, I had to suppress my own laughter. I had been totally caught by surprise, but I appreciated getting the insight. Homo sapiens is, in reality, the only species that has a need for pornography.

When the group's laughter finally began to simmer down, Senator Hatch said, "I suppose that movie was made to satisfy the demands of the animal rights people."

"That's correct," Senator Simpson added. "Saving animals' lives is no longer enough. They need *culture*."

I felt like I was imprisoned in the boys' locker room, but I was getting ready to force myself to leave anyway, and it would have ended right there for me if the subject matter hadn't returned to Anita Hill.

"I'm glad nobody considered calling *her* to testify against me, even for a closed-door session," Judge Thomas said. "But you fellas will really love this. Anita Hill was a very opinionated young lady. Actually, she and I once had an *extremely* animated discussion on the decriminalization of abortion. Can you imagine what the Democrats would've done with *that*?"

And that was the precise instant I made the decision to leak Professor Hill's statement to the press. Although I have constantly been sexually *hassled*, I have never really been harassed in the *legal* sense of the word. However, I *have* had an abortion, and I was totally outraged by the blatant hypocrisy I'd overheard. I had never leaked a document before, but my anger overshadowed my fear.

I chose Nina Totenberg because I had come to trust her reporting about the Supreme Court on National Public Radio. I honestly had no idea what leaking the affidavit would accomplish. I certainly did not envision that it would literally embarrass the Senate into delaying the vote until public hearings were held, though that probably was my secret desire.

But Judge Thomas *testified under oath* that he had never discussed the subject of abortion. However, in response to a question by Senator Hank Brown, Professor Hill testified that she had disagreed with Judge Thomas in a discussion about *Roe v. Wade*. Unfortunately, then-Senator Joseph Biden quickly interrupted her.

"That is not the subject of these hearings," he said.

Personally, I feel quite disappointed about that particular aspect of the testimony, but I have not the slightest regret over leaking Anita Hill's affidavit, and I would gladly do it all over again.

I certainly set a higher moral standard for myself than did the staffer for Senator John Danforth who wrote Judge Thomas's statement that began, "Nobody helped me with this."

PAUL KRASSNER

President Clinton's
Private Confession

The following is a leaked transcript of a closed-door, secretly taped prayer breakfast that Bill Clinton hosted for a group of religious leaders after the impeachment trial failed to remove him from office.

GENTLEMEN — and lady (I guess you must be the Episcopalian) — thank you for being here. It's too bad Reverend Moon isn't among us this morning, so he could perform a mass impeachment of all the senators who swore under oath that they would be impartial. But seriously, folks, I'd like to begin with an epiphany I had yesterday, one that truly humbled me. Strangely enough, it happened while I was watching *The Roseanne Show*. I had never seen it before, but she was interviewing Paula Jones, and, as my mother used to say, curiosity got the best of me.

Ms. Jones was telling Roseanne about the first time she saw me in that hotel. She was working at the courtesy booth for the governors' conference. She described me as funny-looking, the way my hair was styled, being overweight, how my suit was out of fashion and didn't fit. So, she was sitting at the registration desk with her girlfriend, pointing at me and giggling. Somehow, I perceived her through the filter of arrogance that people with power develop, and I assumed that she was giving me a come-hither look. That simple misperception is what triggered this whole long ordeal. I took her willingness for granted.

It was different with Monica Lewinsky. I mean to say, she flashed the strap of her thong underwear — it made my heart go *thump* — and, you know, I'm a prisoner at the White House. I can't go to a motel, but Monica appeared like a gift from Heaven, and I succumbed to temptation. I was fully cognizant that this was a very delicate situation — I even asked for permission to kiss her — yet I blocked out my foresight. Way back in college, when I tried to avoid military service, I was already thinking ahead to campaigning for president, but now I found myself ignoring the likelihood that Monica would not keep our relationship a secret.

I certainly didn't consider the possibility that she would become so seriously involved with me. It was embarrassing to hear the tape that Linda Tripp made, where Monica told her what she had said to me on the phone: "I love you, Butthead." I remember thinking when it happened, "Hey, I'm the president of the United States, you can't call me Butthead." However, I immediately decided to treat the situation with humor. But she hung up before I could say, "I love you, Beavis."

Surprisingly, I was *not* embarrassed about the infamous cigar incident. I felt that it had been an act of restraint from *actual* intercourse. Kind of tender and playful. Now, if it had been a Cuban cigar, *that* would have been illegal. But this was not the sort of intimacy that I would have felt comfortable performing with the First Lady. Hillary and I are really close, but, as I'm sure you understand, no cigar.

For her, the most revealing thing in *The Starr Report* is Monica's fantasy about our — Monica and me — being together more often when I'll be out of office; where she quotes me as saying, "I might be alone in three years." Hillary was furious, not only because it had provided a young intern with false encouragement, but also because it implied that we — Hillary and me — don't have sex, and she felt it divulged our agreement that if we were to separate, it would not occur before we left the White House.

For me, the most revealing section — in that same section of the report — is Monica's testimony that I jokingly said, "Well, what are we going to do when I'm 75, and I have to pee 25 times a day?" True, I did say that, but I really *wasn't* joking. In fact, it was my fear of old age that kept drawing me to Monica. She was my direct link to youth. So, I was being *literal* about peeing 25 times a day when I'm 75. Hell, I drink at least eight glasses of water a day *now* — just like I'm supposed to, for my health — but then I have to pee at least eight times a day. Ironically, the TV commercials warn that if you have to pee eight times in 24 hours, it's a symptom of an overactive bladder.

Indeed, irony has permeated this long-running scandal, beginning to end. It was ironic that my sexual appetite helped put me in office — the Gennifer Flowers allegation originally placed me in the media spotlight — and it was my sexual appetite that almost tossed me out of that same office. And it's ironic that, although Kathleen Willey *enjoyed* our brief encounter, to prove it we would have had to resort to obtaining testimony from her confidant, the wonderful Linda Tripp.

Now, there are things that I've done as president of which I'm *truly* ashamed. Even before my inauguration, I made it a point to stop in Arkansas to oversee the execution of a mentally retarded prisoner. At his last meal, he said he'd wait to have his dessert, a slice of pecan pie, until after the execution — that's how much he understood what was going on. I'm ashamed of *under*-protecting the rights of gays and over-protecting children from the internet. I'm ashamed of being *against* medical marijuana and for requiring a urine test as a prerequisite to obtaining a driver's license. I'm ashamed of bombing Iraq, Afghanistan, and Sudan. I'm ashamed of *in*creasing the military budget and *de*creasing the welfare budget. I'm ashamed of dropping cluster bombs and continuing to plant land mines.

But the Republicans didn't dare attack me for any of those positions because those are *their* positions, too.

I'll tell you how I survived this past year, how I maintained such high approval ratings, while Newt Gingrich fell by the wayside. How I managed, in short, to remain president. It was partly the state of the economy, and it was partly the state of the culture. Pornography is a 20-billion-dollar-a-year business in this country. Steven Spielberg told me that's more than Hollywood's entire domestic box-office receipts. Because it's what the American public *wants*. And the TV networks exploit that dirty little secret. It's why sweeps weeks are always so raunchy. So, then, what *I* did wasn't considered such a big deal after all.

Mainly, though, I have survived because, one sunny afternoon, Monica was positioning herself on the carpet under my desk in the Oval Office *while* I was on the phone with Benjamin Netanyahu. I was telling him about the time that Monica was performing oral sex on me while Yasser Arafat was waiting in the Rose Garden for our appointment. I *didn't* tell Netanyahu that she was just about to perform the same act on me while I was on the phone with *him*. Anyway, at that point, Monica found a big old dusty Mason jar under my desk. There was a label on the side which read, "Property of Ronald Reagan."

That Mason jar was filled with Teflon, and I have rubbed it on myself every day since.

I began my talk this morning with an epiphany, and I'd like to end with another. This epiphany also occurred while I was watching television — *Larry King Live* — and, once again, Paula Jones was the guest. At one point she said, "I've never voted in my life." And I was astounded. Then she said, "I'm so apolitical, it's unreal." And I realized what an incredibly great country America really is, that somebody who was just a plain citizen, who was never even *interested* in politics — somebody who had never even *voted* for a president — had nearly succeeded in toppling one.

Well, this has been a catharsis for me. I just want to say once more how much I appreciate your presence here. And finally, I would like to share with you a little witticism that Hillary came up with last night, an idea for what my epitaph should be: "Here lies Bill Clinton, but that depends on what you mean by lies." Isn't she wonderful?

Oh, and one more thing. Now listen carefully. I did *not* have sexual assault with that woman, Ms. Broaddrick. I'll be honest with you, it may have been *rough* sex, but it was totally consensual. That, I can guarantee. Thank you, and God bless you all.

The Autobiography of
Monica Lewinsky

The following is an exclusive excerpt from an autobiography-in-progress by Monica Lewinsky, titled Going Down in History. *The manuscript was leaked to* The Realist *by, of course, a reliable source.*

I AM NOT AN AIRHEAD. I'm a victim, partly of my own making. And mostly, I'm a political pawn of the spin doctors. There are several books being written about the White House scandal, but only a few individuals know what really happened, and only I know who *I* really am, which is why I have decided to write this book. I would write it even if I didn't need the money for legal expenses. My life may be ruined — at least my reputation will be forever tainted — but the truth must be told.

I don't like being a one-dimensional symbol. If anybody were to take a free-association test, the psychiatrist would say "Monica Lewinsky," and the patient would immediately respond "Oral sex." Maybe soon my name will be in a crossword puzzle — the clue: eight letters across — and the correct word will be "fellatio."

Back home in Brentwood, I've been listening to talk radio a lot. Ronn Owens on KABC had listeners phone in with nothing but jokes about me for a solid hour. First, he warned the audience that if they were easily offended, they should tune out. I have never felt so objectified in my life, and yet, at the same time, I found the program quite riveting.

The best call came from a 9-year-old who said, "Bill Clinton violated the Eleventh Commandment: Thou shalt not put thy rod in thy staff." The worst call came from a man who asked, "What do the *Titanic* and

Monica Lewinsky have in common?" The answer was, "They both have dead seamen (semen) floating in the hull."

And remember that awful piece of gossip — the one Lucianne Goldberg initiated in order to get attention from the press for *her* — that I kept a blue dress stained with Clinton's dried ejaculation as a souvenir? Well, Jonathon Brandmeier on KLSX invited listeners to call in and suggest euphemisms for presidential semen. My favorite was "Bubba butter." Apparently, my role is to serve as a vehicle for the destruction of taboos.

I have also become an automatic comedy reference. So, to Jay Leno, David Letterman, and Conan O'Brien, I'm very useful in punch lines. To *Saturday Night Live*, I'm just a character in their sketches, and never without that beret from my famous hugging-Bill TV footage. But I did think it was hilarious to cast John Goodman in drag as Linda Tripp. That cheered me up. I've been simultaneously depressed, scared, and, strangely enough, exhilarated.

As an instant celebrity, I've learned that everybody always sees everybody else through their own particular filters. Democrats, Republicans, men, women, the other interns — all perceive me subjectively. For a manufacturer of novelty items, I was simply a disembodied inspiration for the marketing of "Presidential Kneepads." And for *Penthouse* magazine, I would only be considered their next notorious masturbation enhancer.

In the eyes of the media — from NBC News to Nightline, from *Time* magazine to *People*, from *The New York Times* to the *National Enquirer*, from *The Washington Post* to *Entertainment Tonight* — I am purely a commodity. Naturally, I believe in the First Amendment, so I'm against censorship. All I'm saying is that while America is achieving adolescence publicly, the tabloids have won the war.

The battleground is like an ongoing contemporary Shakespearean tragicomedy, but there is no script, there is no producer, there is no director. There is only the process of everyone's karma interacting. I recall the words of Terence McKenna when he was a guest lecturer at Lewis and Clark. He said, "Chaos is the tail that wags the dog."

Damage control is the name of the game. It was Dick Morris who advised Clinton to get a dog. Buddy, huh? They should've named him Photo Op. It was also Dick Morris who suggested taping that ostensibly candid scene of the First Couple dancing on the beach. And I would bet my entire book advance that both Hillary and Bill *knew ahead of time* that

Dick Morris was going to release a trial balloon that *if* the rumor about Hillary being a lesbian were true, *then* it would be perfectly reasonable that her husband would need to seek sexual gratification elsewhere.

In fact, the reason I think that Clinton's approval ratings have been so high is because people can *identify* with him fooling around. I mean, when Jimmy Carter admitted that he had lust in his heart, it was the adultery vote that helped get him elected. And that was only lust in his *heart*. Bill Clinton is an *activist*.

I've been reading a book, *Spin Cycle* by Howard Kurtz, and there's a story in there about that time in 1996 when the president said that he "might like to date" a shapely 500-year-old mummy whose remains were on display at the National Geographic Society. Later, chatting after a few cocktails, Press Secretary Mike McCurry told a dozen journalists on the press plane that he could understand Clinton's remark. "Compared to that mummy he's been fucking," McCurry chuckled, "why not?" Poor Hillary.

Without bothering to mention that it was off the record, McCurry assumed his joke wouldn't be reported, and it wasn't — until that book. Washington is a very cynical place. Everything is stated carefully and deliberately, with the *intention* that it will be repeated. When McCurry told the *Chicago Tribune* in an interview that Clinton's relationship with *me* could turn out to have been "complicated," it was no slip of the tongue. He was fully aware that his observation would appear in print.

Unlike Richard Nixon, who never dreamed that *his* words would be published in a book. In *Abuse of Power: The New Nixon Tapes*, edited by Stanley Kutler, Nixon is quoted from one of his tapes as saying, "Bob [Haldeman], please get me the names of the Jews, you know, the big Jewish contributors of the Democrats.... Could we please investigate some of the cocksuckers?"

My mom is a member of the Book of the Month Club, and in their brochure, they printed it "c*cks*ck*rs." Anyhoo, that's how everybody thinks of *me* now. I'm the nation's official c*cks*ck*r laureate.

The image of me on my knees giving head to the president has become a cultural icon. The irony is that *it never happened*. When Wolf Blitzer from CNN asked Clinton at a press conference what he would like to say to me, Clinton smiled and said, "That's good, that's good" — referring sarcastically to the *question* — but it was extremely ironic, because that's *exactly* what I *imagined* he *did* say to me: "That's good, that's good." And I replied, "I gave you a blowjob, but I didn't swallow." He started laughing hysterically, just like that time he did with Boris Yeltsin. Bill liked my sense of humor. That's why we went from flirtation to friendship.

However, the reason I visited the White House 37 times was not for Bill — it was to be with Hillary — *she* was the one who desired me physically. The rumor about her being a lesbian was *true*. And so, my relationship with Bill *was* complicated. He just acted as a middleman for Hillary, and now, by denying an affair with *me*, he's telling the truth *and* taking the fall for *her*. In that sense, he's an incredibly loyal husband. Despite what the public may think, Bill is absolutely devoted to Hillary.

Everybody is watching so closely for him to commit the next indiscretion, but it would have to be with somebody he can *totally* trust, somebody who could suck the leader of the Western World's dick and *not* confide to a friend, or to somebody who *pretended* to be a friend. So, for a while, Bill is left with only Buddy's tongue for sexual companionship. At least, Buddy won't lick and tell. And if I know my president, while Buddy is pleasuring him, Clinton will fantasize that it's a *female* dog.

Subcultures

And Whose Little Monkey Are You?

SOMETIMES I THINK I'M DREAMING when I read the news. But there are places where the inhabitants have never seen a magazine or a newspaper, and it is simply not a part of their psyche to dream about lines of type. In a spurt of generosity, the United States shipped surplus battery-operated TV sets across the sea to one group of islands in the Pacific Ocean, so that those natives could pass directly from a preliterate society to a post-literate society without having to read a single book in the process.

They watched in amazement as so-called psychic Uri Geller bent forks on *The Merv Griffin Show*. The strange thing was that even though Geller accomplished this feat by trickery, there were young children back in America who hadn't yet been taught about the self-fulfilling rules of 20th-century physics, and to their parents' dismay, *they* were able to bend various kitchen utensils by means of sheer willpower.

AS MORE AND MORE deadly conflicts around the world continue to escalate, more and more people are saying, "Boy, the shit's really gonna hit the fan now." That phrase, incidentally, did not come into the language until after there was electricity. People who say that are not referring to a lovely Japanese lithograph showing a kimono-clad woman whose long shiny black hair is twisted up into a bun and who is coquettishly providing her own personal breeze with a colorful rice-paper fan. Then *splat!* — right in her porcelain-like face. So, no, it has to be an *electric* fan, which revolves so fast it protects you from the shit — or spreads it, depending which side you're on — or what's a fan *for*?

Meanwhile, even as all that shit is hitting all those fans, the laxative industry continues to blossom. New brand names are constantly competing in the open marketplace. Ex-Lax has even come out with a "milder" version for women — certainly an indication of rampant male chauvinism in their Research and Development section. What's the implication of this trend? Do females have different digestive systems than males? Is it perfectly acceptable for macho men to have chocolate-covered sandpaper coursing through their intestinal tracts?

And yet credit must also be given to those friendly folks at Ex-Lax. They were the very first sponsor on television to include a sign-language translation of a commercial — a long-overdue service for the constipated hearing-impaired. Indeed, this had been an early demand of the Deaf Liberation Front. You've probably seen their frontline members on the street and in airports, selling little cards with the sign-language alphabet. Some have been getting arrested for being deaf without a license. Naturally, the police recite their Miranda rights, shouting, "*You have the right to remain silent!*"

Anyway, this particular Ex-Lax commercial features a pleasant, matronly woman reminiscing through her family photo album while a young fellow in the corner of the screen ostensibly translates the message into sign language. Actually, he can say whatever he wants. Nobody monitors his translation. He can indulge in private jokes for all the deaf viewers, and only they will know.

The matronly woman in the Ex-Lax commercial says: "Thank God my family is *normal*." The young fellow shifts the emphasis slightly in his translation: "Thank God *her* family is normal." She continues: "Of course, once in a while somebody in our family will be troubled by irregularity." He translates: "No shit." She concludes: "So then we do what we've done in our family for generations — we turn to an old friend, Ex-Lax." He translates: "Jimmy Hoffa knows too much."

And while the hearing-impaired at home giggle at this mistranslation, all over the globe the shit continues to hit the fans.

❋ ❋ ❋

THESE ARE ROUGH TIMES, but it's extremely important to develop a sense of optimism. The *Bulletin of the Atomic Scientists* periodically updates a clock on their cover to indicate how close we're moving toward nuclear war. Recently, they moved it from four minutes to midnight to three minutes to midnight, with midnight representing total annihilation. I don't know exactly what their time scale is — whether one minute represents a month or a year or a decade — but, whichever, they're saying that we are all now only three minutes away from the ultimate holocaust.

That's the bad news.

The good news is that atomic scientists are just as fucked up as the rest of us. They overeat, they forget to floss, they don't have time for serial orgasms, or they suffer from premature ejaculations, and they set their clocks fifteen minutes ahead so that if they need to mail a letter by 6:00, and their clock says it's 6:10, it means they still have five minutes to get to the mailbox. So that clock on the cover of the *Bulletin of Atomic Scientists* is fifteen minutes fast. We don't have just three minutes till doomsday; we have *eighteen* minutes.

LIFE REMAINS PEACEFUL on a certain island off the coast of Japan. Here, humans and animals live in peace and harmony.

There are monkeys who for eons have subsisted entirely on sweet potatoes. They would pick the sweet potatoes right out of the dirt in which they grow — eating them, dirt and all. This is the way they have always done it. But one day, for whatever mysterious reason, an individual young female monkey carried her sweet potato to the shore, washed the dirt off in the ocean, and proceeded to eat the sweet potato.

Who knows why it was this particular monkey? Any explanation will suffice. Maybe she was an Aries, with a strong pioneer spirit. At any rate, once this monkey broke the ice, other monkeys began to wash the dirt off their sweet potatoes before they ate them. But only the young monkeys.

It was not until the 100th young monkey had washed the dirt off a sweet potato in the ocean — not exactly the 100th; it could've been the 93rd or the 108th; the 100th monkey is merely a metaphor for reaching critical mass — but not until then did the first *adult* monkey wash the dirt off a sweet potato. This was a case of reverse generational influence.

And then *other* adult monkeys started to imitate this behavior. Washing the dirt off sweet potatoes even began to occur on adjoining islands, indicating that there was some kind of psychic communication in the air.

Now, how can this living New Age parable be applied to *human* behavior? Well, whatever you do personally to help further the cause of justice and the pursuit of ecstasy, even though you might get discouraged, you must always remember that you might be the one who turns the tide — you have to act as though *you* are the 100th monkey — and this gives us reason to hope.

That's the good news.

The bad news is, those monkeys *needed* that dirt in their diet for roughage. So now there were all these monkeys on this island who weren't able to shit.

But it just so happened that this was one of the islands where we shipped our surplus TV sets. Across the island, monkeys were gathered around those TV sets, all watching a program that was sponsored by Ex-Lax. Moreover, here was that commercial with the sign-language translation. And, fortuitously enough, these monkeys had relatives trained at Stanford University, where they learned how to communicate in sign language, and had been returned to the island to teach others of their species how to sign.

That's the good news.

The bad news is that this was the Ex-Lax commercial where the brand name of the product was not translated. The message in sign language was "Jimmy Hoffa knows too much." These monkeys — serving as shock troops of the Deaf Liberation Front — took that private joke to be their marching orders. So, even though you may have heard the propaganda that Hoffa was killed because he was prepared to speak out about the alliance between military intelligence and organized crime, the truth is that he was eaten to death by hordes of constipated monkeys.

The good news is, they washed the dirt off him first.

IT IS SEVERAL YEARS later now. Things have returned to normal.

The monkeys on those islands off the coast of Japan still watch TV, but they no longer wash the dirt off their sweet potatoes, and they are just as regular in their defecation as they used to be.

But in America, those children who once bent kitchen utensils to the dismay of their parents have grown up. One such young man now works on the assembly line in a missile factory, and he is able to bend certain working parts out of shape through the use of sheer willpower. Soon others will follow suit. Already the intelligence agencies are training their operatives in methods to counteract this kind of psychic sabotage.

PAUL KRASSNER

The Mime and The Pacer

I FOUND MYSELF walking around and around in a counter-clockwise circle on the stage of the Wallenboyd Theatre in downtown Los Angeles — just as a young man known as The Pacer does for several hours every day, always in the same direction, at the exact same spot in the middle of the boardwalk in Venice Beach. He is an inspiration to me, and I sometimes talk about him in my performances.

The boardwalk in Venice is both literally and figuratively on the edge of this country. T-shirts are the hieroglyphics of our time. Here, a grungy wino (who needed a shave long before Don Johnson made stubble fashionable) is wearing a T-shirt that says, "Yes, I Am a Model." There, a nerdy tourist is trying not to let the pizza drip on his T-shirt that says, "I Choked Linda Lovelace" (the porn star of *Deep Throat*).

The boardwalk resembles one of those double-page-spread montages in a children's book showing many different modes of transportation being used simultaneously. Airplanes fly by, trailing printed messages such as "The New Dating Game Wants You," and "Scientology, Give Us Our Money Back," while below, roller skaters and skateboarders mingle with cops riding bicycles and Hare Krishnas preparing for their annual parade featuring an elephant nourished entirely on trail mix.

A lone Jesus freak walks along and yells at them — "Antichrist! Antichrist! Antichrist!" — trying to drown out their chant. "Repent, Krishna! People are starving in India every day because these foolish Krishnas refuse to eat the cow! Eat the cow and believe in Jesus Christ! Repent, Krishna!"

You can buy all types of stuff along the boardwalk — rainbow sunglasses and fake Rolex watches and falafel-shaped yo-yos. "But," complains a flower vendor who pays $600 a month for a ten-by-two-foot space, "rent will be going up to $800 and then to $1,200 by summer. Venice will eventually be inhabited by a bunch of wealthy lot owners and a population of slaves who work for them."

However, the performers pay no rent, dependent upon voluntary donations. There is a poet who speaks professional gibberish; an artist who draws on the ground with colored chalk; a fellow who juggles an electric chainsaw, a bowling ball, and an apple, for which strangers put money into his hat because they're grateful to God that they don't have to do such a bizarre thing to earn a living.

There is a woman who plays the violin while standing on her head. There is a man who has a table covered with wineglasses of different sizes filled to varying heights with water, and he plays this musical instrument by rubbing his fingers around the tops of those wineglasses. Audiences gather spontaneously to hear his rendition of a Mozart sonata or a ragtime melody or the theme from *Chariots of Fire*.

There are break-dancers who bring their own personal linoleum-floor sections, and a jogger who jumps hurdles over the endless row of garbage cans lined along the boardwalk. He has to avoid one garbage can because a homeless person is foraging for lunch.

If I had to choose my favorite moment on the boardwalk, it would have to be the time a Rastafarian yogi was standing on the very top of a wooden chair, preparing to jump barefoot onto a pile of freshly broken bottles. "This is serious shit," he reminded the large semicircle of onlookers. And then, during the anticipatory silence, along came that Jesus freak. Upon seeing this crowd, he edged his way in. Now the Rastafarian yogi was poised upon that unseen edge between "Look before you leap" and "He who hesitates is lost." Suddenly the Jesus freak called out, "Hey, wait, before you commit suicide there, how do you feel about abortion?"

IN FRONT OF THE SIDEWALK CAFÉ on the boardwalk, The Mime, a black man wearing white gloves along with a tuxedo and top hat, just stands still — often for hours. He is listening to a stereo headset. One might think he was playing music to counteract the boredom, but it's really a tape loop reminding him, "Don't move, stay still, it doesn't matter if your back itches, people are paying you not to scratch ..."

Passersby do indeed put cash in the cardboard box at his feet after they have gaped at him long enough to get their money's worth. Standing still is his job. People pay him not to move. When he goes to the unemployment office, a clerk asks, "Did you look for work this week?" He answers simply, "Yes, I stood on the corner of Hollywood and Vine, and then I stood on the corner of Beverly Boulevard and Sierra Bonita, and then I stood ..."

In contrast to The Mime is The Pacer, who intrigues me most. He doesn't call himself The Pacer. He may not even know that others do. But the circle he walks around and around in is his turf. Even an occasional police car respects the force field he creates, and the cops drive around him.

Obviously, he originally started this strange stint as a matter of choice. "I think I'll walk around in circles on the boardwalk today." And the next day. And the next. But somewhere along the way, walking around in circles became a compulsion, and it started doing him. When you play a role long enough, the role can begin to play you if you're not careful.

I've been out at 6:00 in the morning and there was The Pacer walking in circles. I've been out at 6:00 in the evening, and there was The Pacer walking in circles. He does stop to eat — which indicates that at some level he is still acting voluntarily. He walks in a straight line to a greasy-spoon diner nearby on the boardwalk and sits at the counter, but he does not twirl on his stool, nor stir his coffee, nor roll his eyes.

Once he talked about his obsessive activity: "I'm in control of walking, but out of control, too. When I walk, I'm in a trance. If I slow down at night, I see colors. I see millions of faces — some with Pilgrim hats, some with cowboy hats — modern faces and prehistoric faces."

There must be some kind of spiritual path that the sweating, red-faced Pacer keeps treading, even if it's circular — some unique relationship with the universe by which he justifies his existence to himself. Everybody has to feel they're making some contribution to society, if only to maintain self-esteem. Even those who work in a missile factory must rationalize, "Well, the United States needs to have a strong defense."

It's an absurd age we live in. *Future Shock* is already an outdated book. Children whose shoes stay on their feet by the grace of Velcro may never experience the thrill of tying their shoelaces in the dark. They have developed a fast-food approach to perceiving time because all they know is digital clocks. Time goes click, click, and if the power goes off, they think that 12:00 — 12:00 — 12:00 is appliance language for "Help! Help! Help! Turn me back to the right time! Help! Help! Help!"

Kids have lost that certain sense of time in motion, going around and around, eternally. That concept is endangered, just like the whooping crane. But we can all be grateful to The Pacer, for he is the Keeper of the Counter-Clockwise. That is his spiritual calling. But The Pacer doesn't have a cardboard box for people to drop money into — he walks around in circles out of the goodness of his heart.

THE MIME AND THE PACER provide a perfect metaphor for the two-party system in America. The Republicans are like The Mime, standing absolutely still while the world passes them by — Iran, Iraq, Nicaragua, El Salvador — and they get paid for it, just like The Mime. The Democrats are like The Pacer, walking around in circles while the world passes them by — Israel, Libya, Cuba, Honduras — and they don't get paid for it, just like The Pacer.

But recently The Pacer did something that hurled that comparison right into the metaphor graveyard, along with "bringing coals to Newcastle" (for Newcastle finally did run out of coal) and "good as gold" (since the government now prints money without the benefit of the gold standard). The Pacer had put a cardboard box down on the ground and started walking around it. And now people began giving him money.

By the mere presence of that cardboard box, The Pacer had transformed his personal perversion into a marketable talent. Just like so many of us. And I could no longer feel superior to him. He was not just some nut walking in circles. Now he was earning a living.

I still "do" The Pacer in my act, but with increased respect. "His job is no less dignified than anything we do," I tell the audience. "He works hard all day, and then, just like you and me, he goes home and unwinds." And I proceed to walk around and around in a circle onstage, only now in a clockwise direction.

Johnnie Cochran Meets Dr. Hip

TRAGEDY AND ABSURDITY were two sides of the same coin: On one side, O.J. Simpson's "suicide" note with a smiley face in the "O" of his signature; on the other side, the woman who pinched Simpson lawyer Robert Shapiro's ass because "I wanted to be part of history." And somewhere along the ridge of that coin was Simpson himself, walking into the courtroom humming the melody of "Touch Me" from the Broadway hit *Cats* and explaining to reporters that he was thinking about his children.

That was at Simpson's criminal trial. Shortly before his civil trial began in 1997, I met his lead attorney, Johnnie Cochran. He was the guest of honor and luncheon speaker at a national convention of criminal defense attorneys held in a huge banquet hall at a hotel in Santa Monica. No media people were allowed entry.

One of the attendees was Dr. Eugene Schoenfeld, also known as Dr. Hip from his days as a syndicated columnist for the underground press. He now testifies occasionally as an expert witness and was at this event for that reason. My wife Nancy and I were his guests.

Cochran's speech reassured the enthusiastic audience: "In the Simpson matter, we just did what *you* do every *day*" — that is, defend their clients by any means necessary and chalk up a bunch of billable hours in the process — and he got a standing ovation.

In the afterglow of his speech, colleagues came up to Cochran to shake his hand and get in a little banter. One well-wisher shared this joke: "If [prosecutor] Chris Darden spent as much time trying to nail O.J. Simpson as he did trying to nail [prosecutor] Marcia Clark, he might've won the case." The other defense attorneys within hearing distance all had a good laugh at that one.

Dr. Schoenfeld joined the line of lawyers waiting to have photos taken of themselves standing alongside Cochran. When it was Schoenfeld's turn, Nancy focused her camera. For this particular occasion, Schoenfeld had stashed a hand-printed card underneath the standard, plastic-encased ID lapel card. As in the previous poses, Cochran and Schoenfeld put their arms around each other, although they were looking, not at each other, but straight ahead and smiling at the camera.

Thus, Cochran didn't notice how, just before Nancy snapped their picture, Schoenfeld subtly managed to pull away the ID card and reveal the hand-printed card, which declared, in large printed letters, "O.J. DID IT!" I published that photo on the front cover of *The Realist* that spring. It was the result of a good old-fashioned guerrilla action.

Jealousy at the Swingers Convention

THE 24TH ANNUAL LIFESTYLES COUPLES CONVENTION has filled three hotels in Palm Springs, California. The convention center is connected to one of them, the Wyndham, which surrounds a large outdoor pool and patio populated by couples busy socializing in 116-degree dry heat. Women and men alike are wearing thongs. From afar, they appear like so many eyeless smiley faces among the bathing suits. The law that Sonny Bono signed when he was mayor, banning thongs in public, does not apply to this event, or, for that matter, to Cher.

The convention is for couples only. Except for me. I've been hired to perform stand-up comedy at their Friday luncheon, and I'm here alone. On the small propeller plane from Los Angeles to Palm Springs, the right side consists of two-seat rows, occupied entirely by couples on their way to the convention — horny with the expectation of getting laid by the spouse of a stranger, perhaps sitting in front of or behind them — and the left side of the plane consists of one-seat rows, occupied entirely by me. I'm afraid that the plane might tip over upon trying to land.

At the convention center, even the plastic-encased lapel nametags are coupled off: "Ken and Barbie" on his, "Barbie and Ken" on hers. Not all the couples are paired off in real life, though. One person can simply bring along another — known in swinger circles as a "ticket" for gender balance — in order to get into the convention. So everybody has entered two by two, and I feel like a unicorn stowaway on Noah's Ark, surreptitiously balancing on the cusp of love and lust.

There are 3,000 participants at this convention, mostly upper-middle-class, in their 30s, 40s, and 50s. They consider people in the outside world to be "straight," even though one would ordinarily consider *them* straight. I mean, there are suburban soccer moms here, openly celebrating their secret lifestyle at an oasis of supportiveness. There's a man in a suit with a flesh-colored penis necktie, another wearing a T-shirt declaring, "I'm Not Going Bald, I'm Getting More Head," and another dressed only in a leather jockstrap, who recognizes me and introduces himself.

"I'd give you my card," he says, "but I have no place to keep them."

Inside the 100,000 square-foot convention center, the exhibit hall has been turned into an "Adult Marketplace," buzzing with commercial activity. I overhear one shopper's complaint: "But we've *already* spent $400." There's a multitude of merchandise on display — pornographic videos, naughty lingerie, fetish paraphernalia, edible lotions — plus booths galore. At the Golden Nipples booth, women are cheerfully having exact duplicates of their nipples created in sterling silver or 14-karat gold, which can be used as pendants, key fobs, money clips or — yes, of course — nipple covers. At the Penimax booth, an Asian vendor is selling disposable cock rings, which, he promises, will maintain my erection even after I ejaculate.

There are several booths dedicated to booking vacations especially designed for swingers — at nude beaches, clothing-optional resorts, and ocean cruises. I follow around an elderly woman who is busy picking up brochures at every such booth. It seems incongruous, but I try not to indulge in stereotypes. Finally, I engage her in a conversation, and she explains that her boss told her to get as much material as she could, because he owns some property surrounded by government land, and he wants to start a new business.

At the Erotic Massage Wear table, a woman uses my arm to demonstrate a device that turns her fingertip into a vibrator, not intended for nose picking. Then she puts Jergens lotion on my right hand, dons a pair of Love Mitts — made of vinyl with little nubs all over — and proceeds to massage my hand while on the VCR there's a tape of a woman wearing Love Mitts and massaging a man's lubricated penis. This is a bizarre mixed-media sensation. Although I don't get a hard-on, the lobes of my brain seem to fuse, and for the next few hours my left hand persists in feeling neglected.

Checking out the functional furniture, I merely eavesdrop on a (fully clothed) couple testing out the "rocking torso feature" on a Love Table, but I actually *climb into* the Love Swing, assuming a position ordinarily assumed by a woman while the man stands up, crotch to crotch. My body is suspended half upside-down in mid-air with legs spread and feet up in stirrups. I'm feeling mighty vulnerable. As I hang there, the inventor hands me my tape recorder, then proceeds to show me how "the woman can place the man's penis on her G-spot by moving her legs from a position of being out front like this to being in the fetal position" and how "the man, instead of just going in and out like that, he can make his penis a joystick, so every step he takes is a movement inside of her, more like a dance step." He guarantees, "You'll never use a bed again."

Next, I inspect the Bungee Sexperience — a harness designed by a company that makes bungee cords. It bounces in the air, so the "rider" can enjoy weightless sex in a variety of positions. I ask the woman demonstrating this how many hours a day she bounces up and down. "At an event like this," she responds, without missing a bounce, "I'd say eight to twelve hours." She tells me that her circulation is excellent, and that her 18-year-old son refers to the contraption as a "bungee humper." In addition to bouncing, it can also create "the illusion of bondage, yet the person can actually be comfortable while restrained."

The Auto Erotic Chair, however, provides *real* bondage. It's equipped with leather restraints and panic snaps for arms and legs and comes complete with a power box and pneumatically operated anal and vaginal plugs. "Our power source unit is designed to stimulate nerve fibers throughout the genital areas by delivering controllable electro-pulse energy through conductive electrodes on our sex toys. Our precision-engineered technology gives you safe and pleasurable electric play." So, for example, in the Electro-Flex Penile Ring/Anal Plug Configuration, "A single conductor butt plug is used in conjunction with a single conductive cock ring to complete the circuit. With a single conductive cock ring, one side of a double conductive butt plug can be used to stimulate either the prostate or the sphincter."

If you'd prefer something, well, less electric, there's always the Crystal Wand, a 10-inch-long, *S*-shaped co-ed tool, hand-carved from pure crystal-clear acrylic, that doubles simultaneously as a G-spot stimulator and prostate massager. I'm reminded of a swing party I heard about, one that took place at the Whispers Club in Michigan. Couples removed from the refrigerator 12-inch summer sausages and cucumbers that the hostess had planned to use for food that evening. When she walked into the "party room," she couldn't help but notice that although the food was being consumed, it was not exactly in the fashion she had originally envisioned. Instead, the sausages and cucumbers were being utilized as organic sex toys.

As I continue to wander around the Adult Marketplace, I realize that the name of the game is penetration. All paths lead to penetration. But I'm not referring to penetration of the sexual kind, although that's an implicit goal — pick an orifice, any orifice, and there's always a corresponding appendage or gadget that can fulfill its desire for penetration — no, I'm talking about penetration of the *market*. There's lots of money to be made here. The persistent question is, how can I penetrate this market? Maybe I could come up with a combination FM radio and vibrating dildo.

I'M BEGINNING TO FEEL like I'm experiencing an alien encounter, only *I'm* the alien here. Nevertheless, I'm aware that swingers and comedians do have something in common. We both like to have a good opening line. As a performer, I always try to slant my opening line toward a particular audience.

My opening line at the World Hemp Expo was, "Last night, for the first time in my life, I used a hemp condom." My opening line at a Skeptics Conference, attended by the Amazing Randi and the Amazing Kreskin, was: "The is the first conference I've been to where there were two people with the same first name of Amazing. But the Amazing Randi was born with that name — it's on his birth certificate — whereas the Amazing Kreskin changed his name for showbiz. His real name is the Obnoxious Kreskin." And my opening line at a luncheon during the Los Angeles County Bar Association conference was, "I'd like to begin with a moment of silence, so that you can think about your client's problem, and then you can make this a billable hour."

Now I find myself in a lavish hotel suite, trying to crystallize an opening line while contemplating the bald spot on the back of my head, infinitely cloned in the mirrors of the hotel-room bathroom — actually the only place I ever get to *see* that bald spot as others do. This will be a serious opening line, since I have been told that, in the introduction to my performance, I will be presented with the Lifestyles Freedom Award. I decide that my opening line will then be, "I just want to say that freedom of expression existed long before the First Amendment." Though it's not my motivation, I realize that this opening line will undoubtedly please Robert McGinley, the bearded co-founder and president of the Lifestyles Organization.

"We hate government intervention in our lives," he has assured me. "We hate censorship. We're against laws that require helmets for cyclists. It's good that a law was just passed allowing women to breastfeed in public, but we shouldn't need permission from the government to do it." He admits to being "libertarian, but not Libertarian Party." He draws his philosophy from Jack London — "The proper function of man is to live, not to exist" — and, more specifically, his credo is "Adult sexuality is normal." Dr. McGinley (he holds a Ph.D. in counseling psychology) tells me a riddle: "What do you call an Italian swinger?" I give up.

The answer: "A swop."

At the luncheon, it turns out that I will *not* be presented with the Freedom Award after all, and I have to come up immediately with a replacement opening line: "I'm delighted to be at the Lifestyles Convention — this is the first convention I've ever been to that was named after a condom."

Indeed, condom consciousness (if not condom use) is present at the convention. In one workshop, "The ABC's of Swinging," condom etiquette is described as bringing "the right safety equipment, just as you would for scuba diving or parachuting." Another presentation on "Safer Sex" covers new drug therapies for AIDS, information on other sexually transmitted diseases that are increasing among heterosexuals, and "things you should be doing to protect yourself."

Originally, herpes had caused a certain panic in swinger circles. Some swing clubs closed, though private parties increased. But, paradoxically enough, with the advent of AIDS, *new* clubs opened, as if the disease were anti-climactic. Currently, there's a surge of growth in this subculture — thanks to the internet — with estimates ranging from two thousand to three million participants. And, according to Dr. McGinley, "There's been very little increase in condom use. It's the woman's choice."

Nonetheless, at the Adult Marketplace, a woman in a black lace negligee roams around giving out free samples of condoms. There are also Crème Cookie Condoms for sale. They appear to be vanilla and chocolate Oreo-style cookies, individually wrapped in cellophane. I ask the vendor whether these are condoms that look like cookies, or cookies that look like condoms. She tells me that they are edible cookies, but each one has a condom inside.

"They're only a dollar each," she says, adding, as I edge away from her booth, "It's a great joke."

❀ ❀ ❀

THE ART GALLERY at the convention center, featuring the Lifestyles Convention's seventh annual Sensual and Erotic Art Exhibition, almost didn't happen. The state's Department of Alcoholic Beverage Control had tried to prevent it from opening. When their authority was challenged, an ABC representative became an alchemist, transforming logic into absurdity. Legally, he said, you can't even have sex in a hotel room that has a mini-bar. Sure, pal, just try to enforce *that* one.

Two days before the convention, the ACLU obtained a restraining order against ABC's interference with the art exhibit. But ABC didn't just give up and assume the fetal position in a Love Swing. Rather, the agency threatened to revoke the Wyndham Hotel's liquor license if they allowed a special two-hour session, the convention's traditional Evening of Caressive Intimacy, to take place in the Wyndham Ballroom on Friday as scheduled. This popular, closed-door, clothing-optional massage clinic, limited to the first 200 couples who sign up, would include the "human car wash," involving, as one veteran swinger portrays it, "a lot of naked bodies and some serious rubbing."

But the ABC regulations on Attire and Conduct — behavior "deemed contrary to public welfare and morals, and therefore no on-sale license shall be held at any premises where such conduct or acts are permitted" — includes this clause as a no-no: "To encourage or permit any person on the licensed premises to touch, caress or fondle the breasts, buttocks, anus or genitals of any other person." The Wyndham chickens out, the massage clinic is canceled, the money is refunded, Lifestyles will sue the hotel for breach of contract, and next year's convention (in 1998) will be held in Las Vegas.

A lawyer, standing on the border of cynicism, suggests, "Just buy a town in Mexico and buy off all the officials."

In the previous year, 1996, the convention was held at the Town and Country Hotel in San Diego (for the fourth time), but two ABC officers claimed that they witnessed oral copulation in the convention hall, and the hotel's liquor license was suspended for five days, hence Lifestyle's move to Palm Springs this year. Lately, ABC has been spreading its particular brand of paranoia in Los Angeles, where the agency has raided gay, black, and Latino bars in Los Angeles and in Hermosa Beach, where it has imposed restrictions on restaurants, requiring patio patrons to order food with their drinks, and forbidding customers to dance. Proprietors now play less upbeat music so that nobody will be tempted to dance. Those who can't resist are asked to stop.

Incidentally, I find out that, instead of giving the Freedom Award to me, convention officials have decided to present ABC with an Anti-Freedom Award, but that notion gets lost somewhere in award limbo, along with my original unspoken opening line.

On Friday night, the massage clinic that doesn't take place is followed by the Wild West Casino and Dance. One man comes attired in a sheriff's outfit with a rubber penis drooping almost to the floor. A security guard tells him that he'll have to check it. Fake knives, guns, and bullets are acceptable, but not a fake sex organ. Another cowboy, with a *real* (unloaded) gun, is stopped by a security guard, but he resists, asserting in his best John Wayne manner, "This is an 1887 pistol, and I'm not about to check it."

Several folks leave the dance at midnight to attend an unofficial third annual spanking party. It ends at 3:00 a.m. with a bout of fist-fucking. Dear Abby was right. One thing *does* lead to another.

I'VE BEEN SAMPLING many workshops at the convention center, and I notice that whenever I sit down on a chair next to a chair with someone else's stuff on it, and the owner of that stuff is sitting on the other side of that chair, they always tap the top of their stuff in a subconscious gesture of territoriality. I also observe that a man with one leg (he walks with crutches) and his wife seem to arrive at every single workshop that I attend. Hmmmmm. I'm beginning to get suspicious. Obviously, I've seen too many spy movies.

A cartoon in the 1991 convention program showed two rooms where lectures were being given. The attendees in the room featuring "Do It Yourself Porn: Make Your Own xxx Movies" were overflowing into the corridor, while the room featuring "Socio-Political Ramifications of Current Trends in the Erosion of Civil Liberties" was empty, except for the baffled lecturer. It was a nice touch of self-deprecating humor, an exaggeration not too far from reality. At this '97 convention, porn actress Nina Hartley's "So You Want to Throw a Party: Recipes for a Successful Orgy" attracts ten times more audience than attorney Bob Burke's "Sexual Politics: A Behind the Scenes Look."

Unfortunately, one workshop, "The Undertone of Sexuality in the *Star Trek* Series," has been canceled — "due," someone added to the notice, "to Federation Regulations and Star Fleet Emergency Order 1007-932." Deborah Warner, in describing her presentation, had written: "Paramount and its parent company, Viacom, have a vested interest in presenting the *Trek* franchise as a family-oriented show. To this end, they overtly depict the characters as asexual. Yet there exists erotic subtext. This has spawned a very large community of fans who create volumes of explicit erotica that is enjoying great popularity in print and an explosion of interest on the internet."

Now, outside the room where her workshop would have been, there is disappointment — "Oh, and she was gonna bring a Klingon" — and nostalgia — "Remember the time Quark and Deanna were French kissing?"

That theme continues at "American Tantra: How to Worship Each Other in Bed," This workshop — whose motto, "Orgasm long and prosper," paraphrases *Star Trek's* blessing, "Live long and prosper" — is conducted by Paul Ramana Das and Marilena Silbey. "Interspecies intercourse," he muses. "This can't be the only planet where love is made." A writer for AVN (*Adult Video News*) has reviewed their *Intimate Secrets of Sex & Spirit* and confessed, "I've rarely laughed so hard in my life. No shit, this vid earns a pre-nomination for 'most outrageous sex scene.' Paul actually uses Marilena's pussy as an echo chamber!"

Now, in his regular voice, he is telling our workshop of the need to "approach the body, not for sexual release, but for every single inch of this body, the groundwork, the geography of pleasure. Can anybody name one spot on your body that is not capable of receiving pleasure?"

Nobody can. Later, the entire audience, seated around the perimeter of this extra-large room, is instructed to come stand in the center area and face their partners. I start to slide out, but not inconspicuously enough. Ramana Das, who knows me from a previous incarnation, calls out, "There goes Paul Krassner. Are you afraid to participate?"

"I'm here as a journalist."

"Ah, he can't participate because he's a journalist. See how everybody has excuses?"

Suddenly I'm saddled with a dose of New Age guilt, as though I have aborted my inner child. Meanwhile, there's a lovely blonde who doesn't have a partner, and now I'm tempted to participate, but some guy who's also without a partner links up with her. Unexpectedly, my guilt changes to jealousy. Just a slight pang of jealousy, mind you, but a terrible taboo in this particular world.

Jealousy is an outmoded emotion to be shunned like dandruff. There's even a workshop that advises "How to Handle Jealousy" and another titled "Swing Without Guilt or Jealousy." And so now I not only feel guilty about not participating, I also feel guilty about feeling jealous. I've committed a swinger crime. I can hear security guards shouting "Jealousy alert!" Loud sirens go off. "Jealousy alert!"

Now where will I go? I have been reading about tantra in *Real Magic* by Isaac Bonewits: "Energy control is a very important part of the exercises; it is essential, for example, that during *Kama-kali* the male be able to refrain from ejaculating under the most harrowing circumstances." I decide to drop in on a workshop, "How to Prevent Premature Ejaculation," but everybody has already been there, and they all left early.

Sorry. I blurted that out before I could stop myself.

THERE ARE SWING CLUBS all around the country, from "Shenanigans" in Indiana to "Liberated Christians" in Arizona ("for Christians seeking liberation from false sexual repression based on mistranslation of scripture who wish to explore responsible non-monogamy and polyfidelity"). Many clubs designate themselves as Equal Opportunity Lifestyle Organizations, where membership is open to all races, and they belong to NASCA (North American Swing Club Association).

The Spring 1997 issue of NASCA *Inside Report* editorializes, "There are political attacks on freedom that citizens should be aware of. It is far too easy to lose, through complacency and ignorance, the freedom that we Americans cherish. These attacks include the proposed censorship of the internet now under review by the U.S. Supreme Court, the recently court-upheld attempts by states to keep 'harmful' literature from the eyes of children by controlling street news racks, the reintroduction in Pennsylvania of legislation to outlaw swing clubs and a similar measure in California. Regarding the latter two, do we smell a conspiracy here?" If there is one, it's bi-partisan.

In Pennsylvania, Richard Kasunic, a Democratic state senator, failed in his 1996 attempt to outlaw "sex clubs." This year, he has reintroduced legislation to outlaw "swinger clubs." He states, "My bill will outlaw these immoral establishments in every community in Pennsylvania and provide significant penalties for those who choose to continue this offensive practice." The penalty for operating a swing club, even in one's own home: up to two years in jail and $5,000 in fines. For a second conviction: up to seven years and $15,000. For patronizing a swing club: $300 plus court costs.

In California, Tim Leslie, a Republican state senator, has introduced a bill which would provide that "every building or place which, as a primary activity, accommodates or encourages persons to engage in, or to observe other persons engaging in, sexual conduct including, but not limited to, anal intercourse, oral copulation, or vaginal intercourse, is a nuisance and shall be enjoined, abated and prevented, and for which damages may be recovered, whether it is a public or private nuisance."

Swinger periodicals range from *New Friends* to *Fuck Thy Neighbor*. Patti Thomas, author of *Recreational Sex: An Insider's Guide to the Swinging Lifestyle*, is editor at *Connection*, which publishes thirteen titles, including *Cocoa 'n Crème*, catering to interracial swingers (not to be confused with *Black 'n Blue*, catering to sadomasochist swingers). Connection is suing the federal government over a bill that Ronald Reagan sent to Congress in 1987, the Child Protection and Obscenity Act, an outgrowth of the Meese Commission on Pornography.

The specific statute being challenged — known as the recordkeeping and labeling law, or the ID law — was supposed to be aimed at child pornography but has been applied to adults-only swing publications.

It requires anyone placing an explicit photo ad to provide a photo ID, nicknames, maiden names, stage names, professional names, and aliases. These records must be available for inspection by the attorney general's office.

Connection had attempted to comply with the law by cutting out every explicit photo ad from its magazines and sending them with a letter to those advertisers, explaining the new law and its requirements, asking that they submit the proper ID or send a "soft" photo that didn't require ID. Out of 500 advertisers, only 26 responded with IDs. Patti Thomas spoke about this in her keynote speech at the Conclave '97 Convention in Chicago:

> It definitely makes it difficult to produce the magazine our readers and subscribers have come to expect, when you don't have enough so-called "legal" ads to fill all those pages. And considering that *swinging itself is not illegal*, why should we have to "register our sexual choices" with the government just to place a personal ad in a magazine? ... I've never really thought of myself as an activist, or as one who was "politically involved," but over the last few years, I think I've finally come to realizing that it's going to be *necessary* to be involved, even if it does mean "exposing" my lifestyle to those who would repress it. I am *fucking sick and tired of do-gooders* trying to tell me how I should live my life!

In 1995, *Connection* filed a suit challenging the constitutionality of the law and seeking a permanent injunction. In 1997, the motion was denied. Attorneys filed an appeal along with a motion for a temporary injunction relieving *Connection* from complying with the act during that appeal. The motion was granted.

"The justice system in this country just makes no sense to me whatsoever," Patti Thomas tells me. "As far as I know, once we do present our case to the Court of Appeals, if our decision isn't favorable, we will make every attempt to go to the Supreme Court. Our attorneys are the best First Amendment attorneys anywhere. Our lawsuit has been very costly, as you can imagine, but our company believes very strongly in fighting for our constitutional rights. Our suit was filed not only for the benefit of our company but because we felt that this outrageous law was totally infringing on the civil rights and freedoms of people involved in alternative lifestyles. Obviously, the average person involved in swinging would have no way of combating this law on their own."

I ask her whether attempts at repression have resulted in politicizing the swinger community.

"I'm afraid we haven't been very successful," she replies. "We try to inform our readers about political issues threatening our lifestyle and attempt to get them involved. Unfortunately, many in the lifestyle either don't believe that the government will actually take away their rights or are too afraid to make a stand. Swingers who have been 'exposed' as active participants in the lifestyle have lost jobs, family, community standing, and friends as a result.

"People I've personally known who have lost their jobs when their swinging activities were discovered just wouldn't fight back because of the fear of further exposure through the publicity that could have been generated. As a matter of fact, my ex-husband was fired from a management position back in 1980 when someone discovered his photo in one of our magazines and brought it to the attention of his superiors. Luckily, he was able to find a position with one of *Connection*'s affiliate companies. So we pretty much remain an 'underground minority'."

That point is underscored by a 29-year-old woman at the convention. "None of us like publicity," she says. "None of us want to be out in the open. The business world is very conservative." She is wearing an American flag bikini, although she has never heard of Abbie Hoffman. She was born the same year that he got arrested for wearing an American flag shirt. Nor did she have any way of knowing that when he wore another American flag shirt on *The Merv Griffin Show*, his half of the TV screen was blocked out all across America. She was, in short, unaware of the roots of her own, limited freedom.

IT'S SATURDAY NIGHT, and the Carnival Masquerade Ball is being held in the huge convention center ballroom. On the wall behind the stage are gigantic masks. Above the tables are gold and purple balloons, fashioned after either somebody's school colors or a Chinese restaurant's little hot mustard and soy sauce plate. The taped music is loud, and the dancing is raunchy, enhanced by gaudy yellow, blue, and red lights. Pheromones are flying, and the costumes are kinky.

"Costumes," the program states, "may be anything of fertile imagination (genital areas must be covered) for an exotic night of adult social fun." Hey, look who's here: Superman. The Phantom of the Opera. The devil. Mickey Mouse and Minnie Mouse (in a see-through top). An executioner. An Arabian potentate. A gold-plated pharaoh. A chicken lady covered with big yellow feathers. A guy in a dog collar being led around on a leash. And the one-legged man, who is wearing a roller skate as his costume.

At one point, an announcement is made that the next dance number will be filmed, so anybody who doesn't wish to be recognized should get off the dance floor. About 80% of the dancers leave. Similarly, taking part in the costume-judging means that permission to be photographed is automatically granted, which results in many contestants not making themselves available to be chosen as possible finalists.

The Best Male Costume goes to a 75-year-old man dressed as a biker stud. The Best Female Costume goes to his 75-year-old wife, dressed as a biker slut. The Best Couple's Costume goes to a woman with papier-mâché breasts the size of beach balls and her mate with matching enormous testicles but covered by pillowcases and a sign that warns, "Censored by the hotel and ABC."

A marriage ceremony is performed onstage. The blissful pair have written their own vows; nothing is mentioned about forsaking all others. The newlyweds, their party, and a few other couples are invited to a gathering in the suite of a three-time Emmy Award-winning TV producer and his wife. It turns out to be a tantra-filled wedding night. All the women massage the groom, and all the men massage the bride. One woman, a computer animator who wants to become a sexual surrogate, predicts that, as the millennium comes to an end, tantric men will be popping up everywhere.

A retired chairman and CEO of a title and escrow company, who attended another tantra party, tells me, "The difference between the tantra party and the party next door is the fact that at the beginning of the wedding tantra party there was a lot of ceremony and shared tantra ritual, but once we had experienced that, it was every person for themselves. It was like the party next door." These were closed parties by invitation only. But you didn't need an invitation for open parties. All you had to do was find them.

The Wyndham Hotel is permeated by a sense of uninhibitedness. In the elevator, a beautiful black woman is looking in the full-length mirror and admiring her new Clit Clip — non-piercing, adjustable, genital jewelry — "not designed to be painful," I learned at the Adult Marketplace, "just very sensual and aesthetically attractive. The Clit Clip is a long narrow, U-shaped piece of metal, designed to fit around the clitoris hood, with some light-catching Austrian crystals, in your choice of clear, red, blue, and purple, dangling from the ends."

The woman in the elevator turns toward me and asks, "Isn't it nice?" Her husband smiles proudly.

"It's charming," I reply, "but what are you gonna do if the metal detector goes off at the airport?"

I leave them giggling in the elevator as I get off on a floor where I've heard there would be lots of action. I follow one group, but only the couple in front really knows where they're going. But they happen to be on the way to their own room, and when they get there, they go in, close the door, and we are all left out in the corridor, looking like a perplexed ant farm. Everybody turns around. I am now at the front of the line, so I let them all pass by me as they head in the opposite direction, strolling briskly, except for the one-legged man with the roller skate and crutches, who is gliding gracefully along the carpet. Passersby are asked, in vain, "Where's the party?" We finally find a room with a porn photo on the door, which is slightly open.

Inside, there are around 50 people in semi-darkness. Exhibitionists and voyeurs, together again. Here a blowjob, there a copulation, everywhere an undulating juiciness. There is an unspoken homophobia — no man is relating sexually to another man — but there is lots of lesbian libido. In order to keep a low profile, I have ripped several pages out of my notebook and folded them in half so that I can take notes unobtrusively.

However, a woman with a feather duster asks me to hold on to her panties. She is about to join a threesome on the king-sized bed near the bureau that I'm leaning against. I marvel at the choreography of this foursome. But they're playing, and I'm working. Their moans become my background music.

I wasn't *always* a wallflower at the orgy. I flash back 30 years to 1967 ... I was at a Sexual Freedom League couples-only party on New Year's Eve at a large theatrical studio in San Francisco. There were about 150 people dancing in the nude. Behind the closed curtains on the stage, there were fifteen small mattresses in constant use by different couples.

I remember making love on one of those mattresses with a sweet flower child only fifteen minutes after we'd met. It was an exhilarating experience. We were on the front lines of the Sexual Revolution. We had to hold back from screaming out political slogans at our moment of climax. The seeds of contemporary swinging were planted at that party, but who could have known it would blossom into an industry?

IF IT'S TRUE that, as Bill Maher once stated so poetically, "The real problem with marriage is that it's just very difficult to bump your uglies with the same person every night your whole life," then for some people, swinging is the answer. To them, cheating is not an issue, unfaithfulness is obsolescent, and adultery is merely a concept that deprived former Air Force Lieutenant Kelly Flinn of her opportunity to drop a nuclear bomb.

The Lifestyles Convention provides a nurturing environment for these couples the same way a convention of crossword-puzzle enthusiasts or barbed-wire collectors would provide for *those* folks. Yet, in the case of swingers, one is left with a puzzle. Is impersonal intimacy an oxymoron? I ask that question of psychologist Stella Resnick, sex therapist and author of *The Pleasure Zone*. Her reply:

> We can't put a value judgment on this. These are all consenting adults. It doesn't really matter that it's rather impersonal because they are in long-term relationships, so they're getting their intimacy needs met, but not necessarily their needs for excitement in sex, and this is certainly a way to do it. Often, they are sexually identified in the sense that they're sexual people, they have strong desires, they're not necessarily into politics or other causes, but this is a good cause — being in the body, being healthy — and it's a way of relaxing and enjoying their bodies. Whatever turns you on, as long as you're not doing any damage to anybody else and you're taking care of yourself, fine, enjoy.

When Tom Arnold was a guest on *Late Show*, David Letterman pressed him about his friendship with Kathie Lee and Frank Gifford. This was shortly after the *Globe* had entrapped and videotaped Frank Gifford in an extramarital tryst with a flight attendant in a hotel room. Letterman insisted, "I don't revel in the miseries of others," but Arnold reminded him of his monologues with jokes about Gifford. Letterman defended himself: "It's part of the job." Arnold stammered, searching for just the right words. He finally found them: "Frank Gifford took a bullet for a lot of us." And the audience applauded the accuracy of his assessment.

Certainly, non-celebrities don't have to worry about supermarket tabloids revealing infidelities to *their* spouses. Such exposure could never occur with swinging couples, not only because, as a rule, they are honest with each other, but also because they party *with* each other, so there are no surprises. They are sharing a secret lifestyle, one with an ethic that transcends ordinary romance. Sneaky affairs are for straight people, but swingers can eat their wedding cake and have their fantasies, too. Which explains why there have been no hookers hanging around *this* convention.

Life Among the Neo-Pagans

IN THE SUMMER OF 1997, I performed at the 17th annual Starwood Neo-Pagan Festival in Sherman, New York — Amish country on the border near Ohio and Pennsylvania. This event — a female-oriented celebration of the sensual and the spiritual — took place on private campgrounds where clothing was optional. Many women were bare-breasted, and several men and women walked around fully naked, a practice known as the "sky clad" experience.

Instead of camping out, I stayed at a nearby bed-and-breakfast. Downstairs in the living room, I asked a woman — falsely assuming that she was the proprietor — where the key would be left if I came back late at night.

"I don't know," she replied. "I'm here for the festival."

"Oh. In what capacity?"

"I'm in the craft."

"Which craft?"

"That's right," she said.

She had been a Wiccan for twenty years, but now she complained, "Witchcraft has become trendy. I mean, ever since *Buffy the Vampire Slayer* ..."

At the festival, on Merchants Row, there was an inviting banner over one of the booths: "Stop by for a Spell." A positive perspective on witchcraft was a theme at this event, along with such workshops as "Privacy Rights and Drug Policy," "Cultivating Consciousness in Your Child," "Live Meditations in Drumming and Dance," "The Supreme Court and the Free Exercise of Religion," "A Procession to Honor the Earth Goddess," "Safer Sex," and "Dark Ecstasy: The Ritual Use of Pleasure, Pain, and Sensory Deprivation as Psychedelic Experience."

When I walked onto the outdoor stage, my opening line was, "I'm gonna start with two words that have been *thought* year after year at these festivals, but which have never actually been uttered out loud, and those two words are: "Nice tits."

The audience hesitated a second, because in that context this could be a politically incorrect observation — I had deliberately taken that chance — but then they laughed and applauded, because they knew it was true.

I was invited back to perform at Starwood again in the summer of 1998. The previous month, two Amish men had been arrested for distributing cocaine they'd bought from a biker gang, the Pagans, one of whose members was a police informer. The two men were from a particularly conservative Amish sect, where not only electricity and tractors were forbidden, but even zippers. Did the sight of those Amish-tempting zippers on the Pagans' leather motorcycle jackets serve as a gateway drug to cocaine?

Speaking of illegal drugs, at the festival I came across the only individual I've ever met who had actually hallucinated on toad slime. I pictured him as a young lad with a tadpole in his pocket, and now as a grown man with a frog in his pocket.

I also met Reverend Ivan Stang, leader of the infamous Church of the SubGenius. He talked about "how to milk the internet for all it's worth, and get away with murder, before the Conspiracy figures out how to spoil it for us." But Stang was in deep embarrassment mode, since this was only a couple of weeks after the failure of his widely circulated prediction that, on July 5th at 7 a.m., Pleasure Saucers would descend to Earth as part of the great "Rupture" and take away all those SubGeniuses who had paid $30 for the privilege.

The festival climaxed with its traditional 50-foot-diameter, 25-foot-high bonfire, constructed during the week with the aid of a derrick. On Saturday night, several dancers with torches ritualistically teased this pyramid of logs, encircled at a distance by 2,000 enthusiasts, although one impatient woman yelled, "Just *do* it!" The neo-pagans danced and pranced and cavorted around the bonfire late into the night.

My own personal highlight occurred when a beautiful woman named Pearl approached me. She was in the process of transforming her breasts from fetish to functional by nursing a baby that had been conceived there the year before. During that festival, she had walked in on my performance, bare-breasted, at the precise moment that I uttered the words, "Nice tits." She assumed that I was referring specifically to her, and, I had learned, she was flattered, so now I didn't have the heart to disillusion her. But I did write about it in my *High Times* column, "Brain Damage Control," ending with this sentence: "I hope she doesn't read this."

Furthermore, at the 20th annual Starwood Festival in 2000, I found myself in front of a microphone on that same stage, and I told that story. Pearl was in the audience, and she was laughing heartily. This time, though, when I said, "Nice tits," I added, "Okay, now *everybody*," and the words came booming back at me: *'NICE TITS!'*" Later, as I was leaving the stage, Pearl called out, *"Nice dick!"* I was fully dressed, but it didn't matter. This was a perfect example of tit for tat. Or dick for tit.

My old friend Steve Gaskin and I were staying at a bed-and-breakfast where there were angels all over the place. Stuffed angels, plastic angels, plaster-of-paris angels, embroidered angels, stained-glass angels, papier-mâché angels, teddy-bear angels, and origami angels. There were angel dolls and angel paintings and angel sculptures and even an angel mobile hanging from the ceiling. In the bathroom, there was an angel tissue-dispenser and an angel nightlight. On a table in the hallway, there was a pile of *Angels on Earth* magazine. On the bureau in my room, there was a copy of *Whispers From Heaven*, featuring such articles as "Feeding Angels," "When Angels Kiss," and "Rescued by Angels: The Amazing Story of a Kidnapping Survivor."

Gaskin's room had a door that led to the roof, and the first night we sat out there and smoked a joint. The next day there was a note taped to the door: "The roof is to be used only as a fire escape. Please use the patio." The next night we smoked a joint in my room. The next day there was a "No Smoking" sign on the inside of my door, and the electric fan was on, aimed toward the now-open window.

At breakfast the next morning, I was just about to apologize to the kindly Christian woman whose home this was and explain that a doctor had recommended marijuana for my arthritis, but *she* apologized to *me* because she hadn't told me in advance that smoking wasn't allowed. "Some people are allergic to cigarette smoke," she explained.

I almost blurted out, "That wasn't tobacco, that was pot."

I hope she doesn't read this.

PAUL KRASSNER

Swimming in the Dead Pool

WHEN KEN KESEY'S SON JED was killed in an accident — the van carrying his University of Oregon wrestling team had skidded off a cliff — I immediately flew to Oregon. "You were his favorite," Kesey said as we embraced, sobbing. "I feel like every cell in my body is exploding,"

A few days later, several of us old friends were sitting around the dining-room table there, and someone mentioned that the Dead Kennedys were on tour.

"I wonder if Ted Kennedy is gonna go see 'em," I remarked.

Kesey, standing in the kitchen, responded, "That's not funny."

"You're right. I apologize. It's not very abstract right now."

"It's *never* abstract."

I recalled that little dialogue as I began to explore The Game, now in its 34th year [2004], the longest-running dead pool in America, currently with 125 players. Before January 1, everyone submits 68 names of people who might die that year. (Dr. Death, co-founder of The Game, liked to work on a legal pad — 34 lines, two columns, hence 68 names.) Points are awarded according to the age of each dead person — anybody in their 50s is worth five points; 60s, four; 70s, three.

Each participant gets one wild card per year worth five points no matter how old the deceased. Gamesters generally pick one-pointers for their wild card to get four extra points. Last year, most picked Bob Hope. When he died, one Gamester said, "My father was shot during World War II. While recuperating in England, Mr. Hope came up to his bedside and stuffed a half-dozen golf balls into his [own] mouth. It cheered my old man up."

Deaths become official when mentioned in *The New York Times* or any two major newspapers. One player "is extremely frustrated," I was told.

"He has Idi Amin, who is on life support in a Saudi hospital. Now there have been death threats, and armed guards have been posted." Since the listees are all on various rungs on the ladder of celebrityhood, The Game is understandably rife with abstraction.

"After all, the dead pool has probably been around since the phenomenon of fame itself," write Gelfand and Wilkinson in the book *Dead Pool*. "It has certainly been around as long as gallows humor has. In the heyday of hard-boiled journalism (*The Front Page* days of the 1930s), reporters who covered a country ravaged by organized crime and engaged in a world war found respite in the dark humor of the dead pool. Even before the internet, the dead pool was slowly emerging from the shadows of our culture."

As with dead pools, ranging from business offices to Howard Stern's radio show, that book is a guide to profiting from money bets. But members of The Game play solely for the fun of it. Whoever has the most points at the end of the year wins — "bragging rights only" — slightly ironic since Gamesters (lawyers, ad people, educators, psychology professors, writers, everyday working folks) all play under aliases like Frozen Stiff, Fade to Black, Worm Feast, Decomposers, 2 Dead Crew, Johnny B. Dead, Wm. Randolph Hearse, Daisy Pusher, Silk Shroud, Necrophiliac Pimp, Legion of Doom, Gang Green, Habeas Corpse, Die-Uretic, Shovelin' Off, Blunt Instrument, Rig R. Mortis, Flatliners, Unplugged, Toe Tag, Clean Underwear, and Gratefully Dead.

One couple, the Moorebids, insist, "We play for honor, not bragging rights. It has to do with honoring who you get the hit on."

Another player told me, "I compare playing The Game to my day job, science. We do a lot of data collection and data analysis; play our hunches. Our reward is not financial, but peer recognition. One selects some names to acknowledge the person. Other names are selected because earning you points is their last opportunity to do something productive and honorable in their otherwise useless life. My most missed hit was Spiggy [Nixon's disgraced vice president, Spiro] Agnew; I was distressed at missing him."

Each Gamester pays ten dollars to Pontius, official coordinator and editor, to keep score and report the hits. There are players in over 30 states (23 in New York), plus one each in Quito, Kuwait, England, and Australia. You can become a Gamester only by being recommended by another Gamester. They're mostly baby boomers, attracted by a whimsical, informative style of reporting.

Forty-nine Gamesters "hit" Buddy Ebsen. Obituaries mentioned that after ten days of filming *The Wizard of Oz*, Ebsen fell ill because of the aluminum makeup on his skin and was replaced as the Tin Man by Jack Haley. (A suspicious player wondered, "Did Jack Haley add something to the aluminum makeup at the *Wizard* set?") Conversely, there have been "solos" on the unexpected demises of Princess Diana and JFK, Jr.

"A solo I am proud of," one Gamester told me, "is the hit on Christian Nelson, who invented the Klondike Bar."

"Yes, it's sick," another player admitted, "but c'mon, *it's just a game!* The Game is a lighthearted way of spitting in death's eye — your opportunity to pick a Generation-X rock star who ODs on heroin, a geriatric blue-hair who finally kicks the bucket, a fascist totalitarian in the Middle East who is assassinated. I'm not doing great this year because I invested too heavily in Hamas, but I'm still in the top ten. The IDF [Israel Defense Forces] is doing its job — I just guessed wrong. Last year I scored on Khattab, a Chechen rebel leader who was killed by a letter he opened that was poisoned. Our first poison-pen-letter death."

But isn't it somewhat ghoulish?

"Ghoulish?" a participant replied. "No more so than fantasy baseball. We can get up in the morning, and either pick up the newspaper or turn on the internet to see if we scored, every day. It's like baseball stats — you want to move up in the standings of the veterans. The reason we Gamesters play, I would say it's about *style*. Style involves who you pick. Some concentrate on music, some on politics, some on sports."

As for social significance, one player explained, "The pastime has been going on for more than four hundred years, so I don't think it's reflective of any given time or society. Every Gamester comes with their own perspective. The Game is irreverent, even a bit shocking, and some take pleasure in that. It's a poke to the ribs that lie beneath stuffed shirts, a tweak of bluenoses. The Game is a competition — challenging, engaging, and energizing. The Game heightens awareness and helps us to recognize our kinship with those whose deaths we note. The Game is a way of sharing and staying in touch with friends, whether near or far. It gives people a reason to call and correspond."

Pontius's predecessor, Ghostwriter, had thanked many folks in his farewell message, including "Persephone, who enabled me to say, 'Yes,' when a friend here in Central New York said, 'Do you know a good adoption lawyer in Arkansas?' It was my greatest cameo role, my finest hour as a networker, and I couldn't have done it without The Game and this wise, wonderful woman."

The Game's listserv emails are titled "It's a Hit!" They can be poignant, respectful, even sentimental: "July 4th — A score of swaying Gamesters were heard singing 'I Can't Get Enough of Your Love, Babe' as each collected a five-note from velvety-voiced singer Barry White ..."

Or they can sound like a warhorse race: "July 22nd — Mosul, Iraq. Qusay and Uday, the brutal and powerful sons of former Iraqi dictator Saddam Hussein, were ambushed by Special Forces and the 101st Airborne that resulted in a deadly four-hour firefight. Enjoying the best day of his career was Tomb Essence who had a 14-point Daily Double ..."

But the Game giveth and the Game taketh away: "August 21st — British and American armed forces in Iraq announced today that they had arrested Ali Hasan al-Majid, a.k.a. Chemical Ali. Back in April 2003, the British armed forces announced they had killed him. Tomb Essence celebrated then, but is crying like a baby now."

Animals have also been "scored," from Morris the Cat to Dolly the cloned sheep to Keiko the killer whale. Choices can get personal, though. A player told me, "I purposely left off a good friend [former *New York Post* editor Jerry Nachman] who I knew was dying, and one of our game mates refused to list a friend's [famous] mother who knew she was dying. Sometimes we just don't want to 'cash in' on our friends' pain. How un-American of us."

Gamesters have scored on all the Kennedys as well as Lorraine Petersen, the model on the Sun-Maid Raisins box. But, under the title "It's *Not* a Hit!" came this email: "August 9th — The entire Game failed to list dancer and actor Gregory Hines, 57." In The Game's 2001 Hit List, under the subhead "Other Notable Deaths That No One Picked," included was "Ken Kesey, 11/10/2001, author, *One Flew Over the Cuckoo's Nest*."

I had a visceral reaction. This was not abstract.

"I never could decide if leaving Kesey off my list was the right thing to do," one Gamester told me. "The Merry Pranksters obviously inspired my *nom de plume*, the Bury Pranksters."

Trashing the Right to Read

BEFORE KENNETH FOSTER'S DEATH sentence was revoked at the last minute in August 2007, he had read a book, *Welcome to the Terrordome*, and he wrote a letter to the author, Dave Zirin:

> I have never had the opportunity to view sports in this way. And as I went through these revelations, I began to have epiphanies about the way sports have a similar existence in prison. The similarities shook me.... Facing execution, the only thing that I began to get obsessive about was how to get heard and be free, and, as the saying goes, you can't serve two gods.
>
> Sports, as you know, becomes a way of life. You monitor it, you almost come to breathe it. Sports becomes a way of life in prison, because it becomes a way of survival. For men that don't have family or friends to help them financially ... it becomes a way to occupy your time. That's another sad story in itself, but it's the root to many men's obsession with sports.

Zirin writes, "It didn't matter if he was on Death Row or Park Avenue — I felt smarter having read his words. But even more satisfying was the thought that thinking about sports took his mind — for a moment — away from his imminent death, the 11-year-old daughter he will never touch, and the words he will never write. I thought sending him my first book, *What's My Name, Fool?: Sports and Resistance in the U.S.*, would be a good follow-up."

But a form titled "Texas Dept. of Criminal Justice, Publication Review/Denial Notification" announced a ban on Zirin's book from Death Row because "It contains material that a reasonable person would construe as written solely for the purpose of communicating information designed to achieve the breakdown of prisons through offender disruption such as strikes or riots."

Two pages were specifically mentioned.

Page 44 includes a quote from Jackie Robinson's autobiography referring to the blatant racism he suffered early in his rookie season: "I felt tortured and I tried to just play ball and ignore the insults, but it was really getting to me. For one wild and rage-crazed moment I thought, 'To hell with Mr. Rickey's noble experiment. To hell with the image of the patient black freak I was supposed to create.' I could throw down my bat, stride over to that Phillies dugout, grab one of those white sons of bitches, and smash his teeth in with my despised black fist. Then I could walk away from it all."

And page 55 includes a passage about Jack Johnson's defeat of the "Great White Hope," Jim Jeffries: "Johnson was faster, stronger, and smarter than Jeffries. He knocked Jeffries out with ease. After Johnson's victory, there were race riots around the country in Illinois, Missouri, New York, Ohio, Pennsylvania, Colorado, Texas, and Washington, D.C. Most of the riots consisted of white lynch mobs attacking blacks, and blacks fighting back. This reaction to a boxing match was one of the most widespread racial uprisings in the U.S. until the 1968 assassination of civil rights leader Dr. Martin Luther King, Jr."

Zirin points out, "There was a time in Texas when it was illegal to teach slaves to read. The fear was that ideas could turn anger often directed inward into action against those with their boots on black necks. It is perhaps the most fitting possible tribute to Jackie Robinson and Jack Johnson that they still strike fear into the hearts of those wearing the boots."

In the Dallas County jail, one of the largest in the country, *all* publications are refused, including daily newspapers such as *The Dallas Morning News*. "They seem to have a rather callous disregard for the Constitution," said Paul Wright, publisher of Seattle-based *Prison Legal News*, with a circulation of 9,000. He filed a federal lawsuit challenging the ban on First Amendment grounds and won. His lawyer, Scott Medlock, prisoner-rights attorney with the Texas Civil Rights Project, points out that some jails have argued that prisoners can watch TV news in jail, so they don't need access to publications.

Prison Legal News is also preparing a lawsuit against the Utah Department of Corrections for a policy that bars all books except those that are shipped directly from Barnes & Noble. Generally, prisons require that books be sent directly from the publisher or a major distributor, for security reasons. Otherwise, a spokesperson for one jail explains, "There's a possibility something could be in one of the pages that we don't want. There could be little bits of drugs in the pages."

"We have not yet sued them." Wright told me, "since they only sporadically censor us and aren't letting us develop a good fact pattern."

A spokesperson for the Los Angeles County Sheriff's Department said that its jails allow inmates to receive books from booksellers after checking to see whether they can be fashioned into a weapon, promote violence, or have sexually explicit content. Across the country, only paperbacks are accepted. Hardcovers are rejected because they provide "source material" for fashioning weapons. When the Supreme Court ruled that law libraries did not have to be provided to prisoners, jails in Montana not only removed the entire contents of the law library, but they also removed the typewriters.

Washington State has tried to keep *Prison Legal News* itself out of prisons. First, the Department of Corrections prohibited inmates from receiving free publications. PLN sued and won. Next, the state issued a rule that inmates couldn't receive publications that were paid out of their trust accounts. PLN managed to get that rule overturned, too. Then the prisons adopted a policy of not delivering subscription-renewal notices. PLN took that to court and succeeded in getting the policy reversed. PLN has won similar lawsuits or settlements in Alabama, California, Michigan, Nevada, and Oregon.

While serving five years in a California prison for growing medical marijuana, Todd McCormick contributed a couple of stories — about his experiences with psilocybin and ketamine — to my anthology, *Magic Mushrooms and Other Highs: From Toad Slime to Ecstasy,* and when it was published, I immediately sent him a copy. But the warden rejected it "because on pages 259-261, it describes the process of squeezing toads to obtain illicit substances which could be detrimental to the security, good order and discipline of the institution."

This was pure theater of cruelty. Federal correctional facilities do not have a toad problem, and outside accomplices have not been catapulting loads of toads over barbed wire fences to provide the fuel for a prison riot. McCormick wrote to me, "Can you believe this shit! I wonder how much we pay the guy/girl who actually sits and reads every book that comes in for offending passages. How about you tear out pages 259-261 and re-send this book back with a copy of the rejection and a notation that the offending pages have been removed."

Which is exactly what I did. This time, though, my cover letter to the warden was ignored, and the book was returned, stamped "Unauthorized." I had called their bluff. Obviously, McCormick was being punished simply because he could be. I then corresponded with several prison correspondents around the country to find out what inmates had not been allowed to read. I wanted to see other examples of arbitrary and frivolous censorship by prison personnel. Here are some results of my informal survey:

- "The Texas Department of Corrections blocked Bo Lozoff's *Breaking Out of Jail*, a book about teaching meditation to prison inmates."

- "Disallowed: *Trainspotting* because of its 'glorification of drug use'; Tom Robbins's *Still Life With Woodpecker* because it has a chapter that 'contains information about bombmaking'."

- "An inmate couldn't get nude pictures of his wife sent to him, but he could get a subscription to *Playboy*. The rationale: A wife deserved more respect."

- "They kept out *The Anarchist Cookbook*. And no kiddie porn, no tales or photos suggesting sex with a guard, no photos showing frontal or rear nudity — not even a wife or friend."

- "The Utah prison system banned *Rolling Stone* as being an anarchist publication."

- "*A Revolution in Kindness* is banned from the Louisiana State Penitentiary at Angola as 'a threat to internal security.' It was intended for Herman Wallace, who contributed an essay about how he organized a chess tournament on his cellblock as a way of easing tensions and minimizing violence between inmates. Wallace is one of the Angola Three, Black Panthers who have been in solitary confinement for [more than three decades] trying to improve conditions in the 'bloodiest prison in America' in the early 1970s."

- "All hardback books forbidden, because the covers could be fashioned into weapons. Educational textbooks — a new rule precludes prisoners on Death Row [including this particular prisoner] or in lockdown from taking correspondence courses — and I've had a couple of books returned to sender on the claim they appeared to be for a course. MAPS [Multidisciplinary Association for Psychedelic Studies] — their publication was sent back several times because maps are not allowed in here. *High Times* was repeatedly denied because it posed a danger to the safe, secure, and orderly operation of the institution. 'Smut mags' like *Hustler* are reviewed monthly."

- "There's a whole new genre of men's magazines — *Maxim, Stuff, For Him* — which show it all except for nipples and beaver. Now the feds want to ban *Maxim* due to 'security' reasons. The 'rejected mail' slip they send you when some verboten material arrives has boxes to check (to specify offending matter), one of which says 'pubic hair'."

- "Peace activist William Combs spent eight days in solitary confinement for receiving and sharing with other inmates what federal authorities consider disruptive, if not subversive, political literature. The offending 'propaganda' included commentary by such extremists as Bill Moyers and Ellen Goodman, and included an article published in *Reader's Digest*. The common thread was that they all questioned the wisdom of government policy."

The name of the game is control in the guise of security — a microcosm of the nation outside prison walls — the practice of power without compassion.

After *Magic Mushrooms and Other Highs* was rejected for the second time, I appealed to the Regional Director of the Bureau of Prisons (as instructed by the warden) for an independent review. I also wrote to the ACLU. I heard back from neither. Todd McCormick was released from prison in December 2003. Among so many other things to catch up on, he would finally be able to read what he had written. However, he was discharged to a halfway house, where all his books and magazines were confiscated as "paraphernalia."

POSTSCRIPT

PRISONERS AT A JAIL in South Carolina are being denied any reading material other than the Bible. In May 2011, the ACLU asked a federal judge to block enforcement of that policy. A staff member at the prison told plaintiff *Prison Legal News*: "Our inmates are only allowed to receive soft-back Bibles in the mail directly from the publisher. They are not allowed to have magazines, newspapers, or any other type of books." There is no library there, and since 2008, all copies of *Prison Legal News* that were sent to prisoners have been "returned to sender."

In July 2017, the national Human Rights Defense Center organization filed a federal lawsuit against the Kentucky Department of Corrections for violating free speech. It has unconstitutionally blocked the delivery of many books to state prisoners, including the *Prisoner Diabetes Handbook*, the *Merriam-Webster Dictionary of Law*, and the *Prisoners' Self-Help Litigation Manual*.

Welcome to Camp Mogul

MY IRREVERENT FRIEND, Khan Manka, Chairman and CEO of Manka Bros. Studios, had broken his ankle and was afraid he wouldn't be able to attend the 26th annual gathering of the nation's most powerful executives and their trophy wives in Sun Valley, Idaho. I really wanted to spy on this 2008 summer camp for billionaires, so I suggested that Manka get a wheelchair, then I could serve as his official wheelchair pusher, and he immediately went for the idea.

This by-now traditional five-day extravaganza for 300 guests was hosted by Wall Street investment banker Herbert Allen, President and CEO of Allen & Company. There were moguls all over the campground, overflowing with the country's most influential leaders in business, entertainment, and media. I could feel myself developing a severe case of imposter syndrome.

Saturday was Talent Night, and it was absolutely hysterical. Part-time Sun Valley resident Tom Hanks served as the emcee. Warren Buffett was the opening act, performing a medley of Jimmy Buffett songs, all rendered out of tune. Amazon founder Jeff Bezos skillfully juggled five Kindles (wireless electronic books). Edgar Bronfman from Warner Music — dressed like the character Tevye in *Fiddler on the Roof* — sang with zest, "If I Were a Rich Man." Yahoo CEO Jerry Yang — who had previously turned down an offer from Microsoft to buy Yahoo — sang a duet with the ex-CEO of Microsoft, Bill Gates, harmonizing on a song from *Annie Get Your Gun*, "Anything You Can Do, I Can Do Better." Meg Whitman of eBay did a striptease, auctioning off each item of clothing, one at a time, and over $3 million was raised for an unnamed charity. Oracle Corp. CEO Larry Ellison gave a hilarious lecture on "How to Destroy Evidence and Make False Statements."

There had been a lot of drinking in the evening, and it was obviously too much booze that loosened up Fox mogul Rupert Murdoch's tongue. He was shouting at the moon: "Who says there are 27 million slaves around the world? And where the fuck can I get one? How would anybody know it's 27 million, anyway? Do they have census takers or *what*? You tell me! I'll decide!"

Also, a screaming match broke out between Google co-founder Sergei Brin and Google CEO Eric Schmidt over the infamous cover of the *New Yorker*, which depicted Barack and Michelle Obama as the new President and First Lady, a terrorist couple doing that fist-bump gesture in the Oval Office. Sergei thought it was a brilliant satirical illustration, but Eric thought it was racist and irresponsible.

Last year, the surprise guest was former British Prime Minister Tony Blair. This year, it was Steven Beschloss, the editor of a new magazine, scheduled to be launched in October 2008 and be delivered to 100,000 U.S. households with an average net worth of $25 million. There were piles of preview copies scattered about.

While Beschloss was holding court in an outdoor area, annoying mosquitoes kept buzzing around the crowd. Mark Zuckerberg, the founder of Facebook, yelled at him, "I guess we'll never hear *your* readers whining about a mental recession. And those of your subscribers who were in the sub-prime mortgage industry — these mosquitoes are *their* fault, because, along with all the home foreclosures they're responsible for, the stagnant water in abandoned pools turns into new breeding grounds for mosquitoes."

Someone yelled out, "Where are you from, In-Your-Facebook?" Others drowned out Zuckerberg's apparently serious rant by singing the mogul version of a couple of good old-fashioned camp songs, "This Land Is *My* Land, This Land Is *My* Land" and "KumBuyYahoo." I couldn't help but notice that billionaire activist Carl Icahn snapped his fingers as if having an epiphany; a week later he ended up on Yahoo's board of directors.

Khan Manka explained that the bigwigs at these events have so-called "informal" meetings that always take place where a pair of individuals can have their discussions alone without any interruption — on the golf course, hiking along an isolated trail, fly-fishing at Silver Creek — but Manka had been privy to only one specific example that he could share.

"Back in 1995," he told me, "Disney honcho Michael Eisner met with Robert Iger, who was then the head of ABC. And exactly one month later, these two giant companies merged into one media megamonster. Coincidence? I don't think so. Their deal had been sealed when Eisner and Iger exchanged friendship bracelets that they had worked on at Camp Mogul."

PAUL KRASSNER

The Itinerary of
FBI Agent Bates

WHEN THE SANTA CLARA, CALIFORNIA, district attorney's office tried to locate stolen documents for an investigation of FBI-sponsored political burglaries, a member of that office testified that FBI agent Charles Bates had "categorically denied" having any of them. But after being confronted with the testimony of one of his own subordinates, Bates ultimately turned over the documents. Some of the stolen documents, according to *Sundaz*, a Santa Cruz weekly, ended up with Catherine Hearst's pet project, Research West.

In 1969, Charles Bates was a Special Agent at the Chicago office of the FBI when police killed Black Panthers Fred Hampton and Mark Clark while they were sleeping. Ex-FBI informer Maria Fischer told the *Chicago Daily News* that the then-chief of the FBI's Chicago office, Marlon Johnson, personally asked her to slip a drug to Hampton; she had infiltrated the Black Panther Party at the FBI's request a month before. The drug was a tasteless, colorless liquid that would put him to sleep. She refused. Hampton was killed a week later. An autopsy showed "a near fatal dose" of secobarbital in his system.

In 1971, Bates was transferred to Washington, D.C. According to Watergate burglar James McCord's book, *A Piece of Tape*, on June 21, 1972 (four days after the break-in), White House attorney John Dean checked with acting FBI Director L. Patrick Gray as to who was in charge of handling the Watergate investigation. The answer: Charles Bates — the same FBI official who in 1974 would be in charge of handling the SLA investigation and the search for Patty Hearst. When she was arrested, Bates became instantly ubiquitous on radio and TV, boasting of her capture.

And, in the middle of her trial — on a Saturday afternoon, when reporters and technicians were hoping to be off duty — the FBI called a press conference. At 5:00 that morning, they had raided the New Dawn collective — supposedly the aboveground support group of the Berkeley underground Emiliano Zapata Unit — and accompanying a press release about the evidence seized were photographs still wet with developing fluid. Charles Bates held the photos up in the air.

"Mr. Bates," a photographer requested, "real close to your head, please."

Bates proceeded to pose with the photos like Henry Fonda doing a camera commercial. Was there a search warrant? No, but they had a "consent to search" signed by the owner of the house, Judy Sevenson, who later admitted to being a paid FBI informant.

Not only did the raid seem timed to break into print simultaneously with the Sunday funnies, but the investigative technique also smacked of comic-strip morality. In *Dick Tracy*, the "Crimestoppers Textbook" depicted a trio of stereotypical hippie terrorists preparing a time bomb, underscored by the question, "Would you deny police access to knowledge of persons planning your demise?"

Almost six weeks after that Saturday-morning raid, I received a letter by registered mail on Department of Justice stationery:

> Dear Mr. Krassner:
>
> Subsequent to the search of a residence in connection with the arrest of six members of the Emiliano Zapata Unit, the Federal Bureau of Investigation, San Francisco, has been attempting to contact you to advise you of the following information:
>
> During the above indicated arrest of six individuals of the Emiliano Zapata Unit, an untitled list of names and addresses of individuals was seized. A corroborative source described the above list as an Emiliano Zapata Unit "hit list," but stated that no action will be taken, since all of those who could carry it out are in custody.
>
> Further, if any of the apprehended individuals should make bail, they would only act upon the "hit list" at the instructions of their leader, who is not and will not be in a position to give such instructions.
>
> The above information is furnished for your personal use and it is requested it be kept confidential. At your discretion, you may desire

to contact the local police department responsible for the area of your residence.

> Very Truly Yours,
> Charles W. Bates
> Special Agent in Charge

But I was more logically a target of the government than of the Emiliano Zapata Unit — unless, of course, they happened to be the same. Was the right wing of the FBI warning me about the left wing of the FBI? Did the handwriting on the wall read *COINTELPRO Lives*? (COINTELPRO was their Counter-Intelligence Program.) Questions about the authenticity of the Zapata Unit had been raised by its first public statement in August 1975, which included the unprecedented threat of violence against the Left.

When a Safeway supermarket in Oakland was bombed by the Zapata Unit, they claimed to have called radio station KPFA and instructed them to notify police, so they could evacuate the area, but KPFA staffers insisted they never received such a call. Now *The Urban Guerrilla*, aboveground organ of the underground NWLF (New World Liberation Front), commented:

> Without offering any proof, the FBI has claimed that [those arrested] were members of the Emiliano Zapata Unit and mistakenly claimed that the Zapata Unit was part of the New World Liberation Front (NWLF). These FBI claims and lies had been widely repeated by the media.
>
> As soon as they were arrested, Greg Adornetto, whom we knew as Chepito, was separated from the others and disappeared ...
>
> A close analysis of all the actions and statements ... by Chepito leads [us] to the inescapable conclusion that he is not just a weak informer, he is a government infiltrator/provocateur. No other conclusion is possible when one considers that he led our comrades to a house he *knew* was under surveillance ... carrying along things like explosives and half-completed communiqués ...
>
> He recruited sincere and committed revolutionaries who wanted to participate in being a medium for dialogue with the underground, got a bunch of them in the same room with guns, communiqués, and explosives, or even got some of them involved in armed actions, and then had ... Bates move in with his SWAT team and bust everybody ...

In addition, a communiqué from the central command of the NWLF charged that "the pigs led and organized" the Zapata Unit. "We were reasonably sure that it was a set-up from the beginning and we *never* sent one communiqué to New Dawn because of our suspicions."

After publishing the FBI's warning letter to me in the *Berkeley Barb*, I received letters from a couple of members of the Emiliano Zapata Unit in prison. One stated:

> I was involved in the aboveground support group of the Zapata Unit. Greg Adornetto led myself and several others to believe we were joining a cell of the Weather Underground, which had a new surge of life when it published *Prairie Fire*. I knew nothing about a hit list or your being on one and can't imagine why you would have been. When we were arrested, FBI agent-provocateur Adornetto immediately turned against the rest of us and provided evidence to the government.

Another Zapata Unit prisoner advised:

> You shouldn't have believed the boys in the black shiny shoes (FBI) about being on a Zapata hit list. They just found some addresses, and Bates and his running partner Hearst wanted to build up some sensationalism to take the heat off of Patty's trial. They had over 75 people (politicians and corporate execs) under protection, thinking all of us didn't get arrested.

Jacques Rogiers — the aboveground courier for the underground New World Liberation Front who delivered their communiqués — told me at my house that the reason I was on the hit list was because I had written that Donald DeFreeze was a police informer.

"But that was true," I said. "It's a matter of record. Doesn't that make any difference?"

It didn't.

If the NWLF asked me to kill you," Rogiers admitted, "I would."

"Jacques," I replied, "I think this puts a slight damper on our relationship."

So my daughter Holly and I moved to another home.

Higher Than Thou

Checkmating With Pawns

IT WAS A HOT DAY at the chess tournament in Phoenix, Arizona — 103 degrees, to be exact — and 14-year-old Nathaniel Dight was elated over his custom-made chess set. Those carved wooden pieces had been weighted precisely for the smooth moves he liked to make. Each one had been lacquered and, for this extreme heat, carefully protected by matte acrylic spray. But before the game could begin, young Nathaniel was ordered to take a urine test.

"I know why you're doing this," he snarled. "It's because I've won three tournaments in a row, isn't it?"

"No, son, that's just a coincidence. This is a random drug test."

"I don't do any drugs. I mean like when I get a headache from playing chess too long, I won't even take an aspirin."

"Look, here's a cup. I need you to go fill it, right now ..."

All right, I confess, I made all that up, but consider the implications of something that I *haven't* made up:

> America's drug czar, Barry McCaffrey, wrote in an article published in *Chess Life* magazine: "Research proves that mentoring youngsters and teaching them games like chess can build resilience in the face of illegal drug use and other destructive temptations. Drug testing is as appropriate for chess players as for shot-putters, or any other competitors who use their heads as well as their hands."

Accompanying the television image of a couple of eggs sizzling in a frying pan, the phrase, "This is your brain on drugs" has always carried negative connotations, but apparently General McCaffrey has changed his mind about that. He now seems to believe that drugs can actually *improve* the way your brain functions.

There was an infamous chess player named Alexander Alekhine who held the world championship longer than anybody else. His games often had superb surprise endings, known in chess circles as "brilliancies." For instance, he would checkmate with a pawn move that no sane and sober mind could ever imagine. However, he was a notorious alcoholic, and McCaffrey is only referring to illegal drugs.

"Just when I thought I'd heard it all from McCaffrey," was the reaction of Allen St. Pierre, executive director of the NORML (National Organization for the Reform of Marijuana Laws) Foundation. "Drug testing for chess players? What's next from this overreaching drug czar? Drug testing for tiddlywinks players? How about bingo players?"

Moreover, McCaffrey's proposal smacks of subliminal racism. Social psychologist Walli Leff tells me, "I think most of the movement to involve young people in chess is directed toward the African-American community, and the assumption is, if the kids are black, they're going to be drug users. I think white middle-class suburban parents would have a fit if their kids had to take drug tests for their extracurricular activities. Or am I out of it, and am I missing a new, white middle-class suburban submissiveness?"

McCaffrey had been influenced by Chesschild, a group sponsored by the Office of National Drug Control Policy (ONDCP). Chesschild is a substance-abuse prevention program conducted in libraries and schools, promoting a combination of drug-free lifestyles and chess.

"Policy recommendations like this one from ONDCP," said St. Pierre, "demonstrate a deep and disturbing pathology that goes well beyond opposing drug-law reform efforts."

Maybe the drug-law reformers should follow the example of gay-rights activists by having celebrities come out of the pot-smoking closet. Already, veteran stand-up comic George Carlin — in an interview by *The Daily Show*'s Jon Stewart following Carlin's HBO special — admitted that he smokes a joint to help him "fine tune" his material. "One hit is all I need now, and it's punch-up time."

At the Shadow Convention that took place while the Democrats were in Los Angeles, Bill Maher revealed to the audience, "I'm not just a pot reformer, I'm a user" — something which ABC forbids him to say on *Politically Incorrect* — then quickly added, "Just making a light remark there, federal authorities."

Actor and hemp activist Woody Harrelson has stated, "I do smoke." Willie Nelson confirmed in his autobiography that he smoked pot in the White House. And on KRLA, radio talk-show host Michael Jackson's program, Michelle Phillips, actress and former member of the Mamas and the Papas, said that she still enjoys smoking marijuana.

Just as Ellen DeGeneres appeared on the cover of *Time* magazine saying, "Yep, I'm gay," there might come a day when a presidential candidate will appear on the cover of *Newsweek* saying, "Yep, I'm stoned." Isn't that what young pot-smokers need — good role models — so they won't be ashamed of their private pleasure-seeking?

Meanwhile, drug czar McCaffrey would continue his crusade, not only against illegal substances, but perhaps also against certain food supplements, such as a popular herbal mixture with a reputation for aiding memory and concentration. Who could ever have dreamed that chess players might get in trouble for using ginkgo biloba as a performance enhancer?

Tim Leary, Ram Dass, and Me

IN 1964, I ASSIGNED Robert Anton Wilson to write a front-cover article in *The Realist*, which he titled "Timothy Leary and His Psychological H-Bomb." When that issue was published, Leary invited me to visit the Castalia Foundation, his borrowed estate in Millbrook, New York.

The name Castalia came from *The Bead Game* by Herman Hesse, and indeed, the game metaphor permeated our conversation. Leary talked about the way people are always trying to get you onto their game boards. He discussed the biochemical process "imprinting" with the same passion that he claimed he didn't believe anything he was saying, but somehow, I managed to believe him when he told me that I had an honest mind.

"I have to admit," I said, "that my ego can't help but respond to your observation."

"Listen," he assured me, "anybody who tells you he's transcended his ego ..."

Leary and his research partner, Ram Dass (then Richard Alpert) were about to do a lecture series on the West Coast. At the University of California in Berkeley, there was an official announcement that the distribution only of "informative" literature (as opposed to "persuasive" literature) would be permitted on campus, giving rise to the Free Speech Movement, with thousands of students protesting the ban in the face of police billy clubs.

Leary argued that such demonstrations played right onto the game boards of the administration and the police alike, and that the students could shake up the establishment much more if they would just stay in their rooms and change their nervous systems. But it wasn't really a case of either-or. You could protest *and* explore your 13-billion-cell mind simultaneously.

I became intrigued by the playful and subtle patterns of awareness that Leary and Alpert manifested. If their brains had been so damaged, as mythologized by mainstream media, how come their perceptions were so sharp? I began to research the LSD phenomenon, and in April 1965, I returned to Millbrook for my first acid experience. Tim Leary was supposed to be my guide, but he had gone off to India.

Dick Alpert was supposed to take his place, but he was too involved in getting ready to open at the Village Vanguard as a comedian-philosopher. I chatted with him for a while. He was soaking his body in a bathtub, preparing his psyche for the Vanguard gig. He had taken 300 acid trips, but there I was, a first-timer, standing in the open doorway, reversing roles and comforting him in his anxiety about entering show business. When I told my mother about taking LSD, she was quite concerned. She warned me, "It could lead to marijuana." And she was right. It did.

After Leary got arrested in Texas for possession of pot, the notoriety of his research in Millbrook spread. Law enforcement in nearby Pough-keepsie, led by Assistant District Attorney G. Gordon Liddy, raided the estate. In the summer of 1966, Leary and his associates ran a two-week seminar on consciousness expansion, culminating in a theatrical pro-duction of Hesse's *Steppenwolf* legend that weaved its way around the Millbrook grounds and buildings. Leary invited Liddy and members of the grand jury that indicted him, but none showed up.

Leary told me about prominent people whose lives had been changed by taking LSD: actor Cary Grant, director Otto Preminger, think-tanker Herman Kahn, Alcoholics Anonymous founder Bill Wilson, *Time* magazine publishers Henry and Clare Boothe Luce. Of course, it wasn't so difficult to drop out when you had such a stimulating scene to drop into. On the day that he announced the formation of a new religion, the League for Spiritual Discovery (LSD), I signed up as their first heretic.

Alpert and I enjoyed what he called "upleveling" each other with honesty. On one occasion, we were at a party. I was particularly manic, and he pointed it out, choosing an eggbeater as his analogy. I appreci-ated his reflection and calmed down.

On stage at the Village Theater, Alpert was sitting in the lotus position on a cushion, talking about his mother dying and how there

seemed to be a conspiracy on the part of relatives and hospital personnel alike to deny her the realization of that possibility. He also talked
about some fellow in a mental institution who thought he was Jesus
Christ. Conversely, I teased him about discussing his mother openly
but concealing the fact that the man who thought he was Christ was
his brother — death obviously carrying more respectability than crazi-
ness. At his next performance, Alpert identified the man as his brother.

THE ESSENTIAL DIFFERENCE between Tim Leary and G. Gordon Liddy was
that Leary wanted people to use LSD as a vehicle for expanding consciousness, whereas Liddy wanted to put LSD on the steering wheel of
columnist Jack Anderson's car, thereby making a political assassination
look like an automobile accident. But who could have predicted that,
sixteen years after the original arrest, Leary would end up traveling
around with Liddy in a series of debates?

I attended the debate in Berkeley in April 1982. Leary warned the
audience that Liddy was a lawyer — "trained in the adversary process, not to seek truth. I was trained as a scientist — looking for truth,
delighted to be proved wrong." He confessed that "Liddy is the Moriarty
to my Sherlock Holmes — the adversary I always wanted — he is the
Darth Vader to my Mr. Spock."

"As long as it's not Doctor Spock," said Liddy. He argued that "the
rights of the state transcend those of the individual." Not that he was
without compassion. "I feel sorry," he admitted, "for anybody who uses
drugs for aphrodisiacal purposes."

"Gordon doesn't know anything about drugs," countered Leary. "It's
probably his only weakness." He looked directly at Liddy. "It's my duty
to turn you on," he said, "and I'm gonna do it before these debates are
over." Then he made a unique offer: "I'll eat a rat if you'll eat a hashish
cookie."

Liddy turned down the offer — one can carry machismo only so far,
and he had to draw the line somewhere — but he did provide appropriate grist for my own stand-up comedy mill. According to Liddy's
book, he actually ate a rat. He did it to overcome his fear of eating rats.
Certainly a direct approach to the problem. None of that *gestalt* shit.

Now, I'm not sure how he ate the rat, whether he just stuck it between a couple of slices of bread, or barbecued it first, or chopped the rat up and mixed it with vegetables in a stew.

But there were rumors that when Leary and Liddy were on tour, the Psychedelic Liberation Front found out their itinerary and began feeding hash brownies to rats and releasing them, one by one, in Liddy's room at the various motels he stayed at, while he was debating, in the hope that nature would sooner or later take its course, and one night Liddy would feel in the mood for a midnight snack, catch the rat that was left in the room, eat it and, by extension, the hash brownie the rat had eaten, and then Liddy would think he got stoned from eating the rat. This would, of course, be right on the borderline of the ethics of dosing.

EACH TABLET OF OWSLEY WHITE LIGHTNING contained 300 micrograms of LSD. I had purchased a large enough supply from Alpert to finance his trip to India. The day before he left to meditate for six months, we sat in a restaurant discussing the concept of choiceless awareness while trying to decide what to order on the menu.

In India, he gave his guru three tablets, and apparently nothing happened. Alpert's postcard to me beckoned, "Come fuck the universe with me." Instead, I stayed tripping in America, where I kept my entire stash of acid in a bank vault deposit box.

Richard Alpert returned as Baba Ram Dass. Eventually, he dropped the Baba. He was now just plain Ram Dass. His father called him Rum Dum. His brother called him Rammed Ass. One afternoon he was visiting me, and I taped our conversation.

"In 1963," I said, "I predicted, as a joke, that Tiny Tim would get married on the Johnny Carson show, and in 1969, it happened. You and I talked about that, and you called it 'astral humor,' but I never knew exactly what you meant by that phrase."

"Well, it's like each plane of reality is, in a sense, a manifestation of a plane prior to it, and you can almost see it like layers, although to think of it in space is a fallacy because it's all the same space, but you could think of it that way. And so there are beings on upper planes who are instruments of the law. I talk about miracles a lot, but I don't live in the world of miracles, because they're not miracles to me. I'm just dealing with the humor of the miracle concept from within the plane where it seems like a miracle, which is merely because of our very narrow concept of how the universe works."

Ram Dass knew of my involvement with conspiracy theory. "I'm just involved in a much greater conspiracy," he continued. "You can't grasp the size of the conspiracy I understand. But there's no 'conspirator' — it's the wrong word. That's why I say it's just natural law. It is all perfect."

"Would you agree with the concept — what William Blake said, that humans were created 'for joy and woe' — the implication of which is that there will always be suffering?"

"I think that suffering is part of man's condition, and that's what the incarnation is about, and that's what the human plane is."

So I asked Ram Dass, "If you and I were to exchange philosophies — if I believed in reincarnation, and you didn't — how do you think our behavior would change?" He paused for a moment. "Well," he said, "if you believed in reincarnation, you would never ask a question like that."

And then his low chuckle of amusement and surprise blossomed into an uproarious belly laugh of delight and triumph as he savored the implications of his own Zen answer. I would find myself playing that segment of the tape with his bell-shaped spasm of laughter over and over again, like a favorite piece of music.

PAUL KRASSNER

Remembering Scott Kelman

SCOTT KELMAN HAD SEEN ME perform stand-up satire at Town Hall in New York in 1962, and again twenty years later at the L.A. Stage Company in Hollywood. He moved to Los Angeles, and, in 1984, he launched an alternative theater in the grungy, old, industrial skid-row area of downtown. He named it the Wallenboyd (at the corner of Wall and Boyd) Theater and invited me to open there as soon as it was completed.

In fact, on the first night of my performances, the crew was still banging in the final nails. At the time, I was living in San Francisco, so Scott slept at his office, and I stayed at his apartment in Venice Beach. A year later, I moved to an apartment on that same block. Scott became my producer and my close friend. We never had any need for a signed contract.

As my producer, he would occasionally give me suggestions, and I would follow those that I felt worked for me. He'd say in his distinctive gravelly voice (he was addicted to cigarettes), "It doesn't matter if you fuck up — it's how you recover." That was theatrical advice, but it also applied to life.

And it was a two-way street. For Scott, whatever happened in life automatically became grist for his theatrical mill. He was an exemplary explorer. Knowing I was an unbeliever, he once asked me, "What do atheists say during sex when they come?"

"Oh, *no*-God!" I responded, interspersing those words with moans and groans. "Oh, *no*-God! Oh, *no*-God! Oh, *no*-God!" He suggested that I expand that concept into a stage piece, and it evolved into a ten-minute meditation on the relationship between religion and orgasms.

Scott conducted theatrical workshops, and one of his students was John Densmore, the former drummer for The Doors. "I stumbled into the downtown art scene," Densmore told me, "after a big peak in rock 'n' roll. It felt as creative as the '60s. I now get off on the *process*, and it doesn't matter if it's 50 people at the Wallenboyd or 20,000 at Madison Square Garden. It's the work that rings my bell."

Scott also produced Peter Bergman, of the Firesign Theatre. Scott thought that *Peter, Paul, and Harry* would be a great title for an evening of political satire at the Museum of Contemporary Art. He asked the curator if she knew of an appropriate performer named Harry. She suggested Harry Shearer. Scott asked me about him. "He's brilliant," I said, "let's do it." And so he produced a completely sold-out series that was extended for two weekends.

But if Harry had been named after his *other* grandfather, there wouldn't have been a *Peter, Paul, and Harry*. Each of us prepared to perform in our own particular way. Peter stared at himself in the mirror and made strange sounds to exercise his vocal cords. Harry sat in a separate room where his makeup woman, who had flown in from Iowa, transformed him into Derek Smalls from the mockumentary *Spinal Tap*.

And I was off hiding behind some boxes, toking away on a joint of the marijuana that served as my creative fuel. Scott was sure that I performed better when I wasn't high, and he was under the impression I was straight when he told me one night, "That was the best show you've ever done." I confessed that I had smoked a giant doobie before I went onstage. The irony was that Scott sold pot to help pay the rent, and that was exactly the stash that got me stoned that night.

The 20th Anniversary of the Summer of Love

I NEVER WENT to any of my high school or college reunions, but I couldn't resist attending the 20th anniversary of the Summer of Love in San Francisco. At noon on the summer solstice of 1987, young and middle-aged hippies — gray hair and potbellies, but not having erased a certain gleam in their eyes — were marching in an All Beings parade down Haight Street. Costumes ranged from a giant snail to Zippy the Pinhead.

One fellow still in civilian clothes explained, "I was supposed to be Tarzan, but I had to wash the dishes."

Local countercultural fixtures were all there: The Mime Troupe, Rosie Radiator and her fleet of tap dancers, the Automatic Human Juke Box, and a panhandler asking, "Can you spare a hundred dollars?" The buses now had posters that suggested *Shop the Haight.*

The charm of that entrepreneurial urge was not to be confused with the mission of the Haight-Ashbury Preservation Society, whose targets were symbolized by a walking Big Mac cheeseburger, a prisoner of Thrifty's in chain-store chains, mock pallbearers carrying a casket to mourn the wished-for death of Round Table Pizza, a sign warning *Don't Mall the Haight!* and somebody in a Merlin the Magician outfit with a placard, *You don't need magic to fight the franchising.* A lone, sad-faced clown bore a banner with a white dove in a red heart.

In Golden Gate Park, an emcee asked the crowd a series of rhetorical questions to rev them up: "How many people were here in the '60s?... How many are here now?... How many don't know?... How many don't care?" A musician announced, "We were told not to have amplifiers, but we decided to break the law today." Hog Farmer Sharon

Share-alike offered her roll of hard candy to novelist Herb Gold, which immediately aroused his fear of dosing. He asked, "These really are Life Savers, right?"

The Summer of Love reunion continued at the I-Beam, a disco on Haight Street. On stage, I compared the decades:

- In the '60s, marijuana was ten dollars an ounce. In the '80s, it's 300. In the '60s, teenagers used to hide their pot smoking from their parents. In the '80s, parents have to hide it from their kids. In the '60s, the favorite chemical drug was LSD. In the '80s, it's Ecstasy. In the '60s, Ken Kesey wasn't allowed to donate blood because he had ingested acid. In the '80s, there are those who are afraid to get a blood transfusion because of AIDS. In the '60s, Lenny Bruce got arrested for saying "cocksucker" on stage. In the '80s, Meryl Streep got an Academy Award for saying it in *Sophie's Choice*. Now, almost the entire audience at a Grateful Dead concert is younger than the number of years the band has been together — but these kids have less deconditioning to go through than we did. They have less innocence to lose.

- When a group of students and other protesters, including Abbie Hoffman and Amy Carter (the president's daughter), won their case against CIA recruiting on campus by using a "necessity defense," attorney Leonard Weinglass told me that the turning point for the jury was the testimony of Ralph McGehee, who revealed how he had been recruited right off the football field by the CIA, only to become a star player in their assassination-squad program. Members of the jury would not have voted that way in the '60s because they weren't prepared to believe such testimony as they are in the '80s.

- In the '60s, we knew that the CIA was smuggling heroin from Southeast Asia. And in the '80s we know that they're smuggling cocaine from Central America. The same planes that fly weapons for the *contras* to airports in Panama, Honduras, and Costa Rica come back to Florida, Louisiana, and Arkansas with their cargoes filled to the brim with cocaine, even though the administration is carrying on its anti-drug campaign. The pilots only have to be careful to evade the radar screen. So while Nancy Reagan is saying, "Just say no," the CIA is saying, "Just fly low."

- Meanwhile, the quality of co-option had not been strained. The slogan "Today is the first day of the rest of your life" was used in a TV commercial for Total breakfast cereal. Tampax promoted its tampon as "Something over thirty you can trust." Beatles songs were used to sell cars, or, if you preferred to walk, they also sold sneakers. *Time* magazine was being peddled by the Byrds' version of Pete Seeger's song, "Turn, Turn, Turn" — based on Ecclesiastes — there's a *time* for this and a *time* for that, get it?

- The Youngbloods once sent a copy of their song "Get Together" to every member of Congress and the Senate, with a suggestion that it be established as the new national anthem, but who could ever have guessed that it was really destined to become a jingle in a jeans commercial? Or that a Jefferson Airplane song would be used in a bank commercial? Or that Timothy Leary would model a Gap shirt for a full-page ad in *Interview*, and Ram Dass would peddle a rejuvenating skin cream at a Saks Fifth Avenue counter? *People* magazine was selling the 20th anniversary of the Summer of Love with a feature story set off by a double-paged cover with psychedelic artist Peter Max's signature on both pages.

- In red spray paint, on a brick wall just off Haight Street, standing out among the graffiti like John Hancock's signature on the Declaration of Independence, this message summed it all up: *Love Is Revenue.*

Politics

Election 2008

THE REPUBLICANS' PARTY LINE that Barack Obama was "palling around with terrorists" didn't work, although some people believed it because then they wouldn't need a racist reason not to vote for Obama. Next, the campaign acted as though his advocacy of age-appropriate sex education for kindergarteners meant putting condoms on cucumbers. That didn't work, either. Then John McCain tried calling him a "socialist." Also didn't work. Ironically, Socialist Party candidate Norman Thomas ran for president six times, and never won, but every one of his platform planks were eventually adopted by Democrats and Republican administrations alike. They just didn't *call* it socialism.

In January 2009, Christian broadcaster Pat Robertson stated that God told him America is headed for veritable socialism as well as an economic rebound under President-elect Obama. "What the Lord was saying," he claimed, "the people are willing to accept socialism to alleviate their pain. Cast off all the gloom and the doom because things are getting ready to turn around. I say with humility, I hope I've heard the Lord. I spend time praying and asking Him for wisdom, and if there's a mistake, it's not His fault, it's mine." Humility in action.

In any case, one of the factors in Obama's win was indeed the confidence-destroying financial crisis, and now he faces a food chain of euphemisms. Hey, is this like the Great Depression? Nah, it's not a depression, it's only a recession. Wait, it's not a recession, it's just an economic downturn. No, it's not an economic downturn, it's a correction. Oops, it's not a correction, it's an adjustment. Hurry, get me a chiropractor. Similarly, there's a food-chain of solutions to the problem. From the Troubled Asset Relief Program to the Bailout Bill to the Rescue

Package to the Emergency Economic Stability Act to Alan Greenspan confessing "My bad" to Free Botox for Everybody.

Perhaps the most bizarre byproduct of the campaign began with an anonymous ad on Craigslist, headlined: "Need Sarah Palin Lookalike ASAP for Adult Film." The pay would be $3,000, and, it was duly noted, "No anal required." This porn flick, it turned out, would be shot by Hustler Video, and no, Tina Fey did not apply for the job. The climactic scene was a threesome with Sarah Palin, Condoleezza Rice, and Hillary Clinton.

Hillary was played by veteran porn star and sex educator Nina Hartley, who told me, "The big hullabaloo over the movie is being generated by feminists from both the pro- and anti-porn sides. They're up in arms that 'women are being non-consensually satirized' by Big Evil Porn, and The Big Bad Larry Flynt. The usual nonsense from the usual suspects. Even some pro-porn feminists are upset at Palin being 'targeted' by porn. They conveniently overlook the fact that most porn satirizes white men in power: politicians, police, professors. Most recent case in point, *The Elliot Splizter Story* ..."

Who's Nailin' Paylin was ready for release before the election, as was an issue of the horror comic book *Tales From the Crypt*, which featured on the cover a painting of Sarah Palin swinging her hockey stick to disperse the Vault-Keeper and other ghoulish characters as she sneeringly asks, "Didn't we get rid of you guys in the '50s?" — a reference to the censorship problems faced decades ago by EC Comics, the original publisher of *Tales From the Crypt*, and concomitantly a criticism of Palin for her "rhetorical question" about removing objectionable books from library shelves.

However, another publisher was producing a comic-book biography of Palin that wouldn't be released until February 2009, so two endings were prepared. But an edition of *South Park* — broadcast the day after the election — took a risk with only one ending, which lampooned Obama's victory. Co-creator Trey Parker explained, "We're just going to make the Obama version, and if McCain somehow wins, we're basically just totally screwed."

Likewise, Garry Trudeau gambled that Obama would win, and his syndicated *Doonesbury* strip — published the day after the election — depicted three soldiers in Iraq watching the returns on TV as a reporter is saying, "And it's official — Barack Obama has won."

Some editors were undecided about whether to publish it. Trudeau encouraged them to choose hope over fear. "If I'm wrong," he told the *Los Angeles Times*, "it'll be my face that'll be covered with eggs, not theirs." *Times* editors had decided, in the interest of accuracy, to wait for the election results, and if Obama won, they would publish the strip on Thursday, but then they must have realized it was just a comic strip, not investigative journalism, and they published it on Wednesday after all.

Trudeau thought that newspapers should run the strip because "polling data gives McCain a 3.7% chance of victory." Indeed, a week after Obama's win, McCain himself admitted to Jay Leno, "I can read the polls — they tried to keep 'em from me." There were dozens of polls, from ABC to Zogby, and, psychographic sophistication aside, they didn't always exactly agree. For example, in Nevada during the last week of October, one poll put Obama's lead at 12%, another at 7%, another at 5%, and two others at 4%, which meant that, given the margin of sampling error, McCain could conceivably have been slightly ahead. This, then, was the last presidential election. In the future, you'll only need to vote for the pollster that you trust the most.

During the 1968 Democratic convention in Chicago, I was among 15,000 protesters who had gathered in Grant Park for a rally when the police, triggered by the actions of one of their own provocateurs, attacked the demonstrators and sadistically beat as many as they could reach. It seemed impossible that we could ever work within the system. But now, 40 years later, there were 200,000 celebrants who had gathered in that same park, giddy with the excitement of Obama's victory. They had worked within the system.

During the past four decades, there has been a linear progression from Jimi Hendrix playing "The Star-Spangled Banner" at Woodstock to Aretha Franklin singing "My Country, 'Tis of Thee" at the inauguration. Is it possible that this event signified the early tremors of a nonviolent revolution? As the late singer/songwriter Harry Chapin once said to me backstage at a benefit, "If you don't act like there's hope, there is no hope." And remember, placebos work. My hope is I don't get disappointed. [But I did.]

Meanwhile, the memorabilia business flourishes as millions of voters seek a variety of tangible items to remind them of the part they played in history simply by voting. Mouse pads, baby bibs, aprons, dog jerseys, bobbleheads, niche buttons ("Ventriloquists for Obama"), T-shirts ("Now I Don't Have to Move to Canada") and, as reported by NPR, Obama condoms. Somebody bid $400 on eBay for the November 5th issue of *The New York Times*. *U.S.A. Today* printed 500,000 extra copies; *The Washington Post* printed 350,000 extras. The only thing I saved was a full-page ad by the 99 Cents Only stores, which included a "Joe the Plumber Special" plunger. There was no limit on how many I could buy.

A Letter to Barack Obama

October 10, 2010
Dear President Obama,

It seems that the theme emanating from the White House is "Eat, Pray, Be Disappointed." And yet, whenever I do feel disappointed, I always realize that the alternative was John McCain, with Sarah Palin just one Halloween "Boo!" away from the presidency, and then I always feel a sense of relief.

Actually, you've kept one big campaign promise — to send more troops to Afghanistan — so I guess we can't fault you for that. In fact, according to Bob Woodward in *Obama's Wars*, all you want to do now is get *out* of Afghanistan. Well, why don't you just do what Osama bin Laden did — cross over to Pakistan? Since we bribe Pakistan to be our ally, you'd think they would never consider harboring bin Laden, though they reek with empathy when our outsourced drones drop those bombs.

Also, during the campaign, you said you believe that the legality of same-sex marriage should be decided by the states, but that you personally think marriage should be between a man and a woman. Which is exactly the position that eventually led to the revocation of Carrie Prejean's Miss U.S.A. crown. And another thing. You promised to end the raids on medical marijuana dispensaries, but they haven't stopped.

[In 2009, Attorney General Eric Holder issued a memo ordering an end to federal raids of medical marijuana dispensaries. In March 2011, there were 28 such raids in a duration of 24 hours.]

Here's how I understand Washington. America's puritanical political process serves as a buffer between the status quo and the force of evolution. For instance, in order to get Republican votes for the children's healthcare bill, Democrats agreed to fund $28 million to *their* abstinence-only program.

And, during your own campaign, you admitted, in the context of healthcare reform, that the multinational insurance conglomeration is so firmly entrenched that you would be unable to dispense with it. So there would have to be compromises. Now, what with the compromises made to help passage of Prop. 19, amnesty becomes the single-payer system of marijuana reform, and growing your own pot becomes the public option. Meanwhile, as long as any government can arbitrarily decide which drugs are legal and which drugs are illegal, then anyone serving time for a nonviolent drug offense is a political prisoner.

In his new book, Bob Woodward writes about Colin Powell's status as an adviser to you. Referring to his previous book, *Plan of Attack*, *The New York Times* then reported, "Secretary of State Colin Powell disputed Woodward's account .... He said that he had an excellent relationship with Vice President Dick Cheney, and that he did not recall referring to officials at the Pentagon loyal to Cheney as the 'Gestapo office'." Who among us would be unable to recall uttering such an epithet? Powell later apologized for it. He has also changed his mind about gays in the military. In my capacity as a stand-up satirist, I used to conduct an imaginary dialogue with Powell.

"General Powell, you're the first African-American to be head of the Joint Chiefs of Staff, and you come from the tradition of a military family. So you know that blacks were once segregated in the Army because the other soldiers might feel uncomfortable if blacks slept in the same barracks. And now that's what they say about gays, that other soldiers might feel uncomfortable about *gays* sleeping in the same barracks."

"Well, you have to understand, we never *told* anybody we were black."

And, Mr. President, that was the forerunner of the same "Don't Ask, Don't Tell" policy that you promised to rescind, only you haven't been acting like a Commander-in-Chief. All you have to do is sign such a directive. Those who serve in the military are trained to follow orders. If they can follow orders to kill fellow humans, they can certainly follow orders to treat openly gay service people with total equality.

Not only is the current guideline counterproductive, but also this display of trickle-down immorality must, on some level of consciousness, serve as a contributing factor to enabling the anti-gay bullying and torturing of innocent victims. I know, you don't want to take a chance that retracting the policy would interfere with your re-election. You've made the point that you don't want Mitt Romney to win in 2012 and turn around all the good things you've accomplished.

Incidentally, Romney had wanted to overturn *Roe v. Wade*, yet, in 1994, when he was running for the Senate, he came out in *favor* of choice for women. However, freelance journalist Suzan Mazur revealed that he admitted to Mormon feminist Judith Dushku that "the Brethren" in Salt Lake City *told* him he could take a pro-choice position, and that, in fact, he probably *had* to in order to win in a liberal state like Massachusetts. Pandering trumps religious belief.

Meantime, since gays and lesbians have waited so long for basic fairness, they might as well just wait for the next election. If you win, then would you kindly do immediately what you believe is right, constitutionally and in your heart, and end this injustice? The ultimate irony is that gays in the military are fighting, being maimed, and dying unnecessarily, supposedly to protect the freedom their own country is denying them.

Sincerely,
Paul Krassner

POSTSCRIPT

I SENT A COPY of the letter to some folks that day. Among the responses, I received a message from a mother: "I am trying to explain this to my 12-year-old son, who wants to know why, if men and women don't share barracks in the military, why gay men and hetero men should share barracks, but then follows with 'They should all sleep in the same place.'"

And that evening I received this email from a seasoned journalist: "I know it's late, but I cannot wait to ask if this letter is a spoof, or you've actually sent it to Obama. If it's a spoof, and you've not sent it to him, would you like to? I've got his fax number, and he's got a great sense of humor. May I have your permission to send this to him?"

"Absolutely."

Two days later, to the dismay of Obama, who wanted Congress to repeal the "Don't Ask, Don't Tell" policy after the November midterm election (and had told a town hall meeting that he was restricted because it was written into law, adding, "This is not a situation where I can, by the stroke of a pen, end this policy"), Federal Judge Virginia Phillips upset that timetable by issuing an immediate and permanent ban on what she considered to be unconstitutional. This ruling was not a spoof, though it was treated as one by an appeals court that set aside her injunction. In December 2010, Congress repealed the 17-year-old law.

Nor was it a spoof when Attorney General Holder — having been pressured by nine former DEA chiefs, plus the president of Mexico — warned that if Prop. 19 was passed, making California the first state to legalize pot, the federal government would not look the other way, as it has done with medical marijuana.

Holder (who wouldn't prosecute the Bush administration for promulgating torture) explained, "Let me state clearly that the Department of Justice strongly opposes Proposition 19. If passed, this legislation will greatly complicate federal drug enforcement efforts to the detriment of our citizens. We will vigorously enforce the [law] against those individuals and organizations that possess, manufacture, or distribute marijuana for recreational use, even if such activities are permitted under state law."

In a truly free society, the distinction of whether marijuana is used for medical or recreational purposes would be as irrelevant an excuse for discrimination as whether the sexual preference of gays and lesbians is innate or a matter of choice.

And so it came to pass that Barack Obama was re-elected. His opponent, Romney, fell to his knees and pleaded, "Oh, dear Lord, you promised that I would win. Why hast thou forsaken me?"

And the voice of God boomed out, *"HEY, MITT, LISTEN — I WAS JUST FUCKIN' WITH YA ..."*

Unsafe at Safeway

IT WAS STEVE ALLEN, and later Lenny Bruce, who said, "Comedy is tragedy plus time." But everything is accelerating. Even the rate of acceleration is accelerating. The time between tragedy and comedy gets shorter and shorter. The more horrible the news is, the more victims there are to involuntarily serve as setups for punch lines.

Reality has long been nipping at the heels of comedy, and it finally caught up. Example: On the same day [April 19, 1993] that people were being burned alive in the fire at the Branch Davidian headquarters in Waco, Texas, Jay Leno did a joke in his Tonight Show monologue about there being two kinds of cult members there — "regular and crispy."

Of course, events like the January 8, 2011, madman massacre outside a Safeway supermarket in Tucson, Arizona, can be challenging. How could made-up humor possibly top the actual absurdity of mass murderer Jared Loughner (who killed six people and injured 13 others, including U.S. Representative Gabrielle Giffords) asking his MySpace friends not to be mad at him? After all, he was merely planning to indiscriminately kill as many innocent human beings as he could, with democracy itself as collateral damage.

The night before Loughner committed his senseless slaughter, he had taken photos of himself posing with his gun while wearing a bright red G-string and displaying his naked ass. Satirist Harry Shearer observed, "The nightmare in Tucson is the inevitable result of a society where a mentally confused young man can purchase a red G-string anywhere at any time and pose with it as he sees fit. Can't we all agree now to lower the temperature on underwear?"

Speaking of lowering the temperature — in the *Pittsburgh Post-Gazette*, editorial cartoonist Rob Rogers depicted the "U.S. Civil Discourse Gun Shop" where a customer is asking the clerk, "Do you have anything versatile enough to go from a campaign breakfast to a protest march to a town hall meeting?" And in the *Orlando Sentinel*, Dana Summers depicted another gun store featuring semi-automatic 31-clip weapons, where the clerk is explaining to a customer, "Say you have thirty-one burglars break into your house."

On the Monday following the tragic weekend, Jon Stewart was unable to find anything funny about it. Nor was Stephen Colbert, although he did present a montage of news clips with various explanations of Loughner's behavior. The final one, from Fox News — "He is also being described as a left-wing political pothead" — managed to evoke laughter from the audience. And Rush Limbaugh called him a "marijuana junkie."

In October 2008, Loughner told an old friend, Bryce Tierney, that he wasn't going to smoke marijuana anymore. Tierney never saw him smoke pot again and was surprised at media reports that Loughner was rejected by the Army in 2009 for failing a drug test: "He was clean ... I saw him after that continuously. He would not do it ... After he quit, he was just off the wall." But Loughner did *not* fail a drug test that day at the processing station. Rather, he admitted on an application form that he had smoked marijuana "hundreds of times." He didn't know that the military has an official maximum of times you can admit to smoking pot.

A journalist I know acknowledges that he tried to join the Air Force at the San Diego recruitment office, but, "When the subject of drugs came up, I figured, okay, I have long hair, I look maybe homeless, they're going to *know* I'm lying if I say I've always been straight. I'll say I've smoked pot seven or eight times — something ridiculously, embarrassingly low. Whatever it was, it was too high. The recruiter said. 'You can't have smoked more than *five* times. Go away, kid. Maybe the Marines will take you.' Two weeks later I was at the Sacramento recruitment office and I had the 'magic number.' I joined the Air Force. One of the stupider things I've done."

Indeed, Chris Hedges wrote on *Truthdig*: "Power does not rest with the electorate. It does not reside with either of the two major political parties. It is not represented by the press. It is not arbitrated by a judiciary that protects us from predators. Power rests with corporations. And corporations gain very lucrative profits from war, even wars we have no chance of winning. All polite appeals to the formal systems of power will not end the wars in Iraq and Afghanistan. We must physically obstruct the war machine or accept a role as its accomplice."

When it comes to bloodbaths, the only difference between such invisible corporations and Jared Loughner is that he did it face-to-face.

Obviously, Loughner is crazy, but not legally insane, because he knew right from wrong, as indicated by his expectation of life in prison or execution for his unspeakable crime. True, John Hinckley was crazy when he tried to assassinate Ronald Reagan — his motivation was to impress actress Jodie Foster, so she would go out bowling with him — yet he was sentenced to serve *his* time in a mental hospital, including occasional outings with his parents, which resulted in public outrage and a weakening of the insanity defense.

Ironically, Hinckley came out for gun control, and Reagan came out against it.

PAUL KRASSNER

The Yippies and
the Occupiers

AS A CO-FOUNDER of the Yippies (Youth International Party) — known for demonstrating against the Vietnam War at the 1968 Democratic convention in Chicago — I find myself comparing and contrasting the Yippies and the Occupy Wall Street protesters.

We had to perform stunts to get media coverage of our cause, so a group of us went to the New York Stock Exchange, upstairs to the balcony, and threw $200 worth of singles onto the floor below, watching the gang of manic brokers suddenly morph from yelling "Pork Bellies" into playing "Diving for Dollars." Then we held a press conference outside, explaining the connection between the capitalist system and the war.

Now, a particular placard, "Wall Street Is War Street," gives me a sense of continuity. Other anonymous Occupier spokespersons carried posters proclaiming: "God Forbid We Have Sex & Smoke Pot. They Want Us to Grab Guns & Go to War!" "I am an immigrant. I came here to take your job. But you don't have one." "$96,000 for a BA in Hispanic transgender gay & lesbian studies and I can't find work!" And a woman in a wheelchair: "Stand Up For *Your* Rights!"

By the sheer power of numbers without the necessity of stunts, the Occupiers have broadened public awareness about the economic injustice perpetuated by corporations without compassion conspiring with government corruption that has resulted in immeasurable suffering. The Yippies were a myth that became a reality. The Occupiers are a reality that became a myth. The spirit of nonviolent revolution is what connects them.

NPR waited until eleven days of Occupy Wall Street had passed before reporting its existence. The executive news editor explained that the

Occupiers "did not involve large numbers of people" (actually, there were already several hundred), no "prominent people" showed up (thus ignoring Michael Moore and Susan Sarandon), the lack of "a great disruption" (the police pepper-spraying protesters trapped in a cage of orange netting finally met that need), "or an especially clear objective" (oh, right, like all those flip-floppy pandering politicians whose clear objective is to get elected).

The Occupiers appear to be a leaderless community — most likely, you can't name a single one; not yet, anyway — whereas Abbie Hoffman, Jerry Rubin, and I served as spokespeople for the Yippies. We had media contacts and knew how to speak in sound bites. If we gave good quote, they gave free publicity for upcoming demonstrations. It was mutual manipulation.

Sample: A reporter asked me about the 1968 counter-convention we were planning, "Will you be staying in tents?" I replied, "Some of us will be intense. Others will be frivolous."

During an interview with Abbie and me for the *CBS Evening News*, taped at his apartment, Abbie paraphrased Che Guevara and said, "I'm prepared to win or die." However, that never got on the air. When the reporter asked me, "What do the Yippies actually plan to do in Chicago?" I smiled at her and said, "You think I'm gonna tell *you*?" That portion of my answer was used to end Walter Cronkite's segment on the Yippies, but my follow-up sentence — "The first thing we're gonna do is put truth serum in the reporters' drinks" — was omitted. They had beaten me at my own game.

The Yippies were inspired by the Buddhist monk in Vietnam who set himself on fire in order to call attention to the war. The photo of that incident traveled around the globe, and I wore a lapel button that featured that flaming image. Similarly, in 2010, a street vendor in Tunisia refused to pay a police bribe, then immolated himself, which inspired a revolution there, and next in Egypt, spreading into Arab Spring, which ultimately inspired American Autumn in 2011.

Inspired by the Yippies' attempt to levitate the Pentagon, pie-thrower Aron Kay wanted to get fellow Occupiers to levitate Wall Street. No interest. Likewise, inspired by the Yippies' nomination of an actual pig named Pigasus for president, Michael Dare tried unsuccessfully to persuade fellow protesters at Occupy Seattle to carry out his notion that "If corporations are people, let's run one for president." I offered myself as Secretary of Greed.

The evolution of technology has changed the way protests are organized and carried out. The Yippies had to use messy mimeograph machines to print out flyers that had to be stuffed into envelopes, addressed, stamped, and mailed. The internet generally — and social media such as Facebook and Twitter — have enabled Occupiers to inexpensively reach countless people immediately.

When the Yippies were being tear-gassed and beaten sadistically and indiscriminately, we chanted, "The whole world is watching!" But now, when a bloodbath was expected to happen if the New York police forced the Occupiers out of the park — and then that didn't happen — Michael Moore asked a cop, "Why don't you think the eviction happened?" The reply: "Because the mayor's afraid of YouTube."

(One month later, Mayor Bloomberg apparently lost that fear — by his order, the eviction happened at 1:00 a.m. The next afternoon, a protester, before being allowed back in, was overheard remarking, "The cops have occupied Zuccotti Park. We're just trying to figure out what their demands are.")

Not only was what occurred in Chicago in 1968 officially labeled "a police riot" by a government-sponsored investigation, but also an undercover police provocateur — who was disguised as a local biker and acted as Jerry Rubin's bodyguard — ultimately stated that he participated in pulling down the American flag in Grant Park, destroying it, then running up the black flag of the Viet Cong in its place.

"I joined in the chants and taunts against the police," he said, "and provoked them to hitting me with their clubs. They didn't know who I was, but they did know that I had called them names and struck them with one or more weapons."

Now, as the Occupy model has spread around the country, police brutality has increased, and it's not surprising that there have been accusations of provocateurs sabotaging the nonviolent principle, not to mention an assistant editor at a conservative magazine who infiltrated a group of protesters in Washington, D.C., later claiming that his purpose was "to mock and undermine them in the pages of the *American Spectator*," and that he helped incite a riot at the National Air and Space Museum, getting pepper-sprayed in the process.

Moreover, a document from the Houston FBI revealed their plan "to engage in sniper attacks" and "kill the leadership" of the Occupy activists "if deemed necessary."

The Yippies were essentially countercultural, an amalgam of radicalized stoned hippies and straight political activists. And, although the Occupiers are essentially mainstream, their demonization by right-wing media pundits has been providing a repeat performance of neutralizing a progressive cause.

Bill O'Reilly called the Occupiers "drug-trafficking crackheads" and "violent America-hating anarchists." Sean Hannity said they "sound like skinhead Nazi psychos." Ann Coulter referred to them as mobs of "teenage runaways" and "tattooed, body-pierced, sunken-chested 19-year-olds getting in fights with the police for fun." Glenn Beck warned that they "will come for you and drag you into the streets and kill you." Andrew Breitbart declared that Occupy Wall Street is "a group of public masturbating violent freaks."

And Rush Limbaugh labeled them "dumbed down" and "propagandized" and asked a rhetorical question reeking with layers of irony: "Whatever happened to the '60s — *Question Authority*?" At this point, Limbaugh is like a castrated canine that is still busy humping the living-room sofa by force of habit.

Porn Again

Remembering Pubic Hair

OKAY, CALL ME OLD-FASHIONED, but I still like pubic hair. Porn sites now present several choices — completely shaved, vertical landing strips that look like exclamation points, heart-shaped, the "Charlie Chaplin" with just a little patch above the clitoris, and a tiny triangle that serves as an arrow *pointing* to the clit. Yet, for a full bush, one would have to search the Web for "hairy" sites that are considered as "specialty," "kinky," or "fetish."

Retired porn stars have commented on this phenomenon. Gina Rome, retired after six years, shaved every day. "It was part of getting ready for work." When she switched from acting to film editing, she stopped shaving and let her pubic hair grow out. "Shaving was work. I don't have to do it anymore, so I don't." And Kelly Nichols says, "I was a *Penthouse* model in the early 1980s, and I posed with a full bush. No one in adult entertainment shaved back then. Now everybody does."

Although Martha Stewart is back on TV, you can be sure that she'll never give any suggestions on what to do about those big red razor bumps that result from shaving your vagina, so here's a helpful hint I'd like to pass along — they can be largely eliminated with, of all things, Visine eye drops. But pubic hair is practical — it serves as a cushion against friction.

The porn industry has played an important part in shaping pubic styles. Jordan Stein writes in an article titled "Has Porn Gone Mainstream?": "Consider the near icon status the female porn star has achieved. She is so mainstream that even *good girls* are imitating her various styles of undress, disappearing hair and all. Porn chic? You bet."

However, Julia Baird writes in *Celebrity Porn*, "The idea that the fashion industry can strip, then exhibit women in the name of 'porn chic,' is a bit silly, frankly. But 'flesh is the new fabric' could be the new catch-cry. Americans call their bush George W. It's fashionable — the curious fact is that it is fueled by the porn aesthetic that celebrities love to love."

Among Hollywood actresses, Gwyneth Paltrow and Kirstie Alley have both admitted favoring Brazilian wax jobs, where most of their pubic hair is removed, leaving a small tuft that remains hidden under a thong bikini. Sara Jessica Parker's character, Carrie Bradshaw, had her pubic hair removed during the third season of *Sex in the City*. Presumably, it's now in the Smithsonian museum along with Archie Bunker's easy chair and the Fonz's leather jacket.

On ABC's *Women's Murder Club*, a medical examiner directs her gaze to the crotch of a female corpse and says, "That's not your mama's bikini wax." On *The View*, Joy Behar said, "No pubic hair creates a wind tunnel." And in a hysterical episode of HBO's dark comedy series, *Curb Your Enthusiasm*, former *Seinfeld* producer Larry David performed oral sex on his wife, and in the process, he sort of swallowed one of her pubic hairs. The next day, he was still choking on it, like a cat trying to get rid of a hairball.

A psychologist at Harvard Medical School and author of *Survival of the Prettiest: The Science of Beauty*, Nancy Etcoff, writes, "There's also an erotic, sexual component to hairlessness because your skin is more sensitive when it's more exposed. Women today are emulating porn stars who have no pubic hair, and I think men like it."

My own resistance to the plethora of bald pussies stems from my pre-adolescent days when pubic hair was such a big taboo that I became obsessed with it. In those pre-bikini days, I would go to Coney Island and stroll around the sand, sneaking glances at ladies in the hope of finding a few stray curlicues of forbidden pubic hair peeking out from their various and sun-dried crotches. And if I was able to discover any, why, it felt as though I had experienced a really productive afternoon.

Betty Dodson, sex educator and producer of *Viva La Vulva*, says, "I think we have changing ideas about what's public and what's private. And now that nudity is more public — nude beaches, routine nudity in film, and the enormous amount of exhibitionism and porn on the Web — I'm not surprised to see a trend toward pubic shaving. I think it's probably here to stay." She told me, "Thanks to the lack of a comprehensive sex education for kids, young girls now want their vulvas to look like porn stars because that's what their boyfriends jerk off to and prefer. It's all they know." But a new study has concluded that pubic hair is returning: "The men don't care, and the women can't bother."

Welcome back, good old bush. Hide and seek a friendly clit.

Ironically, although Arnold Schwarzenegger was only joking when he announced that *he* was going to get a bikini wax, actually Beverly Hills skin care and waxing expert Nance Mitchell has about fifty regular male customers that come for pubic waxing who "are not gay, and they are not porn stars. Some go totally bare, some just do the shaft and up around the pelvic area." She explains, "It depends on what their wives and girlfriends want. Men go along because removing the hair makes the whole package look bigger."

Ah, yes, the *illusion* of size does matter.

PAUL KRASSNER

The Taste of Semen

ONLINE SEXOLOGY COLUMNIST Sandor Gardos was asked, "How do I increase the amount of my ejaculate? I've noticed porn stars seem to ejaculate copious amounts of fluid, and I'd like to be able to wow my partner." Dr. Gardos points out that "the actors in porn films are professionals. Even they often don't ejaculate that much — sometimes movie makers will supplement with synthetic semen shot from a small tube."

Well, I'm just shocked to realize that somewhere in America there must be a group of scientists in a laboratory who earn their salaries by manufacturing fake semen.

Meanwhile, ManNotIncluded.com has become the first cyberspace sperm bank for lesbians and single women who want to become pregnant. They are matched with anonymous donors who have the desired race, eye color, height, and weight, then sent instructions on how to inseminate themselves. John Gonzalez, founder of the website, hopes this service will overcome the hurdles presented by bureaucracies and fertility clinics who are prejudiced against same-sex couples.

"Lesbians hook up with gay men all the time," he says, "either friends or guys they've met through personal ads. We are now simply allowing them to do so safely and without discrimination."

On the other hand, in the movie, *Sarah Silverman: Jesus Is Magic* — a performance by one of the best and raunchiest female stand-up comedians — she describes a sure method of birth control: "cumming all over her face." Of course, that punch line is derived from the ever-popular image on internet porn sites, where I look in vain for the small print with messages warning, "Do Not Try This Particular Money Shot At Home" and "This Is Not Exactly What She Means When She Says She'd Like To Get a Facial For Her Birthday."

Furthermore, in Chelsea, Michigan, Book Crafters has refused to print *Baboon Dooley, Rock Critic*, a collection of John Crawford's comic strip, because his protagonist accidentally drinks from a glass of semen. He spits it out upon learning the content, only to be called a sexist, and challenged: "You'd expect a *woman* to drink it, right?" However, on CNN, author Hugh Prather was a guest, and the subject was couples. A caller revealed his problem: "The trouble is, when I cum in her mouth, she can't really swallow it all." The anchor quickly hung up on this premature ejaculation.

Cartoonist Mary Lawton depicted a character saying, "I just found out that alfalfa sprouts smell like sperm. Does this mean I should practice safe salad?" Yet humorist Jacqueline Shtuyote tells me, "Sperm is basically tasteless. The truth should be out about this. Men seem to think that their white stuff is a culinary delight, yet I know of no culinary courses extolling the flavor of sperm. And if, as rumored, Jack-in-the-Box cooks occasionally spill their cum on an irritating customer's hamburger, how many of us would be pleased with the added ingredient?

"Why can't we find something that changes the flavor of cum? Then men could squirt red stuff that is raspberry-flavored, or brown stuff that is chocolate-flavored. Shy women could finally delight in swallowing their lover's cum. No sperm would ever be spit out again. There could be a pill to make cum taste like fast-food hamburgers. Maybe then we wouldn't mind if we found out that the secret sauce on top of Jack-in-the-Box hamburgers is, after all, sperm."

But let's not forget those who don't eat meat. They face an ethical dilemma — whether or not it's an acceptable practice for a vegetarian to give a blowjob, and if so, is it all right to swallow? The general practice is that, yes, it's definitely okay to give a blowjob because no animal is harmed in the process. And, yes, it's also okay to ingest the semen because it's a good source of protein, something that's often lacking when meat is removed from the diet.

Finally — and this could possibly be an urban legend — in a biology class at Harvard University, a professor was discussing the high glucose levels found in semen, which give the spermatozoa all that energy for their journey. A female freshman raised her hand and asked him, "If I understand you correctly, you're saying there is a lot of glucose, as in sugar, in semen?"

"That's correct," replied the professor.

"Then why doesn't it taste sweet?" the student asked.

She blushed in belated realization of what her question implied, then hurriedly picked up her books and headed for the door, even as he answered, "It doesn't taste sweet because the taste buds for sweetness are on the tip of your tongue and not in the back of your throat — Have a good day."

PAUL KRASSNER

Eating Shit
for Fun and Profit

I AM IN COMPLETE AWE of the democracy of the internet, which presents an infinite menu for individual tastes and ideologies, and in this context, specifically to viewers of online pornography. From golden showers to farm animals, the World Wide Web caters to virtually every imaginable desire. With the privacy provided by a computer screen, you can worship at the fetish of your choice. But, in the process of surfing porn sites — for research purposes only, of course — I realized that I had never come across a site specializing in coprophagia. It means eating shit. Literally.

There's an old saying among nutritionists: "You are what you eat." However, comedian Darryl Henriques, playing the role of a New Age swami, says, "You are what you don't shit."

One of the nastiest things you can say to someone is, "Eat shit." A nonfiction book, *The Pit*, reveals a strange cult in San Francisco where a group of successful businessmen were forced, along with other acts of humiliation, to eat their own shit. Ultimately, they were represented in a lawsuit by flamboyant attorney Melvin Belli. But that was more-or-less involuntary shit eating, and what we're talking about here is the voluntary kind.

For many years I heard stories that comic actor Danny Thomas, the star of *Make Room for Daddy*, was a coprophagiac. I assumed it was just another urban legend until I bumped into an old friend who was now working as a prostitute in Hollywood. Over lunch, she mentioned the names of some of her celebrity clients, including Danny Thomas. She told me how he had hired her to save her solid waste in her panties so that he could rub those panties on his face and gobble up her shit as though it were cotton candy.

When he finished, he would wash his hands and face thoroughly then pay her and, as if coming out of a trance, he'd say, "Where was I?" He was trying to distance himself from what he had just done. Instant denial. Since then, I have believed that Danny Thomas's fundraising for Saint Jude's Hospital was really for the purpose of having secret access to their bedpans.

Anyway, I googled "eating shit." Topping the list was "Shit Eating Grins: In Defense of Adam Sandler." But sure enough, I was soon led to hardcore shit-eating sites, which I found totally disgusting, yet absolutely riveting. You may not want to read any further, but we both know you will.

There are photos of beautiful women shitting. If you click for a close-up, you can spot a yellow kernel of corn in one big brown chunk o' shit. Women are spreading shit all over their naked bodies and inside their vaginas. A pair of lovely lesbians are eating handfuls of shit, then tongue kissing each other. Two women are eating the same lengthy turd, starting from opposite ends. A woman, fully dressed, wearing a miniskirt, is shitting as she walks along the sidewalk. One woman is shitting into another woman's mouth. Mmmm, good to the last dingleberry.

Among the shit-eating sites, there are Asian movies. Here's a couple of descriptions: "A bunch of kinky Japanese guys find some truly hot looking girls and take them down below the streets of Tokyo into a real sewer full of shit." And "Cute Kyoko's diarrhea suddenly acts up again. Her piano teacher becomes a willing student of hot scat games. Lots of shit pours out of her hot ass into his waiting mouth. Then she asks if he would rub it all over her. 'Sure, why not,' he says."

If there is one particular image that remains in my mind's eye, it is an innocent-looking, attractive teenager — she's over 18, of course — and she is cheerfully drinking a shit shake through a straw in an old-fashioned, malted-milk glass.

I thought about her father discovering that video in cyberspace, yet he is unable to confront his daughter about it because he would then have to admit what *he* was doing at that site. I mean, this isn't exactly the type of thing that would be mass emailed by one of those selfless spammers, is it? And even if the father did confess to his daughter, he would undoubtedly hesitate to ask if he could eat *her* shit, because that could be considered a form of incest, and you have to draw the line somewhere, right?

There must be an especially strong bond among coprophagiacs, though, because they have experienced in common a form of liberation from a taboo that can be traced all the way back to infancy, when a parent would cringe and say, "Stop! Don't eat that! I said *no!*"

Who knows, someday coprophagia might even become a religion? Holy shit!

PAUL KRASSNER

"I Fuck Dead People"

YOU DON'T SEE MANY porn sites that feature intercourse with corpses, and if you do, how do you know they're really dead? But say what you will about California Governor Arnold Schwarzenegger, you have to give him credit for signing a bill to forbid necrophilia. Under the new law, sex with a corpse is now a felony punishable by up to eight years in prison.

Age is no barrier. The state's first attempt to outlaw necrophilia — in response to a case of a man charged with having sex with the corpse of a 4-year-old girl in Southern California — stalled in a legislative committee, but the bill was revived after an unsuccessful prosecution of a man who was found in a San Francisco funeral home, passed out on top of an elderly woman's corpse.

Necrophiliacs have been getting away with it all this time, but district attorneys will no longer be stymied by the lack of an official ban. According to Tyler Ochoa, a professor at Santa Clara University of Law who has studied California cases involving allegations of necrophilia, "Prosecutors didn't have anything to charge these people with other than breaking and entering. But if they worked in a mortuary in the first place, prosecutors couldn't even charge them with that."

Whether necrophilia is a victimless crime may still be open to debate. Nevertheless, claiming that the act was consensual will not be considered as a legal defense. It should be noted that the necrophilia community ranges from those who are monogamous and stick with one partner for a lifetime, to those who are promiscuous and hop from casket to casket.

According to his own journal entry, Ralph Waldo Emerson, one of the most revered figures in American literary history, was so devastated by the death of his young wife, Ellen, that, shortly after her burial, he went out to the cemetery one night and dug up her corpse, though he didn't mention exactly what he did with it.

One of the most popular episodes of the police TV show, *Homicide: Life on the Street*, was about the investigation of a lonely old widower, a mortician, who used to party with the corpses, setting them around a table as if they were alive. They investigated him because he shot a neighbor who knew about this practice, and then sat in the garden and waited for the cops. But again, the mortician's relationship with those corpses may have been purely platonic.

Let us now eavesdrop on the dialogue of a few participants in an internet support group, Necrophiliacs Anonymous:

"Obviously, neither a corpse nor a 4-year-old can provide consent, but if you leave permission in your will for your lonesome spouse or significant other to have one last fling with your mortal coil, shouldn't the state of California respect your wishes?"

"I still think that organ donation is a better cause. It's just that I believe the only offense here is really violation of private property. I wonder if someone gives their partner, in a will, the right to have sex with their body after their death, will it be legal?"

"Or, even without that permission, if you are an only heir of somebody, doesn't it mean their body belongs to you? It sounds gross, but isn't it an issue of private rights in the United States of America, that likes so much the idea of individualism and is ready to exploit people and the environment in the name of that ideal?"

"I never understood why people think that having sex with a dead body is worse than raping a living person. To me, that's the worst kind, and then raping poor helpless animals. I really couldn't care less about my *own* dead body."

Conversely, Sam Kinison, the late evangelist who turned into a comedian, had a great routine about necrophilia: "Well, that's it, man — I'm dead. Nothing else bad can happen to me now. Wait a minute — what's that? What's this guy doing? What's going on here? [Screams] Oh oh oh oh oh OH OH OH OH OH *OOOOOOHHHHHH NOOOOOOO!!! LIVE IN HELL!!!*"

The majority of cannibalistic serial killers are motivated by a kind of necrophilia — it's usually a highly sexually arousing experience for them when they eat their victims. Here, from my "Great Moments in Necrophilia" file, is a dispatch from the Associated Press:

The prosecution in the insanity trial of serial killer Jeffrey Dahmer rested its case. Dahmer has confessed to killing and dismembering 17 young males since 1978. A jury must decide if he will be sent to prison or a mental institution. The final prosecution witness, Dr. Park Dietz, a psychiatrist, testified that Dahmer wore condoms when having sex with his dead victims, showing that he could control his urge to have intercourse with corpses.

I smell a public service announcement there: "If Jeffrey Dahmer is sane enough to have safe sex, what about *you*?"

Comedians

Remembering Lenny Bruce

AUGUST 3, 2016, MARKED the 50th anniversary of groundbreaking comedian Lenny Bruce's death from an overdose of morphine, while his New York obscenity conviction at Cafe Au Go Go was still on appeal. On that same day, he received a foreclosure notice at his Los Angeles home.

But it wasn't a suicide. In the kitchen, a kettle of water was still boiling, and in his office, the electric typewriter was still humming. He had stopped typing in mid-word: "Conspiracy to interfere with the 4th Amendment const" Constitutes what, I wondered.

Lenny was a subscriber to my satirical magazine, *The Realist*, and in 1959 we met for the first time at the funky Hotel America in Times Square. He was amazed that I got away with publishing those profane words for which other periodicals used asterisks or dashes. He had been using euphemisms like "frig" and asked, "Are you telling me this is legal to sell on the newsstands?"

I replied, "The Supreme Court's definition of obscenity is that it has to be material which appeals to your prurient interest." He magically produced an unabridged dictionary from the suitcase on his bed and looked up the word "prurient." He closed the dictionary, clenching his jaw and nodding his head in affirmation of a new discovery. "So," he observed, "it's against the law to get you horny."

When we were about to leave the room, he stood in the doorway. "Did you steal anything?" he asked furtively. I took my watch out of my pocket since I didn't like to wear it on my wrist, and, without saying a word, I placed it on the bureau. Lenny laughed one loud staccato "Ha!" and kissed me on the forehead.

We developed a friendship integrated with stand-up comedy. In his act, Lenny had broken through traditional stereotypical jokes about airplane food, nagging wives, Chinese drivers, and annoying mothers-in-law. Instead he weaved his taboo-breaking targets — teachers' low salaries *versus* show-business celebs, religious leaders' hypocrisy, cruel abortion laws, racial injustice, the double standard between illegal and prescription drugs — into stream-of-consciousness vignettes.

In each succeeding performance, he would sculpt and re-sculpt his concept into a theatrical context, experimenting from show to show like a verbal jazz musician. Audience laughter would sometimes turn into clapping for the creative process itself. "Please don't applaud," he'd request. "It breaks my rhythm."

Lenny was writing an autobiography — *How to Talk Dirty and Influence People* — which *Playboy* planned to serialize, then publish as a book, and they hired me as his editor. We met in Atlantic City, where he was taking Dilaudid for lethargy, and he sent a telegram to a contact, with a phrase — DE LAWD IN DE SKY — as a code to send a doctor's prescription.

At a certain point he was acting paranoid and demanded that I take a lie-detector test, and I was paranoid enough to take him literally. I couldn't work with him if he didn't trust me. We got into an argument, and I left.

He sent a telegram that sounded like we were on the verge of divorce. "WHY CAN'T IT BE THE WAY IT USED TO BE?" he wrote. I agreed to try again, and in 1962 I flew to Chicago. Lenny was performing at the Gate of Horn, where he was asking the whole audience to take a lie-detector test.

Lenny was intrigued by the implications of an item in *The Realist*, an actual statement by Adolf Eichmann that he would have been "not only a scoundrel, but a despicable pig" if he hadn't carried out Hitler's orders. Lenny wrote a piece for *The Realist*, "Letter From a Soldier's Wife," namely Mrs. Eichmann, pleading for compassion to spare her husband's life.

Lenny had been reading a study of anti-Semitism by Jean-Paul Sartre. Now, on stage, giving credit to Thomas Merton's poem about the Holocaust, he requested that all the lights go off except one dim blue spot. Then he began speaking with a German accent:

> My name is Adolf Eichmann. And the Jews came every day to what they thought would be fun in the showers. People say I should have been hung. *Nein.* Do you recognize the whore in the middle of you — that you would

have done the same if you were there yourselves? My defense: I was a soldier. I saw the end of a conscientious day's effort. I watched through the portholes. I saw every Jew burned and turned into soap.

Do you people think yourselves better because you burned your enemies at long distance with missiles without ever seeing what you had done to them? Hiroshima *auf Wiedersehen*. [*German accent ends*.] If we would have lost the war, they would have strung Truman up by the balls, Jim. Are you kidding with that? Not what kid told kid told kid. They would just *schlep* out all those Japanese mutants. "Here they did; there they are." And Truman said they'd do it again. That's what they should have the same day as Remember Pearl Harbor. Play them in unison.

Lenny was arrested for obscenity that night. One of the items in the Chicago police report complained: "Then talking about the war he stated, 'If we would have lost the war, they would have strung Truman up by the balls.'" The cops also broke open Lenny's candy bars, looking for drugs. They checked the IDs of audience members, including George Carlin, who told the cops, "I don't believe in IDs." Then they arrested Carlin for disorderly conduct, dragged him along by the seat of his pants, and hoisted him into the police wagon.

"What are you doing here?" Lenny asked.

"I didn't want to show them my ID."

"You schmuck."

Lenny was released on bail, but the head of the Vice Squad warned the Gate of Horn manager: "If this man ever uses a four-letter word in this club again, I'm going to pinch you and everyone in here. If he ever speaks against religion, I'm going to pinch you and everyone in here. Do you understand? You've had good people here. But he mocks the pope — and I'm speaking as a Catholic — I'm here to tell you your license is in danger. We're going to have someone here watching every show."

And indeed, the Gate of Horn's liquor license was suspended. There were no previous allegations against the club, and the current charge involved neither violence nor drunken behavior. The only charge pressed by the city prosecutor was Lenny Bruce's allegedly obscene performance. Nobody's prurience was aroused, but that made no difference. After all, there wasn't any law against blasphemy.

"Chicago is so corrupt, it's thrilling," Lenny said.

Chicago had the largest membership in the Roman Catholic Church of any archdiocese in the country. Lenny's jury consisted entirely of Catholics. The judge was Catholic. The prosecutor and his assistant were Catholic. On Ash Wednesday, the judge removed the spot of ash from his forehead and told the bailiff to instruct the others to do likewise. The sight of a judge, two prosecutors and twelve jurors, every one with a spot of ash on their foreheads, would have all the surrealistic flavor of a Lenny Bruce fantasy.

Since he often talked on stage about his environment, and since police cars and courtrooms had become his environment, the content of Lenny's performances began to revolve more and more around the inequities of the legal system. "In the Halls of Justice," he declared, "the only justice is in the halls." But he also said, "I love the law." Instead of an unabridged dictionary, he now carried law books in his suitcase. His room was cluttered with tapes and transcripts and photostats and law journals and legal briefs.

Once he was teasing his 10-year-old daughter, Kitty, by pretending not to believe what she was telling him. "Daddy," she said, "you'd believe me if it was on tape."

Lenny's jazz jargon was gradually being replaced by legal jargon. He had become intimate not only with the statutes concerning obscenity and narcotics but also with courtroom procedure, and his knowledge would be woven into his performances. But as clubs became increasingly afraid to hire him, he devoted more and more time and energy to the law.

In less than two years, Lenny was arrested 15 times. Club owners were afraid to book him. He couldn't get a gig in six months. On a Christmas day, he was alone in his hotel room, and I brought him a $500 bill. With a large safety pin, he attached it to his denim jacket. When he finally got a booking in Monterey, he admitted, "I feel like it's taking me away from my work."

Lenny lived way up in the hills. His house was protected by barbed wire and a concrete gate, except that it was always open. He had a wall-to-wall one-way mirror in his living room, but when the sun was shining you could see into the room instead of out. He was occasionally hassled by police on his own property. One evening in October 1963, we were talking while he was shaving, when four officers suddenly appeared, loud and obnoxious. He asked them to leave unless they had a search warrant.

One of the cops took out his gun. "Here's my search warrant," he said. Then Lenny and the cops had a discussion about the law, such as the rules of evidence, and after half an hour they left. Lenny tried to take it all in stride, but the encounter was depressing, and he changed his mind about going out that night.

When everything was quiet, we went outside and stood at the edge of his unused swimming pool. Dead leaves floated in the water. Lenny cupped his hands to his mouth. "All right, you dogs," he called out. "Bark for the rich man!" — thereby setting off a chain reaction of barking dogs, a canine chorus echoing through Hollywood Hills.

We ordered some pizza, and he played some old tapes, ranging from a faith healer to patriotic World War II songs. "Good-bye, Mama, I'm off to Yokohama, the Land of Yama-Yama ..."

Back at the Cafe Au Go Go arrest in New York, Lenny had told a fantasy tale about Eleanor Roosevelt, quoting her, "I've got the nicest tits that have ever been in this White House ..." The top of the police complaint was "Eleanor Roosevelt and her display of tits." At the trial, Lenny acted as his own attorney. He had obtained the legislative history of an Albany statute, and he discovered that back in 1931 there was an amendment proposed, which excluded from arrest in an indecent performance: stagehands, spectators, musicians, and — here was the fulcrum of his defense — actors. The law had been misapplied to him. Despite opposition by the New York Society for the Suppression of Vice, the amendment was finally signed into law by then-Governor Roosevelt, but to no avail.

"Ignoring the mandate of Franklin D. Roosevelt," Lenny observed, "is a great deal more offensive than saying Eleanor has lovely nay-nays."

On October 13, 1965 (Lenny's 40th birthday), instead of surrendering to the authorities in New York, he filed suit at the U.S. District Court in San Francisco to keep out of prison, and he got himself officially declared a pauper. Two months before his death in 1966, Lenny wrote to me: "I'm still working on the bust of the government of New York State." And he included his doodle of Christ nailed to a crucifix, with a speech balloon asking, "Where the hell is the ACLU?"

After he died, his mother brought his old faded denim jacket to a séance. That large safety pin was still attached to it. And at the funeral, his sound engineer friend dropped Lenny's microphone into his grave before the dirt was piled on. Lenny's problem had been that he wanted to talk onstage with the same freedom that he had in his living room. That problem doesn't happen to stand-up comedians any more.

As for me, I'm working on my long-awaited (by me) first novel. It's about a contemporary Lenny Bruce–type satirist. Those scenes where my protagonist performs, I've developed onstage myself, although at times it felt like I was actually channeling Lenny, until the day that he said, "C'mon, Paul, you know you don't believe in that shit." Well, this ended *that* wishful-thinking delusion.

I told my friend Avery Corman — author of *Oh, God* and *Kramer vs. Kramer* — how I welcomed the challenge of writing fiction.

"But you know," I added, "it's really hard to write. You have to make everything up."

And he said, "Hey, listen, you've been making stuff up all your life."

"Yeah, but that was journalism."

My Acid Trip with Groucho Marx

LSD WAS INFLUENCING MUSIC, painting, spirituality, and even the stock market. Tim Leary once let me listen in on a call from a Wall Street broker thanking him for turning him onto acid because it gave him the courage to sell short. Leary had a certain sense of pride about the famous folks he and his associates had introduced to the drug.

"But," he told me, "I consider Otto Preminger one of our failures."

I first met Preminger in 1960 while I was conducting a panel on censorship for *Playboy*. He had defied Hollywood's official seal of approval by refusing to change the script of *The Moon Is Blue*. He wouldn't take out the word *virgin*.

At the end of our interview, he asked, "Ven you tronscripe dis, vill you vix op my Henglish?"

"Oh, sure," I replied quickly. "Of course."

"Vy? Vot's drong viz my Henglish?"

I saw Preminger again in 1967. He was making a movie called *Skidoo*, starring Jackie Gleason as a retired criminal. Preminger told me he had originally intended that role for Frank Sinatra. *Skidoo* was pro-acid propaganda thinly disguised as a comedy adventure. However, LSD was not why the FBI was annoyed with the film. Rather, according to Gleason's FBI files, the FBI objected to one scene in the script where a file cabinet is stolen from an FBI building. Gleason was later approved as a special FBI contact in the entertainment business.

One of the characters in *Skidoo* was a Mafia chieftain named God. Screenwriter Bill Cannon had suggested Groucho Marx for the part. Preminger said it wasn't a good idea, but since they were already shooting, and that particular character was needed on the set in three days,

Groucho would be playing God after all. During one scene, Preminger was screaming instructions at him. Groucho yelled back, "Are you drunk?"

I had dinner with Groucho that evening. He was concerned about the script of *Skidoo* because it pretty much advocated LSD, which he had never tried, but he was curious. Moreover, he felt a certain responsibility to his young audience not to steer them wrong. He had read my descriptions of acid trips, so he asked if I could I possibly get him some pure stuff, and would I care to accompany him on a trip? I did not play hard to get. We arranged to ingest those little 300-microgram white tablets one afternoon at the home of an actress in Beverly Hills.

Groucho was especially interested in the countercultural aspects of LSD. I mentioned a couple of incidents that particularly tickled him, and his eyes sparkled with delight. One was about how, on Haight Street, runaway youngsters, refugees from their own families, had stood outside a special tourist bus — guided by a driver "trained in sociological significance" — and they held mirrors up to the cameras pointing at them from the windows, so that the tourists would get photos of themselves trying to take photos.

The other was about the day that LSD became illegal. In San Francisco, at precisely 2:00 in the afternoon, a cross-fertilization of mass protest and tribal celebration had taken place, as several hundred young people simultaneously swallowed tabs of acid while the police stood by helplessly.

"Internal possession wasn't against the law," I explained to Groucho.

"And they trusted their friends more than they trusted the government," he said. "I like that."

We had a period of silence and a period of listening to music. I was accustomed to playing rock 'n' roll while tripping, but the record collection at this house consisted entirely of classical music and Broadway show albums. First, we listened to Bach's "Cantata No. 7." "I'm supposed to be Jewish," Groucho said, "but I was seeing the most beautiful visions of Gothic cathedrals. Do you think Bach *knew* he was doing that?"

"I don't know. I was seeing beehives and honeycombs myself."

Later, we were listening to the score of a musical comedy, *Fanny*. There was one song called "Welcome Home," where the lyrics go something like, "Welcome home, says the clock," and the chair says,

"Welcome home," and so do various other pieces of furniture. Groucho started acting out each line, as though he were actually *being* greeted by the clock, the chair, and the rest of the furniture. He was like a child, charmed by his own ability to respond to the music that way.

There was a bowl of fruit on the dining room table. During a snack, he said, "I never thought eating a nice juicy plum would be the biggest thrill of my life." Then we talked about the sexual revolution. Groucho asked, "Have you ever laid two ladies together?"

I told him about the time that I was being interviewed by a couple of students from a Catholic girls' school. Suddenly Sheila, *The Realist's* "Scapegoat," and Marcia, the "Shit-On" — she had given herself that title because "What could be lower than a scapegoat?" — walked out of their office totally nude. "Sorry to interrupt, Paul," said Sheila, "but it's Wednesday — time for our weekly orgy." The interviewers left in a hurry. Sheila and Marcia led me up the stairs to my loft bed, and we had a delicious threesome. It had never happened before, and it would never happen again.

At one point in our conversation, Groucho somehow got into a negative space. He was equally cynical about institutions, such as marriage — "legal quicksand" — and individuals, such as Lyndon Johnson, referred to as "that potato-head."

Eventually, I asked, "What gives you hope?"

He thought for a moment. Then he just said one word: "People."

I told him about the sketch I had written for Steve Allen, "Unsung Heroes of Television," with the man whose job it was on *You Bet Your Life* to wait for the secret word to be said so that he could drop the duck down, and Groucho told me about one of his favorite contestants on the show. "He was an elderly gentleman with white hair, but quite a chipper fellow. I asked him what he did to retain his sunny disposition. 'Well, I'll tell you, Groucho,' he says, 'every morning I get up and I *make a choice* to be happy that day.'"

Groucho was holding onto his cigar for a long time, but he never smoked it, he only sniffed it occasionally. "Everybody has their own Laurel and Hardy," he mused. "A miniature Laurel and Hardy, one on each shoulder. Your little Oliver Hardy bawls you out — he says, 'Well, this is a *fine mess* you've gotten us into.' And your little Stan Laurel gets all weepy — 'Oh, Ollie, I couldn't help it. I'm sorry, I did the best I could.'"

Later, when Groucho started chuckling to himself, I hesitated to interrupt his reverie, but I had to ask, "What struck you funny?"

"I was thinking about this movie, *Skidoo*," he said. "I mean some of it is just plain ridiculous. This hippie inmate puts a letter he got, which is soaked in LSD, into the water supply of the prison, and suddenly everybody gets completely reformed. There's a prisoner who says, 'Oh, gosh, now I don't have to be a rapist anymore!' But it's also sophisticated in its own way. I like how Jackie Gleason, the character he plays, *accepts* the fact that he's not the biological father of his daughter."

"Oh, really? That sounds like the ultimate ego loss."

"But I'm really getting a big kick out of playing somebody named God like a dirty old man. You wanna know why?"

"Typecasting?"

"No, no — it's because — do you realize that irreverence and reverence are the *same thing*?"

"Always?"

"If they're not, then it's a misuse of your power to make people laugh." His eyes began to tear. "That's funny. I'm not even sad." Then he went to urinate, and when he came back, he said, "You know, everybody is waiting for *miracles* to happen. But the whole *human body* is a goddamn miracle." He recalled Otto Preminger telling him about his own response to taking LSD and then he mimicked Preminger's accent: "I saw *tings*, bot I did not zee myself." Groucho was looking into a mirror on the dining room wall, and he said, "Well, I can see *my*self, but I still don't understand what the hell I'm *doing* here ..."

A week later, Groucho told me that members of the Hog Farm commune who were extras in the movie had turned him on with marijuana on the set of *Skidoo*. "You know," I said, "my mother once warned me that LSD would lead to pot." "Well," he said, "your mother was right."

When *Skidoo* was released, Tim Leary saw it, and he cheerfully admitted, "I was fooled by Otto Preminger. He's much hipper than me."

In 1971, during an interview with *Flash* magazine, Groucho said, "I think the only hope this country has is Nixon's assassination." Yet he wasn't subsequently arrested for threatening the life of a president. In view of the indictment against Black Panther David Hilliard for using similar rhetoric, I wrote to the Justice Department to find out the status of their case against Groucho, and received this reply:

Dear Mr. Krassner:

Responding to your inquiry, the Supreme Court has held that Title 18 U.S.C., Section 871, prohibits only "true" threats. It is one thing to say, "I (or *we*) will kill Richard Nixon" when you are the leader of an organization which advocates killing people and overthrowing the Government; it is quite another to utter the words which are attributed to Mr. Marx, an alleged comedian. It was the opinion of both myself and the United States Attorney in Los Angeles (where Marx's words were alleged to have been uttered) that the latter utterance did not constitute a "true" threat.

Very Truly Yours,
James L. Browning, Jr.
United States Attorney

It would later be revealed that the FBI had published pamphlets in the name of the Black Panthers, advocating the killing of cops, and that an FBI file on Groucho Marx had indeed been started, and he actually *was* labeled a "national security risk." I phoned Groucho to tell him the good news.

"I deny everything," he said, "because I lie about everything." He paused, then added, "And everything I *deny* is a lie."

The last time I saw Groucho was in 1976. He was speaking at the Los Angeles Book Fair. He looked frail and unsmiling, but he was alert and irascible as ever. He took questions from the audience.

"Are you working on a film now?"

"No, I'm answering silly questions."

"What are your favorite films?"

"*Duck Soup. Night at the Opera.*"

"What do you think about Richard Nixon?"

"He should be in jail."

"Is humor an important issue in the presidential campaign?"

"Get your finger out of your mouth."

"What do you dream about?"

"Not about you."

"What inspired you to write?"

"A fountain pen. A piece of paper."

Then I called out a question: "What gives you the most optimism?"

I expected him to say "People" again, but this time he said, "The world."

There was hardly any standing room left in the auditorium, yet one fellow was sitting on the floor rather than take the aisle seat occupied by a large Groucho Marx doll.

Remembering George Carlin

GEORGE CARLIN DIED in June 2008. He was a generous friend. When I performed in Los Angeles, he sent a limousine to pick me up at the airport, and I stayed at his home. And such a sweet man. When I opened for him at the Warner-Grand Theater in San Pedro, we were hanging around in his dressing room, where he was nibbling from a vegetable plate. I watched as he continued to be genuinely gracious with every fan who stopped by. If they wanted his autograph, he would gladly sign his name. If they wanted to be photographed with him, he would assume the pose. If they wanted to have a little chat, he indulged them with congeniality.

I said, "You really show respect for everybody."

"Well," he responded, "that's just the way I would want to be treated."

As a performer, Carlin was uncompromising, knowing that his audience trusted him not to be afraid of offending them. In fact, he was excited by that possibility. The day before one of his live HBO specials, he called and told me to be sure and watch it, because he would devote the first ten minutes of his performance to the subject of abortion.

Carlin had long been vocal in support of the right to smoke and ingest various drugs, and he posed this rhetorical question: "Why are there no recreational drugs in suppository form?" I was pleased to inform him that teenage girls have been experimenting with tampons soaked in vodka, inserting them vaginally or rectally as a way of getting intoxicated without their parents detecting booze on their breath.

No matter what else Richard Nixon accomplished in *his* lifetime, his obituaries always mentioned him as the first American president to resign, and no matter what else George Carlin accomplished in his lifetime, his obits always connected him with the Supreme Court ruling on "The Seven Words You Can't Say on Television."

When asked in the Green Room at the Warner-Grand Theater by producer Dan Pasley why he didn't include the word "nigger" in that list, Carlin replied, "There's nothing funny about it — that really *is* a dirty word — but repressed words about sexual functions and bodily parts were truly funny. I had only been thinking about the 'dirty' words in terms of sex and bodily functions, and how uptight these religious freaks have made us. *That's* fun, that's some funny shit."

At a private memorial for family and friends, Carlin's daughter Kelly read from his burial instructions, written on May 1, 1990:

> Upon my death, I wish to be cremated. The disposition of my ashes (dispersal at sea, on land, or in the air) shall be determined by my surviving family (wife and daughter) in accordance with their knowledge of my prejudices and philosophies regarding geography and spirituality. Under no circumstances are my ashes to be retained by anyone or buried in a particular location. The eventual dispersal can be delayed for any reasonable length of time required to reach a decision, but not to exceed one month following my death.
>
> I wish no public service of any kind. I wish no religious service of any kind. I prefer a private gathering at my home, attended by friends and family members who shall be determined by my surviving family (wife and daughter). It should be extremely informal, they should play rhythm-and-blues music, and they should laugh a lot. Vague references to spirituality (secular) will be permitted.

Kelly added, "There will be no mention of God allowed," and "No one will be allowed to say that 'George is now smiling down at us from Heaven above.'"

Carlin once told an audience of children how to be a class clown as a way of attracting attention. "I didn't start out with fake heart attacks in the aisle," he explained. Ah, if only that's what he was doing *this* time.

But a reporter did once ask him how he wanted to die.

"I'd like to explode spontaneously in someone's living room," he replied. "That, to me, is the way to go out."

And, through his CDs, DVDs, books, and online, George Carlin does indeed continue to explode spontaneously in living rooms across the country and around the world.

Roasting With Robin

THE FIRST TIME I MET Robin Williams was in 1976 at the first annual Comedy Competition in San Francisco. He was sweating profusely, his hairy chest and arms showing, and he wore a brown cowboy hat. I was one of the judges. Although I voted for Williams, he came in second.

I forget the winner's name, but I recall that the lights went off in the middle of his act, so he took advantage of the accident, and, in the darkness, he whispered loudly, "Okay, now, when the lights go back on, everybody shout out, 'Surprise! Surprise!'" The audience laughed and applauded that ad lib.

Robin's disappointment was palpable, but his stardom was inevitable. Our paths continued to cross backstage at benefits where we both performed. He was also a reader of *The Realist*. In 1988, the word got around that I was going to undergo surgery, and he sent me a generous unsolicited check to help.

In 1998, Anita Hoffman, Abbie's widow, dying from cancer, decided to take her life on December 27, so as not to spoil Christmas for family and friends who were visiting and bringing all kinds of food. Her appetite was ravenous, and her humor was dark. After devouring a pastrami sandwich, she remarked, "I'd better brush my teeth, I don't want to get gum pockets."

She was staying at a house in San Francisco owned by actress Wynona Rider, whose godfather was Timothy Leary. He had been Anita's role model during the final months of *his* life. "You couldn't choose how and when and with whom you were *born*," he said, "but you can take charge of your own death." And that's exactly what she was now doing.

Robin Williams learned about Anita's situation from his co-star in *Good Will Hunting*, Matt Damon, who had been told about it by his girlfriend, Wynona. Robin had never met Anita, but he called and offered to pay a visit, in keeping with his benign case of Patch Adams Syndrome. After all, if Patch could travel to Trinidad to entertain murderers who would be hanged three days later, why shouldn't it be appropriate for Robin to make Anita laugh on Christmas day? She hesitated — "I've never really been a fan of his work," she thought — but then invited him to visit....

And so it came to pass in 2014 that Robin Williams would also commit suicide. In the midst of mass mourning for Williams, Rush Limbaugh explained, "Leftists are never happy." And the anti-choice *Lifenews* claimed that Robin killed himself out of guilt over an abortion his girlfriend had in the 1970s.

The last time I saw Robin was in 1986 on a Saturday evening in July, at the Los Angeles Press Club, where we were both participants at a roast for Harlan Ellison. Ellison, also a friend, was a prolific author of fantasy and science/speculative fiction, credited with more than 1,700 short stories, novellas, screenplays, comic book scripts, television scripts, and critical essays. Years later, I compiled a book, *Pot Stories for the Soul* — which included contributions by Hunter Thompson, Michelle Phillips, Wavy Gravy, Ken Kesey — but Harlan wrote a totally anti-stoner story. I felt that would serve as an ironic foreword. "Basically, fuck dope," he began, "No offense, dude, but fuck dope." So I sent him a $100 check. He ripped it up and told me to send a $10 check instead.

Ellison, famously, had a reputation for angry ranting with literary style. My wife Nancy said, "He has a black belt in Mouth."

The roast was supposedly a fundraiser for Ellison's defense costs in a frivolous libel lawsuit brought by comic book writer Michael Fleischer, who wanted $2 million in compensation. In an interview in a 1980 issue of *The Comics Journal*, Ellison had mentioned Fleischer's first novel and called him "crazy" like H.P. Lovecraft and other renowned writers. Ironically, Harlan had intended it to be a compliment.

I say "supposedly," because, coincidentally, the book you're holding now is published by Fantagraphics Books, which, along with its publisher, Gary Groth, were Ellison's co-defendants. During the course of preparing this book, Groth, who had a falling-out with Ellison as the case wound its way to trial, remarked to me "this fund-raiser was a scam; all of [Ellison's] legal bills were being paid by his insurance company."

Anyway, the auditorium at the Press Club was filled, at $25 a head.

Screenwriter David Gerrold remarked, "The fact that Ellison is a self-made man relieves God of a great responsibility. I've been Harlan's friend for six years. Of course, I've known him for eighteen years."

The moderator of the roast, film critic Digby Diehl, read a telegram from Isaac Asimov that concluded, "Kick him in the balls — signed, Frank Sinatra." Onstage, Asimov's fellow science-fiction writer Robert Silverberg announced, "Harlan Ellison is so short that he goes up on his girlfriend." Robin and I were sitting next to each other, and we simultaneously crossed that joke off our imaginary lists.

There were short jokes galore. Have a few free samples: "Short? I carry a life-sized portrait of Harlan in my wallet." "Harlan's parents were normal, but the milkman was a syphilitic dwarf." And the producer of *The Twilight Zone*, Phil DeGuere, complained, "It took Harlan nine months before he figured out how to shoot himself in the foot at *Twilight Zone* and get canned. But of all the people I have worked with, Harlan is by far the shortest. Harlan doesn't have a short fuse. He *is* a short fuse."

My own short joke was, "Actually, this isn't a roast. It's more like a microwave." Robin said, "Harlan is a tall Paul Williams, a white Paul Simon." I pointed out, "Harlan is on the right side of a lot of important fights. He's fought against racism and sexism. That's why this whole panel is white males."

A roast by definition overflows with irreverence, insults, and raunchiness. Examples: "If it's true that you are what you eat, Harlan would be a vagina." Stan Lee of comic-book infamy said, "Harlan is a very difficult person to arouse. Ask any of his former wives." And Robin contributed a metaphorical dick joke: "If you're hung like a field mouse, don't stand in the wind."

I stated, "Harlan is an egomaniac partially because at the moment of sexual climax, he calls out his own name." Robin shouted, "Was it good for *me*?" I responded, "Harlan has a typewriter with only two letters — M and E. And on it he has somehow managed to write 42 books as well as 300 of Steve Allen's songs plus a few of Lyndon LaRouche's speeches."

Robert *Psycho* Block remembered when "Harlan was interested in re-writing other people's work. He took me into a nearby drugstore and showed me how he had erased the M's off all the Murine bottles."

I observed, "Harlan has always refused to get involved with the drug world — as a user. However, he *is* a dealer. In fact, he was the connection for Cathy Evelyn Smith."

A severe groan emanated from the audience, and I realized that I was treating a roaster as a roastee, not an uncommon practice — Robin Williams and Robert DeNiro had been with Cathy Smith and John Belushi on the night of Belushi's death in 1982.

"Oh, that's a good one," Robin said with understandable Sarcasm 101. "Listen," I replied, "if she didn't plea bargain, you wouldn't be here tonight."

Moderator Digby Diehl proceeded to rub salt into Robin's wound that I had unintentionally caused: "Robin Williams has been called the king of improv, and he has proven it tonight by interrupting everybody, stepping on their lines, doing schtick. He's been about as annoying as he can be."

"I loved that review, though," said Robin, referring to Diehl's negative critique of *Club Paradise*.

Diehl: "I was hoping you hadn't seen it, Robin. It's said of you in Hollywood that you don't read your scripts. Anyway, ladies and gentlemen, I'd like to bring you Robin Williams, fresh from *Club Paradise*, his biggest failure yet."

Williams: "Thank you, Gary Franklin [the movie reviewer Diehl replaced]. What can you say about a man who's a TV critic? A man who looks at a good film and letters it like a report card. Is that art? I think not. And I'd like to thank Harlan's lawyer for proving, God, is there a reason for law? I think not. And I'd like to thank Mr. Krassner for all the Cathy Smith references. That's some funny stuff."

Robin confessed, "I really don't know Harlan for shit," then described his house. "It's like Notre Dame done by Sears. There's Harlan, naked, playing in his toys with a beautiful shiksa goddess jumping up and down saying, 'I like him. He's smart.'" Robin morphed into a little boy in the bathroom. "I'm reading Bradbury, Dad." (Roaster Ray Bradbury chortled. Robin suppressed a fake sob.) "It's just taken me so far down to be here. I wish I could cry, but I don't care." (The audience applauded.)

"Well," said Diehl, "it's been basically a really hostile, ugly night, with a lot of lame jokes and sentimental drivel. But we still have the ritual forgiveness to look forward to." He introduced Harlan Ellison, "a man with the milk of human kindness dripping from his fangs."

"Ha, ha. Very funny, I'm sure," Harlan reacted. "I had a friend once, but the wheels fell off. Zip friends. Dust is my friend. And what of these fuckers here? Robin Williams can't even get a pair of pants that fits him."

"There's a reason for that, Harlan!"

"Yeah, sure. It was for you they made up the phrase, 'Is it in yet?' You wanna talk about that, Williams? I've got four words for you: *Club Paradise* and *The Survivors*."

"Yeah, on a double bill with *A Boy and His Dog*!" (Ellison wrote the movie's screenplay based on his own novella.)

Harlan continued to baste the roasters. As for me, he said, "I want to thank my old chum Krassner for being here tonight. I want to commend him on his restraint in the remarks he made. Or perhaps it was only caution on his part because I promised if he fucked around with me, I'd let on that he caught his herpes from Nancy Reagan."

Digby Diehl concluded, "Harlan's only fear is that he'll get in a car accident and have to re-live this event. And in the true tradition of roasting, that tradition being to talk dirty and mention a big name, thank you all for coming. And join us next week when our guest roaster will be Mother Teresa."

I blurted out, "I fucked *her*!"

The audience screamed, hooted, stomped, and Robin jumped out of his chair and ran around in a circle. Then he said, "Gandhi is going, 'Who is this man? He may not get through the gates of heaven for that line.'"

Harlan said, "Thank God Krassner got off one good one."

I explained, "I guess I just fell into the insult mode."

"Basically," said Robert Silverberg, "the roast is a really ugly, repugnant, immature, and childish art form. I hate it. And I will only do one if Harlan is the target."

(Ellison, et al., won the lawsuit later that year. He died in June 2018.)

On our way home, Nancy summed up the irony: "A compliment was originally perceived as an insult, and consequently we've had an evening of insults which were really compliments."

PAUL KRASSNER

Remembering Dick Gregory

I FIRST MET DICK GREGORY when he asked me to interview him for *The Realist* in New York. I saw him again when I was in Chicago. He was performing at the Playboy Club and invited me to his show. Two years previously, Negro comedians performed only in Negro nightclubs, and Gregory was no exception.

But one evening, the regular white comic at the Playboy Club got sick, and Gregory took his place. It made *Time* magazine, and he was invited to perform on *The Tonight Show*, but he declined unless, after doing his stand-up act, he would be asked to sit down and talk with Jack Paar. The gamble worked, and Gregory became an instant celebrity, breaking through the color barrier with humor.

Eventually we became friends and fellow demonstrators. Now he was performing at the Playboy Club, not as a substitute comic but as a star attraction. They had to supply me with a jacket, and a tie that was decorated all over with bunny symbols. Gregory was already on stage.

"How could Columbus discover America," he was asking the audience, "when the Indians were already *here*?"

In his dressing room between shows, Gregory took out his wallet and showed me a tattered copy of his favorite poem, "If," by Rudyard Kipling. I laughed, and he looked offended, until I explained that I was laughing because it was also *my* favorite poem, and "the unforgiving minute" was my favorite poetic phrase.

Gregory visited me on the Lower East Side of New York. The entire side of one building on that block featured a fading advertisement for a cleanser personified by the Gold Dust Twins, a pair of little Negro boys. It had originally been painted right on the bricks.

When he saw it, he said, "They ought to take that whole wall and preserve it in a museum somewhere."

ON A WORK-VACATION in the Florida Keys with Abbie and Anita Hoffman in December in 1967, I followed a neighborhood crow down the road, then continued walking to town by myself to use the telephone. First, I called Gregory, since it was in his city, Chicago, that we were planning to invade the presidential convention in the summer of 1968. He told me that he had decided to run for president, and he wanted to know if I thought Bob Dylan would make a good vice president.

"Oh, sure, but to tell you the truth, I don't think Dylan would ever get involved in electoral politics."

Gregory would end up with assassination researcher Mark Lane as his running mate. Next, I called Jerry Rubin in New York to arrange for a meeting when we returned.

At our counter-convention we all attended an Unbirthday Party for President Lyndon Johnson at the Coliseum, with Ed Sanders, leader of the Fugs, serving as emcee. The atmosphere was highly emotional. Dick Gregory recited the Preamble to the Declaration of Independence with incredible fervor. Fists were being upraised in the audience as he spoke, and I thrust my own fist into the air for the first time.

WHEN MY MARRIAGE BROKE UP in 1971, I moved to San Francisco, and I had my own talk program. Gregory announced on my show that, until the war in Vietnam was over, he was going to stop eating solid foods. I, in turn, announced that, until the war was over, I was going to eat all of Dick Gregory's meals. Actually, my only *real* discipline was being silent one day a week.

When my young daughter Holly came out to stay with me that summer, she decided to join me on my silent day. We communicated with handwritten notes. Holly wrote, *Does laughter count?* Since we were making up the rules as we went along, I answered, *Yes, but no tickling.* Naturally, she tried to make me laugh, but I held it in — and got a rush.

All the energy that normally gets dissipated into the air with laughter seemed to surge through my body instead. I decided to stop laughing altogether, just to see what would happen. The more I didn't laugh, the more I found funny. And, paying closer attention to others, I refined my appreciation of laughter as another whole language that could often be more revealing than words. Sometimes I would get a twinge of guilt if I nearly slipped and laughed, and I remembered what I had always known, that children must be *taught* to be serious. When I mentioned my laugh-fast to Dick Gregory, still on his food-fast, it didn't sound so far-fetched to him.

"That's two things people do out of insecurity," he said. "Eating and laughing."

"Well, what would happen to us if everyone in our audiences realized that?"

"Brother, we'd go out of business."

I WAS INVITED to a Christmas party in 1977 by *Hustler* publisher Larry Flynt. Gregory was at the party, and Flynt asked each of us to perform, but first he would take the microphone himself. To my surprise-shock, he wanted me to publish his magazine beside *The Realist* while he traveled around the country to spread his (temporary) born-again Christianity.

On Thanksgiving Day, Gregory had been arrested in front of the White House for protesting the lack of human rights in South Africa. Larry Flynt had a premonition that there would be an assassination attempt on Gregory. Flynt contacted him a couple of weeks later, and they became friends. Gregory was now staying at Flynt's mansion in Columbus, helping him change to a vegetarian diet. Flynt had already taken off 40 pounds. On the day before the Christmas party, Gregory was in the middle of giving himself an enema when Flynt walked in.

According to Gregory, "Larry said, 'Let me tell you about this fantastic guy I've got comin' out, and I don't know what I'm gonna do yet, but I just wanna talk with him.' And I said, 'Well, who is it?' He said, 'Paul Krassner.' And I just fell out, and said, 'Are you serious? He's one of the hippest minds in the whole world.' Then he came back and said, 'How long you been knowin' him?' and I told him, 'All through the '60s,' you know. And I said it was a fantastic idea."

For the New Year, Flynt flew Gregory and me to the Bahamas. Gregory was in the kitchen, diligently preparing a health drink for Flynt — this must have been the birth of his Bahamian Diet powder — and he was also feeding unfiltered conspiracy theories to his eager student.

At midnight, we all went out on the dock and stood in a misty drizzle as Gregory uttered truly eloquent prayers for each of us. When he finished, Flynt's wife Althea whined, like Lucy in the *Peanuts* strip, "My hair's getting all wet." It was her way of saying, "Amen."

On New Year's Day, we were sitting in the sand, just relaxing. Flynt had bought a paperback novel by Gore Vidal in the hotel store, but first he was reading the Sunday *New York Times* and worrying about the implications of juries with only six members. A moment later he was rubbing suntan lotion on my back.

"I'll bet Hugh Hefner never did this for you," he said.

LARRY FLYNT HAD BEEN TRAVELING around a lot, but he happened to be back in L.A. at the same time that my friend LSD guru Ram Dass was visiting, so I had the unique pleasure of introducing them. Larry, Althea, Ram Dass, and I went to a health-food restaurant, where we discovered that we shared something in common: we were all practicing celibacy — Larry at the suggestion of Dick Gregory, Althea by extension, Ram Dass for spiritual purposes, and me just for the sheer perversity of it.

When Larry got shot down South by a racist nut because *Hustler* had a naked black model, Althea had transformed the Coca-Cola Suite at Emory University Hospital into her office, where she was now studying the slides of the irreverent "Jesus and the Adulteress" feature. Dick Gregory was there, and he said, "This scares *me*." He was concerned about reaction in the Bible Belt, notwithstanding the fact that *Hustler*'s research department had already made certain that the text followed the Bible.

And now Althea was checking for any sexism that might have slipped past the male editors' limited consciousness. The spread was already in page forms, but not yet collated into the magazine, and there was still a gnawing dilemma about whether or not to publish it.

The marketing people were aghast at the possibility that wholesalers would refuse to distribute an issue of the magazine with such a blatantly blasphemous feature. Althea and I voted to publish. Gregory and editor Bruce David voted not to publish. "I'm against it," he said, "because this is an issue that just simply will not be distributed."

Faced with this crucial decision, Althea made her choice on the basis of pure whimsicality. She noticed a pair of pigeons on the window ledge. One of them was waddling toward the other. "All right," she said, "if that dove walks over and pecks the *other* dove, then we *will* publish this." The pigeon continued strutting along the window ledge, but it stopped short and didn't peck the other pigeon, so publication of "Jesus and the Adulteress" was postponed indefinitely.

Of course, Dick Gregory continued to spread his diligent activism until he died. He was a loss to me, and to this country, and around the world, but his powerful inspiration remains.

The Later Years

Words and Phrases
That I've Coined

I REALLY DON'T LIKE TO BOAST, but in my lifetime, on half a dozen occasions, I have actually added words and phrases to the language. It's something I always wanted to do. What a thrill it must have been for Dr. Harold Cerumen, who decided that cleaning out earwax should be known as "cerumen disimpaction." And veterinarian Alice Neuticle who coined the word "neuticles" — cosmetic testicles for a dog that's been neutered.

So I'm not asking for credit. Or cash. Since money had been called "dough" and then morphed into "bread," I figured that "toast" would be the next logical step in that particular linguistic evolution, but my campaign itself became toast, in the sense that "toast" now means history.

Also, I was intrigued by the process of having a body part named after oneself. How proud Casper Bartholin's parents must have been to have a son who christened the source of female lubrication that takes the friction out of intercourse as "Bartholin's glands." But my idea of calling those two vertical lines between your nose and your mouth "Krassner's crease" just never became popular.

Here, then, for better or worse, are my contributions to American culture that did manage to catch on, or at least may be on their way.

1

IN 1958, PORNOGRAPHY was gradually becoming legal, but at that stage of the game, the Supreme Court was unwilling to allow First Amendment protection of "hard-core" porn — as opposed, I assumed, to the term I invented, "soft-core porn," which was obviously more respectable, though it seemed kind of sneaky, pretending to be squeaky clean. So I decided to satirize the concept with a new feature in *The Realist*: "Soft-Core Porn of the Month."

For example, phallic symbolism in newspapers and magazines was a key ingredient of soft-core porn. Sample: A close-up of a stick shift in a 1965 Volkswagen ad was accompanied by the question, "Does the stickshift scare your wife?" Soft-core porn now refers to limited sexuality, as seen in network TV dramas and hotel-room movies that feature jiggling breasts and buttocks but no genitalia. The way to recognize soft-core porn is that it gives men a soft-on.

2

ON THE AFTERNOON of December 31, 1967, several activist friends were gathered at Abbie and Anita Hoffman's Lower East Side apartment, smoking Columbian marijuana and planning a counter-convention for the Democratic Party's event the following summer in Chicago. Our fantasy was to counter their convention of death with our festival of life. While the Democrats would present politicians giving speeches at the convention center, we would present rock bands playing in the park. There would be booths with information about drugs and alternatives to the draft. Our mere presence would be our statement.

We needed a name, so that reporters could have a *who* for their journalistic who-what-when-where-and-why lead paragraphs. I felt a brainstorm coming on and went from the living room to the bedroom so that I could concentrate. Our working title was the International Youth Festival. But the initials IYF were a meaningless acronym. I paced back and forth, juggling titles to see if I could come up with words whose initials would make a good acronym. I tried Youth International Festival. YIF. It sounded like KIF. Kids International Festival? Nope, too contrived. Back to YIF. But what could make YIP? Now that would be ideal because then the word Yippie could be derived organically.

Of course, "Yippie" was already a traditional shout of spontaneous joy, but we could be the Yippies! It had exactly the right attitude. "Yippies" was the most appropriate name to signify the radicalization of hippies. What a perfect media myth that would be — the Yippies! And then, working backward, it hit me. Youth International Party! It was a natural. *Youth*: This was essentially a movement of young people involved in a generational struggle. *International*: It was happening all over the globe, from Mexico to France, from Germany to Japan. And *Party*: In both senses of the word. We would be a party and we would have a party.

Yippie was only a label to describe a phenomenon that already existed — an organic coalition of psychedelic dropouts and political activists. There was no separation between our culture and our politics. In the process of cross-pollination, we had come to share an awareness that there was a linear connection between putting kids in prison for smoking marijuana in this country and burning them to death with napalm on the other side of the planet. It was just the ultimate extension of dehumanization. But now reporters had a who for their lead paragraphs. A headline in the *Chicago Daily News* summed it up: "Yipes! The Yippies Are Coming!" Our myth was becoming a reality.

3

IN 1972, I FOUND MYSELF smoking a combination of marijuana and opium with John Lennon and Yoko Ono. Lennon was absentmindedly holding on to the joint, and I asked him, "Do the British use that expression, 'Don't bogart that joint,' or is it only an American term — you know, derived from the image of a cigarette dangling from Humphrey Bogart's lip?" He replied, with a twinkle in his eye, "In England, if you remind somebody else to pass a joint, you lose your own turn." Since Bogart and Lauren Bacall were a classic Hollywood couple, I was inspired by that snippet of dialogue to say, "Don't *bacall* that joint."

4

INTUITIVELY, I WAS AN ADVOCATE of equal rights and opportunities for both genders long before Women's Liberation became a movement. In 1959, I wrote, "From a completely idealistic viewpoint, classified ads for jobs should not have separate Male and Female classifications, with exceptions such as a wet-nurse." In 1964, that practice became illegal. Masturbation was a powerful taboo for females, a subdivision of the war on pleasure, while it was somehow expected of males. But if it was okay for guys to jack-off, I wrote in a media fable, *Tales of Tongue Fu*, in 1974, then it was also okay for girls to jill-off.

5

IN 1979, I COVERED, for a weekly alternative paper, the trial of ex-cop Dan White for the double execution of San Francisco Mayor George Moscone and Supervisor Harvey Milk, the gay equivalent of Martin Luther King, Jr. In a surprise move, homophobic White's defense team presented a bio-chemical explanation of his behavior, blaming it on compulsive gobbling down of sugar-filled junk-food snacks. This was a purely accidental tactic. Dale Metcalf, an attorney, told me how he happened to be playing chess with one of White's attorneys, Stephen Scherr.

Metcalf had just read *Orthomolecular Nutrition* by Abram Hoffer. He questioned Scherr about White's diet and learned that, while under stress, White would consume candy bars and soft drinks. Metcalf recommended the book to Scherr, suggesting the author as an expert witness. In his book, Hoffer revealed a personal vendetta against doughnuts, and White had once eaten five doughnuts in a row.

During the trial, psychiatrist Martin Blinder testified that, on the night before the murders, while White was "getting depressed about the fact he would not be reappointed [as supervisor, after having quit], he just sat there in front of the TV set, bingeing on Twinkies." In my notebook, I scribbled "Twinkie defense," and wrote about it in my next report.

In the wake of the Twinkie defense, a representative of the Continental Baking Company asserted that the notion that overdosing on the cream-filled goodies could lead to murderous behavior was "poppycock" and "crap" — apparently two of the artificial ingredients in Twinkies, along with sodium pyrophosphate and yellow dye — while another spokesperson couldn't believe "that a rational jury paid serious attention to that issue." Nevertheless, some jurors did. One remarked after the trial, "It sounded like Dan White had hypoglycemia."

Later, the *San Francisco Chronicle* reported: "During the trial, no one but well-known satirist Paul Krassner — who may have coined the phrase 'Twinkie defense' — played up that angle. His trial stories appeared in the *San Francisco Bay Guardian*."

6

TWITTER IS AN INTERESTING PHENOMENON. It's perfect for those folks with a short attention span, and it's scary for paranoids who don't want to be followed. It appeals to minimalists, such as, say, Bob Dylan. I once asked him, "How come you're taking Hebrew lessons?" He replied, "I can't speak it." And when I mentioned the Holocaust, he responded, "I resented it."

Tweets range from the trivial (David Gregory announcing that he was going to eat a bagel before moderating *Meet the Press*) to international conflicts (Iranian citizens reporting on the uprising against their repressive government). It occurred to me that there could be classic haiku tweets — three lines consisting of five syllables, seven syllables and five syllables — adding up obviously to no more than 140 characters — and so I decided to embed the phrase I coined in the following (also) twaiku:

What's worth sharing now?
World War Three or stubbed my toe?
I have Twitter's Block.

PAUL KRASSNER

My Brother's Secret Space Communication Projects

WHEN MY OLDER BROTHER George and I were kids, I could recite the alphabet backwards, whereas he read the entire dictionary. We both played the violin, and when he was 9 and I was 6, we performed at Carnegie Hall. I was the youngest concert artist in any field to perform there.

Our younger sister, Marge, was four years younger than me. My mother had wanted to have a boy and a girl, but I was her second boy. If I had been a girl, Marge wouldn't have been born. Marge took piano lessons and became a legendary figure at Boys and Girls High School in Brooklyn, teaching music and running the chorus. After she retired, she and two women — one played the cello, the other the flute — performed at the Salvador Dali Museum in St. Petersburg, Florida, playing music connected to various phases of Dali's life. She also taught Tai Chi. She died in 2018 from pancreatic cancer. I'm happy she was born, for her whole lifetime.

Marge was the only one in our family who stuck with classical music. Although I was considered a child prodigy, I merely had a technique for playing the violin, but I had a real *passion* for making people laugh. I put my violin in the closet when I was 12, and, several years later, I used it essentially as a prop when I began performing stand-up comedy. George went to the High School of Music & Art and was offered a four-year scholarship at the Juilliard School's renowned Music Division, but he really preferred Math and Science. He surprised our parents, announcing his decision to be an electrical engineer, but they were totally supportive.

He turned down the scholarship and instead attended CCNY. "Because," he says, "I thought then that the violin was good for my avocation, not my vocation. With so many brilliant musicians then, you really had to know somebody to get anywhere in that world. It's not like YouTube today." While at CCNY, he played with a square-dance group and became Official Fiddler for the New York/New Jersey Square Dance Callers Association. He learned that a caller earned twice as much as he did, so he put down his fiddle and took up calling square dances. He was also captain of the varsity boxing team.

George went to the University of Michigan for his master's degree. Our mother insisted — and to please her — he mailed his laundry home in a light aluminum case she had purchased for that specific purpose. To pay for his tuition, basement apartment, and other expenses, he got a teaching fellowship, was a research assistant, sold programs at football games, and bussed tables at a local restaurant, which he quit when the table he cleared was occupied by fellow students.

He won the all-campus boxing championship but had to fight in a heavier weight class since no one else weighed as little as he did. "Being a violinist," he said, "I was worried about my hands. But my opponent in the semi-final match was an oboe player with a concert scheduled for the next day, and he asked me to take it easy on his mouth."

IN OCTOBER 1957, Russia sent Sputnik into space. It was the first orbiting satellite, circling the earth in 96 minutes, and making 1,440 orbits in three months. This astounding technical feat was totally unanticipated by the United States and ignited the era of the space race. At the time, George was working as a civilian scientist for the Army Signal Corps in Fort Monmouth, New Jersey, in charge of the radio relay program. He had been recruited by their senior executive of Research and Development, an alumnus of the University of Michigan.

A week after Sputnik, George sent a proposal to the Commanding General, urging a space communication program. The response: *Do it!* "So," George recalls, "I created the first Space Electronics organization in the country. It was very strange making presentations to generals and top government officials. At age 29, as head of the Astro-Electronics Division, I had the civilian rank equal to a colonel, but I looked like a young kid. It was embarrassing to take them to lunch and be carded by the waiter."

That wasn't his only embarrassment: "At the Signal Corps, I accidentally flushed my top-secret badge down the toilet. It took a lot of official paperwork and the notation 'irretrievably lost' to finally get a new badge. Also, in 1954, the McCarthy paranoia was paramount. I, and fellow civilians — and military personnel, I assume — had to empty our lunchboxes and briefcases for inspection every time we entered the building."

Five months after he had begun as a civilian scientist, George was drafted. In the Army, he was assigned to the 82nd Airborne Division at Fort Bragg, North Carolina. He was a "leg," though. Instead of jumping out of an airplane, his job was to maintain all radios, phones, and electrical equipment. He also started the U.S. Helicopter Square Dance Team to demonstrate the mobility of helicopters. When assigned KP (Kitchen Police), rather than peel potatoes, he scheduled helicopter square-dance practice.

Eight months after Sputnik, his team began working on the design of the world's first communication satellite, SCORE (Signal Communications Orbit Relay Equipment). "There were no reference books, precedents, or Google for information. We were the pioneers. It's interesting that the first known reference to communication satellites was in a 1945 science-fiction story by the British author, Arthur C. Clarke."

It took the team only six months to design and build the satellite, which was launched in December 1958 by an Atlas rocket that weighed 9,000 pounds. "The satellite payload became famous for the tape-recorded message from President Dwight Eisenhower, who insisted that this project remain top secret," George tells me. "He said the launch would be aborted if any word leaked out, because he didn't want a chance of failure to tarnish our image. As it turned out, one of the two tape recorders did fail, but his Christmas message to the world was the very first transmitted message from space."

Eisenhower stated: "This is the president of the United States speaking. Through the marvels of scientific advance, my voice is coming to you via a satellite circling in outer space. My message is a simple one. Through this unique means, I convey to you and all mankind America's wish for peace on Earth and good will toward men everywhere."

IN 1945, in the wake of World War II, the victors launched Operation Paperclip, recruiting a variety of 600 scientists from Nazi Germany to work in the United States. President Harry Truman ordered the exclusion of any "member of the Nazi Party or an active supporter of Nazi militarism," but the Joint Intelligence Objectives Agency created false employment and political biographies to circumvent Truman's command.

Those scientists were then granted security clearances and infiltrated into hospitals, universities, and the aerospace industry, further developing their techniques in propaganda, mind control, and behavior modification. Among them was Wernher von Braun, who had been a member of the Nazi Party and an SS officer who could be linked to the deaths of thousands of concentration camp prisoners. (Fun fact: he married his cousin.) He came to America in 1945 and became a citizen in 1955. He was called the "father of the U.S. space program."

In June 1958, by the time those German importees had become entrenched in a slew of American niche communities, I published the first issue of *The Realist*, including a cartoon that depicted the U.S. Army Guided Missile Research Center with a sign in the window, *Help Wanted*. A couple of scientists are standing in front of that building, and one is saying to the other, "They would have hired me only I don't speak German."

Exactly one year later, Wernher von Braun recruited thirteen scientists to work with him on an ultra-top-secret program, Project Horizon, to build a communication station on the moon. Its purpose was a study to determine the feasibility of constructing a scientific/military base.

"I was one of the lucky thirteen," George remembers. "In fact, you don't have to be a rocket scientist to be a rocket scientist. Von Braun told me that many of his ideas came from science-fiction magazines.

"The project was so secret that the thirteen of us could not even tell our bosses — they didn't have what was called 'need to know.' I would tell [my wife] Judith that I was going to Washington, D.C., and then I would change planes to go to Huntsville, Alabama, where much of the work was done. I made up stories about Washington for her, while I really was in Huntsville, which also was the watercress capital of the world. I'd make up a story about the cherry blossoms, or seeing a senator in the street.

"Unfortunately, when I left the government after nine years (two in the army), I lost my own security rating and need-to-know, so I had no idea if the station was ever built on the moon, and I no longer got cheap watercress."

According to Wikipedia, "The permanent outpost was predicted to cost $6 billion and become operational in December 1966. A lunar landing-and-return vehicle would have shuttled up to 16 astronauts at a time to the base and back. Horizon never progressed past the feasibility stage in an official capacity."

However, just like George had lied to Judith, he in turn learned in 2014 that he was lied to about the *actual* purpose of Project Horizon: "[It] was a 1959 study to determine the feasibility of constructing a scientific/military base on the Moon ... On June 8, 1959, a group at the Army Ballistic Missile Agency (ABMA) produced for the Army a report titled *Project Horizon, A U.S. Army Study for the Establishment of a Lunar Military Outpost.*

"The project proposal states the requirements as: The lunar outpost is required to develop and protect potential United States interests on the moon; to develop techniques in moon-based surveillance of the earth and space, in communications relay, and in operations on the surface of the moon; to serve as a base for exploration of the moon, for further exploration into space and for military operations on the moon if required; and to support scientific investigations on the moon."

"WHEN I HAD BEEN IN THE ARMY, I was assigned to work on top-secret military and satellite work," George tells me. "The FBI did routine checks. One of our neighbors told Judith that the FBI visited them but were told not to let us know of their inquiries. Apparently, you [me, Paul] were on their 'watch list' — based on your 'radical' writings, I assume. I learned from my boss at the Signal Corps that my top-secret clearance was in jeopardy. Granting my clearance took about a month longer than normal, but, eventually, it was granted."

Meanwhile, I was placed on the FBI's RI (Round-up Index), though I had broken no law. Who knows? Maybe it was because I published a cartoon depicting a man sitting at a desk, speaking on the phone: "I'm very sorry, but we of the FBI are powerless to act in a case of oral-genital intimacy unless it has in some way obstructed interstate commerce."

When *Life* magazine ran a favorable profile of me in 1968, an FBI agent using a fake name, Howard Rasmussen, sent a poison-pen letter to the editor: "To classify Krassner as some sort of 'social rebel' is far too cute. He's a nut, a raving, unconfined nut." But in 1969, the FBI's previous attempt at mere character assassination escalated to a more literal approach. This was not included in my own COINTELPRO (Counter-Intelligence Program) files but, rather, a separate FBI project calculated to cause rifts between the black and Jewish communities.

The FBI had produced a "Wanted" poster featuring a large swastika. In the four square spaces of the swastika were photos of Yippie founders Abbie Hoffman, Jerry Rubin, and me, and SDS (Students for a Democratic Society) leader Mark Rudd. Underneath the swastika was this headline — LAMPSHADES! LAMPSHADES! LAMPSHADES! — and this message:

"The only solution to Negro problems in America would be the elimination of the Jews. May we suggest the following order of elimination? (After all, we've been this way before.) *All Jews connected with the Establishment. *All Jews connected with Jews connected with the Establishment. *All Jews connected with those immediately above. *All Jews except those in the Movement. *All Jews in the Movement except those who dye their skins black. *All Jews. Look out, Abbie, Jerry, Paul and Mark!"

(Shades of Wernher von Braun!)

It was approved by FBI director J. Edgar Hoover's top two aides: "Authority is granted to prepare and distribute on an anonymous basis to selected individuals and organizations in the New Left the leaflet submitted. Assure that all necessary precautions are taken to protect the Bureau as the source of these leaflets. This leaflet suggests facetiously the elimination of these leaders." And, of course, if a black militant obtained that flyer and eliminated one of those "New Left leaders who are Jewish," the FBI's bureaucratic ass would be covered: "We *said* it was a facetious suggestion, didn't we?"

On top of that, my name was on a list of 65 "radical" campus speakers released by the House Internal Security Committee. The blacklist was published in *The New York Times* and picked up by newspapers across the country. It might have been a coincidence, but my campus speaking engagements stopped abruptly.

When I was assigned to write a piece for the *Los Angeles Times*, I titled it "I Was a Comedian for the FBI," because I mentioned that I had once recognized a pair of FBI agents taking notes while I was performing at the Community Church in New York. My FBI files later stated that I "purported to be funny about the government." Since when did taxpayers provide the funds to cover the FBI's theater critics squad?

The banner headline on the cover of that *L.A. Times Sunday Calendar* section blared out: "Paul Krassner — 'I Was a Communist for the FBI'." In the *San Francisco Chronicle*, columnist Herb Caen wrote, "Fearing Krassner would sue, the *Times* recalled and destroyed some 300,000 copies at a cost of about $100,000. Krassner would have laughed, not sued." Or maybe I would've sued and laughed my ass off.

BY 1963, GEORGE HAD RISEN to Chief Scientist, Astro-Electronics Division at the Signal Corps, and McGraw-Hill contacted him, asking if he would write a book. And indeed, he began working on *Introduction to Space Communication*, which became the world's first book on that subject.

"The problem was the incredible pace of technology," he says. "While I was writing Chapter 5, the nuggets of wisdom in Chapter 2 were becoming obsolete. The last chapter was called 'Ad Astra' (Latin for 'to the stars'), where I tried to forecast future technology. When the book was published in 1964, most of my future projections were already obsolete. Darwin had no idea about the speed of evolution when applied to technology. By the way, more copies of the book were sold in Russia than in the United States."

On George's last active project, he worked with the original seven astronauts. He was program manager at Simmonds Precision, responsible for the design of the fuel gauging system on the command module where the astronauts were housed. In 1972, Apollo 17, the eleventh manned mission, was the sixth and final lunar landing in the Apollo program. "We were on an extremely tight schedule, and my team worked nearly eighty hours with virtually no sleep to finish on time.

We received a rare commendation and bonus from NASA for superior performance ahead of schedule and below budget."

Gordon Cooper — one of those seven original astronauts — had piloted the longest and final Mercury space flight in 1963, becoming the first American to sleep in orbit. "He gave me a rare souvenir," George reminds me, "a dehydrated oatmeal cookie the size of a large dice that he had on a space mission. During a family dinner, I passed around the cookie for everyone to see. Dad was hard of hearing and didn't hear the story, so he popped the space cookie into his mouth, and it was gone before I could get any words out of my mouth. It was pure grief when it happened, but funny now."

As I write this in 2018, George is 88, and if a movie were to be made about him, he'd like to be portrayed by Matt Damon. In 1988, he was diagnosed with advanced prostate cancer and given three years to live, but his daughter Devra, a naturopath, convinced him to meet with a macrobiotic counselor, and, overnight, he changed his diet and lifestyle.

He played tennis until a few years ago, when he discontinued after a bad fall, because he was playing too aggressively. Currently, his exercise consists of taking walks and lifting dumbbells, though not simultaneously. He remains active, doing business seminars for adult education, providing legal plans for families, small businesses, and employees, and calling square dances. But not for helicopters. Or drones.

The Six Dumbest
Decisions of My Life

I'm TALKING HERE about seriously dumb decisions, not those minor regrets like that time in 1970 when *Esquire* magazine assigned me to fly to New Mexico where director Monte Hellman was filming *Two-Lane Blacktop*, about street racing. Among the actors was a pair of musicians — James Taylor as a driver and Dennis Wilson as a mechanic. They both agreed to be interviewed, as did screenwriter Rudy Wurlitzer and others.

During a conversation with Taylor about not laughing at jokes, he said, "My brother once told me a joke that made me laugh."

"Wait, don't tell me now," I said. "Let's save it for the interview."

I was supposed to reveal the behind-the-scenes of making the movie, but I learned that there were a couple of violations of law: a few members of the cast had been tripping on magic mushrooms; and a 17-year-old actress, Laurie Bird, who played "The Girl," had sex with two members of the crew. Nine years later, she would commit suicide.

Anyway, I decided not to write the article — I was a reporter, not a snitch — and never did get a chance to do any interviews. Nor did I ever hear the joke that James Taylor's brother told him and made him laugh. I was mildly disappointed, but what follows are half a dozen of my really dangerous dumb decisions that continue to make me humble.

1

EARLY ONE MORNING in 1963, at my tiny apartment on the Lower East Side of New York (now the East Village), I was in bed with a young woman I had met at a party when the phone rang. It was her boyfriend, a lower-echelon Mafioso. He asked if I knew where she was. I told him no, even as she was cuddling next to me. He said he would check his source and call me right back. A few minutes later, he did.

"You were seen with her last night. You spent the night with her. She didn't come home last night. You *punk!*"

He said that he was coming to my office a few blocks away — which is where he thought he was calling me — to talk about it. I told her she'd better leave, and I rushed to the office, but he was already waiting outside the "*Mad* building" [where *Mad* magazine was published], peering through the locked outside door into the lobby, expecting the elevator door to open and me to step out and open the door for him. Instead he saw me on the sidewalk coming toward him.

"What are you doing out here?" he said.

"Well, I came out just a minute ago, but you weren't here."

"I was calling you up because you didn't come out."

"Oh — I figured you had the address wrong, so I took a walk around the block."

"Let's go to your apartment."

"Don't you want to come up to my office?"

"I said, 'Let's go to your apartment.'"

"You don't expect to find her *there*?"

"She leaves traces wherever she goes. By the way, do you have a telephone at your apartment?"

"Oh, yeah, well, it happens to be the same number as my office, incidentally."

There was a certain tension between us while we were walking.

"Tell me," he said, "do you have many friends who smoke Tareyton cigarettes?"

I suddenly realized what he meant by "She leaves traces."

At the apartment, she was gone, but the bed was unmade, and he couldn't help but notice the semen stain on the sheet. Which, of course, was no proof that it was *she* who had been there. However, the ashtray was filled with Tareyton cigarette butts.

"Do *you* smoke Tareytons?"

"No," I answered, "I don't smoke any cigarettes."

"I guess I caught you with your pants down, didn't I?"

He picked up the phone and dialed a number. He was calling her mother. "I found him," he said. "What should I do, throw 'im out the window?" I was scared that he might actually do it. He hung up the phone, and I didn't know what to expect. I thought, *How could a realist have gotten himself into such an unrealistic situation?*

We proceeded to have a discussion.

"I got the *horns*," he yelled. "I gotta *do* something! It ain't *manly!*"

"Look, restraint itself can be a form of manliness."

"You know," he said, "I could arrange to have you killed while I was having dinner with your mother and father."

"Well, actually, they're not having too many people over to the house these days."

His low chuckle in response to that wisecrack marked a positive turning point in our conversation. He finally forgave me, and we shook hands. Then he borrowed twenty dollars, which we both knew I would never get back, but it was worth not being thrown out the window. I had known he was her boyfriend, and so I vowed never again to risk sleeping with a gangster's girlfriend, especially if she smoked cigarettes.

2

IN 1979, I COVERED the trial of Dan White, who had assassinated two progressive government officials in San Francisco — Mayor George Moscone (in 1975, as a state senator, he had authored a bill to decriminalize marijuana) and Supervisor Harvey Milk (a dedicated gay activist) — and yet, after an incompetent prosecution and a shrewd defense, White was sentenced to only seven years.

That evening, I was unwinding at home, smoking a joint and preparing to write my final report for the *San Francisco Bay Guardian*. My reverie was suddenly interrupted by a phone call from Mike Weiss. We had become friends during the trial, which he had covered for *Time* and *Rolling Stone*. He was calling from a phone booth across the street from City Hall. I could hear crowds screaming and sirens wailing behind his voice. He had to yell.

"There's a riot going on! You should get here right away!"

Reluctantly, I took a cab. When I arrived at Civic Center, there were a dozen police cars that had been set on fire, which in turn set off their alarms, underscoring the shouts from a mob of 5,000 gay protesters. On the night that Milk was murdered, they had been among the 30,000 who marched silently to City Hall for a candlelight vigil. Now they were in the middle of a post-verdict riot, utterly furious.

But where were the cops? They were all fuming *inside* City Hall — where their commander had instructed them to stay — armed prisoners watching helplessly as angry demonstrators broke the glass trying to ram their way through the locked doors.

I spotted Weiss and a student from his magazine-writing class, Marilee Strong. The three of us circulated through the crowd. Standing in the middle of the intersection, *San Francisco Chronicle* columnist Warren Hinckle was talking with a police official, and he beckoned me to join them. I gathered from their conversation that the cops were about to be released from City Hall. Some were already out. One kept banging his baton on the phone booth where Weiss was calling in his story, and he had to wave his press card before the cop would leave.

I found Marilee and suggested that we get away from the area. As we walked north on Polk Street, the police were beginning to march slowly in formation, not too far behind us. But the instant they were out of view from City Hall, they broke ranks and started running toward us, hitting the metal pole of a bus stop with their billy clubs, making loud, scary *clangs.*

"We better run," I told Marilee.

"Why? They're not gonna hit us."

"Yes, they are! Run! Hurry!"

The police had been let out of their cage, and they were absolutely enraged. Marilee got away, but I was struck with a nightstick on the outside of my right knee. I fell to the ground. The cop ran off to injure as many other cockroaches in his kitchen as he could. Another cop came charging, and he yelled at me, *"Get up! Get up!"*

"I'm trying to!"

He made a threatening gesture with his billy club, and when I tried to protect my head with my arms, he jabbed me viciously on the exposed right side of my ribs. Oh, God, the pain! The cops were running amuck now, in an orgy of indiscriminate sadism, swinging their clubs wildly and screaming, *"Get the fuck outta here, you fuckin' faggots, you motherfuckin' cocksuckers!"*

I managed to drag myself along the sidewalk. It felt like an electric cattle prod was stuck between my ribs. Marilee drove me to a hospital emergency ward. X-rays indicated that I had a fractured rib and a punctured lung.

The City of San Francisco was sued for $4.3 million by a man who had been a peaceful observer at the riot following the verdict. He was walking away from the Civic Center area when a cop yelled, "*We're gonna kill all you faggots!*" — and beat him on the head with his nightstick. He was awarded $125,000.

I had wanted to sue the city, but an attorney requested $75 for a filing fee, and I didn't have it. I was too foolish not to borrow it, and I decided to forego the lawsuit. I must've been crazy.

3

IN 1985, AFTER LIVING in San Francisco for 16 years, I moved south to Venice, a block-and-a-half walk to the beach. I rented a top-floor tiny two-room apartment consisting of a kitchen/office where I could see the ocean and a living room/bedroom which came with a convertible sofa. The bathroom had a bathtub/shower.

One afternoon, I took a bus to Santa Monica to eat at a little soul-food restaurant in a food court and to see a Woody Allen movie. When I returned home, I walked up the steps to the top floor, and when I opened the door to my "penthouse" apartment, it was filled with smoke. I had stupidly, utterly recklessly, left a candle burning in a glass ashtray on the arm of the sofa. I didn't *forget* to do that. I had *chosen* to leave it that way.

The ashtray had broken in half from the heat, and the sofa was burning, although asbestos material had prevented it from being on fire in a way that would spread the flames. I ran down the steps and got the fire extinguisher off the wall in the hall, ran back up, and sprayed the sofa.

"You should be ashamed of yourself," I said to myself.

I was grateful that only the sofa had been destroyed. Also, my pride in expanded consciousness had disintegrated. I've never quite forgiven myself for having endangered the lives and property of the tenants in the other four apartments. I had ignored the concept of cause and effect. My bad. Immensely.

4

ON THE MORNING OF APRIL 1, 1995, I flew to San Francisco. I was scheduled to emcee a benefit for Jack Kerouac's daughter, Jan, who had been on dialysis treatment for the last few years. On that sunny afternoon, I was stoned in Washington Square Park, wearing the *Mad* magazine jacket that my daughter Holly had given me for Christmas. The smiling face of Alfred E. Neuman — stating his renowned philosophy, "What — me worry?" — graced the back of my jacket.

I was waiting for the arrival of the annual Saint Stupid Day Parade, led this year by Grand Marshal Ken Kesey in an open-topped convertible. The event was sponsored by the First Church of the Last Laugh. Their sound equipment was surrounded by yellow plastic tape warning, "Police Line — Do Not Cross." Somebody in a clown costume handed me a three-foot section of that tape.

The celebration featured music, comedy, and a traditional free brunch, along with such favorite rituals as the Sock Exchange and the Leap of Faith. Kesey was also in town to speak at the benefit, which was held only because Jan happened to be the daughter of a groundbreaking literary celebrity, even though he had abandoned her mother when she was pregnant with Jan.

I said to my friend Julius, who drove me there, "It's not enough anymore just to be a sperm donor."

Jan had met her father only twice. The first time, she was 9. The second time, six years later, he sat there, drinking a fifth of whiskey and watching *The Beverly Hillbillies.* Jan would eventually die of kidney failure at the age of 44, never having fulfilled her fantasy of becoming drinking buddies with her father, who died when she was a teenager.

Now, backstage, someone I knew handed me a baggie of what I assumed to be marijuana. I thanked her and put it in my pocket. Ah, yes, one of the perks of the benefit biz. Later, as the final members of the audience were straggling out of the theater, I was sitting with Julius in his car in the parking area at Fort Mason Center.

He was busy rolling a joint in a cigar box on the dashboard with the map light on. There was a police car circling around in the distance, but we unwisely ignored it. Suddenly, there was a fist knocking heavily on the passenger-side window and a flashlight shining in my eyes. Shit! Fuck! Caught!

We were ordered outside and, with our arms outstretched against the side of the car, the face of Alfred E. Neuman was smiling at the cop and asking, "What — me worry?" Indeed, the cop was worried. He asked me if I had anything sharp in my pockets.

"Because," he explained, "I'm gonna get very mad if I get stuck," obviously referring to a hypodermic needle.

"No, there's only a pen in this pocket," I said, gesturing toward the left with my head, "and keys in that one."

He found the coiled-up three feet of yellow plastic tape warning "Police Line — Do Not Cross," and asked, "Where'd you get this?"

"At the Saint Stupid Day Parade."

"What's it for?"

"To keep people away."

But then he found the baggie. And, to my surprise, it contained magic mushrooms. He examined the contents. Then, reeking with sarcasm, he asked, "So you like mushrooms, huh?" Under the circumstances, it was such a ridiculous question that I almost laughed, but I realized that, from his point of view, this was a serious offense.

Julius was given a $50 citation for possession of marijuana, but I was arrested on the spot, handcuffed behind my back, and had my Miranda rights read to me. I stood there, heart pounding fast and mouth terminally dry, trying to keep my balance on the cusp of reality and unreality. Fortunately, attorney Doron Weinberg got me off with a $100 fine and nothing on my permanent record.

But I finally understood what that cop meant when he snarled, "So you like mushrooms, huh?" His question was asked with such archetypal hostility that it kept reverberating inside my head. *So you like mushrooms, huh?* It was not as though I had done anything that might harm another human being. This was simply an authority figure's need to control. But control what? My pleasure? Or was it deeper than that?

What was his *actual* message? Back through eons of ancestors — all the way back to what psychedelic researcher Terence McKenna called "the *unstoned* apes" — this cop was continuing a never-ending attempt to maintain the status quo. He had unintentionally revealed the true nature of the threat he perceived. What he *really* said to me was, "So you like the evolution of human consciousness, huh?"

"Well, yeah," I thought, "now that you mention it, I do. I mean, when you put it like that — *So you like the evolution of human consciousness, huh?* — sure, I do. I like it a whole lot."

Too bad I had remained silent instead of using my instinct and advising Julius, "Let's get the hell out of here."

5

ONCE, IN THE MEN'S ROOM at an airport, I couldn't help but notice a man standing at a urinal a couple of urinals away from me who was urinating without touching his penis. He was allowing his penis to aim itself, because he happened to be busy using both his hands to floss his teeth. It was a monument to multi-tasking.

I'll admit that I occasionally brush my teeth while I'm urinating — at least that leaves me with one hand free to steer — but this guy could possibly be the only human being on Earth who pisses and flosses simultaneously.

I'm embarrassed to admit that, rather than using dental floss, I used to use a dollar bill to clean between my teeth. In doing so, I was actually adding bacteria to my mouth, thereby giving a new, literal meaning to the concept of "dirty money." As a result, my teeth were in terrible shape.

I had known better. Back in 1971, publisher Stewart Brand had invited Ken Kesey and me to co-edit *The Last Supplement to the Whole Earth Catalog.* Our managing editor, Hassler (Ron Bevirt's Merry Prankster name), introduced me to the fine art of flossing.

"I began cleaning between my teeth with dental floss, and then brushing carefully after every meal for the last nine years," he told me. "Dental floss is really important because it removes particles of food from between the teeth that can't be dislodged by the brush. It's this crap between the teeth that really causes decay."

Although I didn't practice what he preached, I immediately assigned him to write a piece about the process of flossing for *The Last Supplement.* After all, the *Whole Earth Catalog* was devoted to informing its readers about a variety of New Age tools. And floss was definitely a useful tool. "Floss comes in two thicknesses," Hassler wrote. "Thin, called Dental Floss; and thick, called Dental Tape. Recently, I found Dental Floss Unwaxed. All the floss and tape I've used in the past were waxed. I find that I prefer the waxed because it slips in and out between my teeth cleanly without leaving any of the floss behind, which I find to be a problem with unwaxed floss. I've realized the importance of my teeth in the service of my habit. Munch, slurp, slobber, drool ..."

In 1987, I was a keynote speaker at the annual International Society for Humor Studies conference, held in Tempe, Arizona. I had dinner with a group of five staffers from the Russian humor magazine *Krokodil* at the Holiday Inn. They all ordered the specialty of the house — pork ribs — which came with huge bibs. The editor was given a bib with the words "Miss America" on it. The art director got a bib with a big iconic "S" for Superman.

They were really getting a dose of our culture. As we walked along the salad bar, one of the Russians stopped at the corn chowder and asked me, "Is this typical American soup?" As the others gathered around, I didn't quite know how to answer. "I'm sorry, I don't know," I said. "I'm sure it's typical *somewhere* in the country." And then I remembered that multitasking man at the airport urinal. "In America," I told the Russian, "corn chowder comes with dental floss that has little pieces of corn embedded in it, so if you get hungry between meals, you can floss and have a snack at the same time."

A few years before I met my wife, Nancy, she had gone to a dentist who required all new patients to take a two-session course in flossing and oral health. Only when he was satisfied that patients would be capable of caring for their teeth properly would he then make their first cleaning appointment. Nancy learned the technique, and recently a friend named her "the Floss Queen." We came across an ad stating, "If you follow a vegan diet, you may opt for Eco-Dent's GentleFloss, which uses beeswax instead of animal products." Who knew?

The irony behind all this is that Medicare doesn't cover any dental procedures, even though dentists emphasize how bad teeth can cause illness in other, internal parts of the body. For example, a research team from Columbia University's School of Public Health released the results of a three-year study of 420 men and women, concluding that the improvement of gum health can help slow the development of atherosclerosis — the build-up of cholesterol-rich plaque along artery walls that can lead to heart attacks and strokes.

I still regret that I would eat candy without flossing afterward. Especially a Clark Bar, which could cause a cavity *and* fill it simultaneously.

6.

I HAD TAPED AN INTERVIEW on an electric recorder-transcriber, plus a battery-operated cassette recorder as a back-up precaution, which turned out to be an absolute necessity when the electric recorder conked out right in the middle.

Later on, I bought a new one to replace it, but first I had to get rid of the old one. My desk consisted of a wooden door supported by a couple of two-drawer filing cabinets. I was just too damn lazy to take all the equipment and books off the desk so that I could move the desk toward me and pull up the wire from behind it.

So I simply cut the wire with a pair of scissors. *Bzzzzzt!!!* I was shocked, but not injured. Though the recorder had conked out, I had incredibly left the wire still plugged into a socket on the surge protector. Where the scissors had cut the wire, parts of the metal had melted away just a couple of inches from my hand. I might've been electrocuted. *Yikes!*

I could've been killed, and the cause would've been a simple lack of the practice of mindfulness that I treasure so much. Instead, I had *emptied* my mind. Oops, wrong discipline. But I was still alive, and I thanked God for that. And then I heard a resplendent voice booming through the clouds: *"SHUT UP, YOU SUPERSTITIOUS FOOL!"*

The Parts Left Out of
Manson's Obituaries

WHEN CHARLES MANSON was a prison inmate, he got introduced to Scientology by fellow prisoners, and his ability to psych out people was intensified so that he could zero in on their weaknesses and fears. In 1967, he was released and went to the Scientology Center in San Francisco. A friend who accompanied him there told me, "Charlie said to them, 'I'm Clear — what do I do now?'"

But they expected him to sweep the floor — shit, he had done that in jail. However, in Los Angeles, he went to the Scientology *Celebrity* Center. Now this was more like it — there he could mingle with the elite. I was able to obtain a copy of the original log entry: "7/31/68, new name, Charlie Manson, Devt. No address. In for processing = Ethics = Type III." The receptionist — who, by Type III, meant "psychotic" — sent him to the Ethics office, but he never showed up.

At the Spahn Ranch, Manson combined his version of Scientology auditing with post-hypnotic techniques he had learned in prison, with geographical isolation and subliminal motivation, with sing-along sessions and encounter games, with LSD and mescaline, with transactional analysis and brainwashing rituals, with verbal probing and sexual longevity that he had practiced upon himself for all those years in the privacy of his cell. He was also raped by fellow inmates.

Ultimately, in August 1969, he sent his well-programmed "family" off to slay actress Sharon Tate, some friends, and her unborn baby. Tate's husband, film director Roman Polanski, was in London at the time. A few months later, when the family members were captured and charged with homicides, Manson was portrayed by the media as a hippie cult leader, and the counterculture became a dangerous enemy.

Hitchhikers were shunned. Communes were raided. In the public's mind, flower children had grown poisonous thorns. But Manson was never really a hippie.

He had grown up behind bars. His *real* family included con artists, pimps, drug dealers, thieves, muggers, rapists, and murderers. He had known only power relationships in an army of control junkies. Indeed, Charlie Manson was America's Frankenstein monster, a logical product of the prison system — racist, paranoid, and violent — even if hippie astrologers thought that his fate had been predetermined because he was a triple Scorpio.

Now, on their black-painted bus, they visited the Hog Farm commune where everyone there was gathered in a circle, chanting "Om," which somehow caused the visiting Manson to start choking and gagging, so *his* family began counter-chanting "Evil." It was an archetypal confrontation. Charlie even tried to get Hugh [later Wavy Gravy] Romney's wife, Bonnie Jean, in exchange for one of his girls. But they finally left, mission *un*accomplished.

Manson had convinced himself and his family that the Beatles' songs "Helter Skelter" and "Blackbird" were actually harkening a race war, which he wanted to hasten by leaving clues to make it appear that black militants had done the killing. Stolen credit cards were deliberately thrown away in a black neighborhood. *Healter* [sic] *Skelter* was scrawled with a victim's blood on the refrigerator, and the word "WAR" was scratched onto a victim's stomach.

Roman Polanski put a $10,000 contract out on Manson's life.

Meanwhile, Black Panther Eldridge Cleaver was still on the lam. He had gone from Cuba to Algeria. Having been arrested for possession of marijuana, Timothy Leary escaped from prison to Algeria with the help of the Weather Underground, only to be imprisoned by his host, Cleaver. Leary escaped from Cleaver's clutches only to be arrested by American agents and taken back to the States, then put in solitary confinement at Folsom Prison, in a cell right next to Manson's. The two "hole-mates" couldn't see each other, but they could talk. Manson didn't understand why Leary had given people acid without trying to control them.

"They took you off the streets," Manson explained, "so that I could continue with your work."

✳ ✳ ✳

Coincidentally, as I was diving into my Manson research, I received a letter from Charlie himself. He had seen in prison a copy of *The Last Supplement to the Whole Earth Catalog*. During the trial, I had published an apocryphal piece in *The Realist* about Manson's stay at Boys Town — "Charles Manson Was My Bunkmate" by Richard Meltzer. A defense attorney read it to Manson, and he got pissed off. He complained, "You know how long I stayed in Boys Town? *Two days!*"

In response to his letter, I mentioned that the article had been intended only as a satire of media exploitation. He replied: "Yes, brother, the world is a satire and I did see all sides of your story, 'Charlie's Bunkmate.' But I think in Now with no cover. Most people take into their minds bad thoughts and call it joking. Some lie and call it funny. I don't lie."

Shades of Trump.

In pursuit of information, I visited Warren Hinckle. He was my editor at *Ramparts*, and after that folded, at *Scanlan's*, which also folded, but he had been planning to publish an article on the Manson case in *Scanlan's*, and now he brought me to former FBI agent William Turner, who had checked out Doris Day. The only connection she could possibly have with the Manson case was that her son, record producer Terry Melcher, had met Charlie and was interested in his music, and that Melcher was a former tenant of the Beverly Hills mansion where the massacre took place. *Aha!* I realized that could be the focal point of my satire — a torrid affair between Doris Day and Charlie Manson — a perfect metaphor for the coming together of the image and underbelly of Hollywood. Just for the hell of it, I wrote to Manson and asked if he had ever had sex with Doris Day.

His reply: "Yes, and I also fucked [the Hollywood dog actor] Rin-Tin-Tin and the Virgin Mary."

I continued to absorb whatever details I could find out about the Manson case. A prison psychiatrist at San Quentin told me of an incident he had observed during Manson's trial. A black inmate said to Manson, "Look, I don't wanna know about your theories on race, I don't wanna hear anything about religion, I just wanna know one thing — how'd you get them girls to obey you like that?"

Manson replied, "I got a knack."

Hinckle also brought me to the renowned private investigator Hal Lipset, who informed me that not only did the Los Angeles Police Department seize pornographic films and videotapes that they found in Sharon Tate's loft, but also that certain members of the LAPD were *selling* them. Lipset had talked with one police source who told him exactly which porn flicks were available — a total of seven hours' worth for a quarter-million dollars. Lipset began reciting a litany of porn videos. The most notorious was Greg Bautzer, an attorney for Howard Hughes, with Jane Wyman, the former wife of then-Governor Ronald Reagan. There was Sharon Tate with Dean Martin. There was Sharon with Steve McQueen. There was Sharon with two black bisexual men.

Lipset recalled, "The cops weren't too happy about *that* one."

He told me there was a videotape of Cass Elliot from the Mamas and the Papas in an orgy with actors Yul Brynner, Peter Sellers, and Warren Beatty. Brynner and Sellers, together with John Phillips of The Mamas & the Papas, had offered a $25,000 reward for the capture of the killers.

I had felt that there was some connection between Charlie's executioners and their victims before the murders took place. I finally tracked down a reporter who told me that when she was hanging around with L.A. police, they showed her a porn video of killer Susan Atkins and victim Voytek Frykowski, even though, according to the myth, they had never met until the night of the massacre.

But apparently the reporter mentioned the wrong victim, because when I asked Manson directly — "Did Susan sleep with Frykowski?" — he replied, "You are ill advised and misled. [Hairdresser victim Jay] Sebring done Susan's hair, and I think he sucked one or two of her dicks. I'm not sure who she was walking out from her stars and cages, that girl *loves* dick, you know what I mean, hon. Yul Brynner, Peter Sellers ..."

I CAME ACROSS Billy Doyle's name in Ed Sander's book, *The Family*. Doyle was Cass Elliot's boyfriend. He was also the drug connection for two of the victims, Voytek Frykowski and his girlfriend, coffee heiress Abigail Folger. Sanders wrote:

> Sometime during [the first week in August] a dope dealer from Toronto named Billy Doyle was whipped and video-buggered at [the Tate residence]. In the days before his death, Sebring had complained to a receptionist at his hair shop that someone had burned him for $2,000 worth of cocaine and he wanted vengeance. Billy Doyle was involved in a large-scale dope-import operation involving private planes from Jamaica.

And Dennis Hopper was quoted in the *Los Angeles Free Press*:

> They had fallen into sadism and masochism and bestiality — and they recorded it all on videotape too. The L.A. police told me this. I know that three days before they were killed, 25 people were invited to that house to a mass whipping of a dealer from Sunset Strip who'd given them bad dope.

Naturally, Billy Doyle felt it was rude of Sebring and Frykowski to tie him to a chair, whip him, and then fuck him in the ass while a video camera taped the proceedings before a live audience. When folksinger Phil Ochs and Yippie Jerry Rubin visited Manson in jail, Ochs asked him if he knew Doyle. Manson, who had been quite glib up to that point, flinched, then hesitated, and said, "No."

Police investigators eliminated Doyle as a suspect in the murders. However, on the Friday evening just a few hours before the massacre took place, Joel Rostau — the boyfriend of Sebring's receptionist and an intermediary in a cocaine ring — visited Sebring and Frykowski at the Tate house to deliver mescaline and coke. During the Manson trial, several associates of Sebring were murdered, including Rostau, whose body was found in the trunk of a car in New York. So it appeared that the Manson family had actually served as some sort of hit squad for a drug ring.

Voytek Frykowski's father had financed Roman Polanski's first film. Voytek and Abigail Folger were staying at the Polanski residence. She was paying the rent and supplying him with the money for their daily drug supplies. In July 1969, Billy Doyle promised Frykowski a new synthetic drug, MDMA [today known as ecstasy], made in Canada. I had tried MDMA a few times — it felt like a combination of mescaline and amphetamine, acting as an extraordinary energizer and, if you were with the right person, a powerful aphrodisiac. The plan was for Frykowski to become the American distributor of MDMA. He was hoping to sell a screenplay, but it's always nice to have something to fall back on.

Peter Folger was the coffee tycoon whose daughter Abigail had been one of the victims. She supported Tom Bradley as the first black candidate for mayor of Los Angeles, despite the objection of her father, who had a reputation as a fierce racist. While Ed Sanders was researching his Manson book, he received a Mafia kiss from a lawyer for Peter Folger.

WITHIN A WEEK after the murders, there was a dawn raid on the Spahn Ranch, with a grand theft auto search warrant. The Manson group had been stealing Volkswagens and turning them into dune buggies. Manson and four family members — Linda Kasabian, Susan Atkins, Patricia Krenwinkel, and Leslie Van Houten — were arrested, then released after three days. But, while they were in confinement, Atkins told her cellmate about the murders, and when the cellmate was released, she informed the Los Angeles police.

By this time, Manson and the others had moved to another ranch in Death Valley, where they were arrested again. Preston Guillory, a former deputy sheriff at the Malibu Sheriff's Department, aided the Los Angeles Sheriff's Department in the original raid of the Spahn Ranch. Guillory had participated in that raid, and I interviewed him at an apartment in San Francisco. He stated:

> We had been briefed for a few weeks prior to the actual raiding of Spahn Ranch. We had a sheaf of memos on Manson, that they had automatic weapons at the ranch, that citizens had complained about hearing machine guns fired at night, that firemen from the local fire station had been accosted by armed members of Manson's band and told to get out of the area, all sorts of complaints like this.
>
> We had been advised to put anything relating to Manson on a memo submitted to the station, because they were supposedly gathering information for the raid we were going to make. Deputies at the station of course started asking, "Why aren't we going to make the raid sooner?" I mean, Manson's a parole violator, machine guns have been heard, we know there's

narcotics, and we know there's booze. He's living at the Spahn Ranch with a bunch of minor girls in complete violation of his parole.

Deputies at the station quite frankly became very annoyed that no action was being taken about Manson. My contention is this — the reason Manson was left on the street was because our department thought that he was going to attack the Black Panthers. We were getting intelligence briefings that Manson was anti-black, and he had supposedly killed a Black Panther, the body of which could not be found, and the department thought that he was going to launch an attack on the Black Panthers.

Manson was a very ready tool, apparently, because he did have some racial hatred, and he wanted to vent it. But they hadn't anticipated him attacking someone other than the Panthers, which he did. Manson changed his score. Changed the program at the last moment and attacked the Tates, and then went over to the LaBiancas and killed them. And here was the Sheriff's Department suddenly wondering, "Jesus Christ, what are we gonna do about this? We can't cover this up. Well, maybe we can."

I bet those memos are no longer in existence. The memos about what Manson was doing. Citizens' complaints. All those things I'm sure have disappeared by now. It shows the police were conscious of the fact that he had these weapons in violation of his parole. You've got at least involvement here on the part of Manson's parole officer, on the part of the Sheriff's Department, probably the sheriff himself, and whoever gave him his orders. Manson should have been [imprisoned] long before the killings, because he was on parole, period. He was living at the Spahn Ranch with an outlaw motorcycle gang. I feel that, to say the least, the sheriff of Los Angeles County is an accessory to murder.

The raid was a week after the Sharon Tate thing, and the intelligence information was coming in for about three weeks prior to the raid. They just didn't want any arrests made. It was obvious they wanted the intelligence information we were gathering for some other reason. Three days after they were arrested, 72 hours later, they were all released — lack of evidence — after this mammoth raid. This raid involved two helicopters, 102 deputies, and about 25 radio cars, and all the charges were dropped against everyone.

It appeared to me that the raid was more or less staged as an afterthought. It was like a scenario that we were going through. There was some kind of a grand plan that we were participating in, but I never had the feeling the raid was necessary or that it required so many personnel. Now, if you were a police official and you were planning a raid on the Spahn Ranch, utilizing 102 deputies and helicopters and all that, one would think that with all the information coming out a month prior to the raid, wouldn't you have them under fairly close surveillance? If you did have them under fairly close surveillance, wouldn't you see them leave the Spahn Ranch to go over and kill seven people and then come back?

So the hypothesis I put forward is, either we didn't have them under surveillance for grand theft auto because it was a big farce, or else they were under surveillance by somebody much higher than the Sheriff's Department, and they did go through this scenario of killing at the Tate house and then come back, and then we went through the motions to do our raid. Either they were under surveillance at the time, which means somebody must have seen them go to the Tate house and commit the killings, or else they weren't under surveillance.

You have to remember that Charlie was on federal parole all this time from '67 to '69. Do you realize all the shit he was getting away with while he was on parole? Now here's the kicker. Before the Tate killings, he had been arrested at Malibu twice for statutory rape. Never got [imprisoned for parole violation]. During the Tate killings and the Spahn Ranch raid, Manson's parole officer was on vacation, so he had no knowledge of Manson being incarcerated, so naturally Manson was released, but why wasn't a parole hold put on him?

It's like Manson had God on his side when all these things are going down, or else somebody was watching every move he made, somebody was controlling from behind the scenes. Somebody saw that no parole hold was placed. Manson liked to ball young girls, so he just did his thing, and he was released, and they didn't put any hold on him. But somebody very high up was controlling everything that was going on and was seeing to it that we didn't bust Manson.

Prior to the Spahn Ranch raid, there was a memo — it was verbal, I would have loved to Xerox some things but there wasn't anything to Xerox — that we weren't to arrest Manson or any of his followers prior to the raid. It was intimated to us that we were going to make a raid on the Spahn Ranch, but the captain came out briefly and said, "No action is to be taken on anybody at the Spahn Ranch. I want memos submitted directly to me with a cover sheet so nobody else can read them." So deputies were submitting memos on information about the Spahn Ranch that other deputies weren't even allowed to see. We were to submit intelligence information but not to make any arrests. Manson was in a fire-free zone, so to speak. He was living a divine existence. We couldn't touch him.

And so it was that the presence of racism had morphed the Sheriff's Department into collaborators in a mass murder. But who was the higher-up that gave them the order to leave Manson alone? I was certainly prepared to believe that's what occurred. I had been gathering piece after piece of a mind-boggling jigsaw puzzle, trying to make them all fit snugly into one big cohesive picture, but without having any model to pattern it after.

Tex Watson, the Manson family member who led the others on the night of the massacre, had played a bigger part in planning the massacre than generally believed. Charlie had instructed the girls to do whatever Tex told them. When Manson was charged, Watson was also charged, but federal authorities held Watson in a Texas prison with no explanation — not even his own lawyers were allowed to see him — while Vincent Bugliosi prosecuted the Manson trial in California.

In order to find Manson guilty, the jury had to be convinced that Charlie's girls were zombies who followed his orders without question. However, in order to find *Watson* guilty, another jury had to be convinced that he was *not a zombie at all* and knew exactly what he was doing.

IN THE COURSE OF OUR CORRESPONDENCE, there was a letter from Manson consisting of a few pages of gibberish about Christ and the Devil, but at one point, right in the middle, he wrote in tiny letters, *Call Squeaky*, with her phone number. I called, and we arranged to meet at her apartment in Los Angeles. On an impulse, I brought several tabs of LSD with me on the plane.

Squeaky Fromme resembled a typical redheaded, freckle-faced waitress who sneaks a few tokes of pot in the lavatory, a regular girl-next-door except perhaps for the unusually challenging nature of her personality plus the scar of an X that she had gouged and burned into her forehead as a visual reminder of her commitment to Charlie.

That same symbol also covered the third eyes of her roommates, Sandra Good and Brenda McCann. "We've crossed ourselves out of this entire system," I was told. They all had short hairstyles growing in now, having shaved their heads completely. They continued to sit on the sidewalk near the Hall of Justice every day, like a coven of faithful nuns being witness to Manson's martyrdom. Sandy had seen me perform stand-up at The Committee in San Francisco some years previously. Now she told me that when she first met Charlie and people asked her what he was like, she had compared him to Lenny Bruce and me. It was the weirdest compliment I ever got, but I began to understand Manson's peculiar charisma.

With his sardonic rap, mixed with psychedelic drugs and real-life theater games such as "creepy-crawling" and stealing, he had deprogrammed his family from the values of mainstream society, but reprogrammed them with his own philosophy, a cosmic version of the racism perpetuated by the prison system that had served as *his* family. Manson stepped on Sandy's eyeglasses, threw away her birth-control pills, and inculcated her with racist sensibility. Although she had once been a civil rights activist, she was now asking me to tell John Lennon that he should get rid of Yoko Ono and stay with "his own kind." Later, she added, "If Yoko really loved the Japanese people, she would not want to mix their blood."

The four of us ingested those little white tablets containing 300 micrograms of acid, then took a walk to the office of Laurence Merrick, who had been associated with schlock biker exploitation movies as the prerequisite to directing a sensationalist documentary, *Manson*. Squeaky's basic vulnerability emerged as she kept pacing around and telling Merrick that she was afraid of him. He didn't know we were tripping, but he must have sensed the vibes. I engaged him in conversation. We discussed the fascistic implications of the movie *The French Connection*, and he remarked, "You're pretty articulate —"

"— for a bum," I completed his sentence, and he laughed.

Next, we went to the home of some friends of the family, smoked a few joints of soothing grass, and listened to music. They sang along with the lyrics of "A Horse With No Name": *In the desert, you can remember your name, 'cause there ain't no one for to give you no pain.*

I was basking in the afterglow of the Moody Blues' "Om" song when Sandy began to speak of the "gray people" — regular citizens going about their daily business — whom she had been observing from her vantage point on the corner near the Hall of Justice.

"We were just sitting there," she said, "and they were walking along, kind of avoiding us. It's like watching a live movie in front of you. Sometimes I just wanted to kill the gray people, because that was the only way they would be able to experience the total Now." That was an expression Charlie had borrowed from Scientology.

Later, Sandy explained that she didn't mean it literally about killing the gray people — that she had been speaking from another dimension. She told me that prosecutor Vincent Bugliosi once snarled at her as she kept vigil outside the courthouse, "We're gonna get you because you sucked Charlie Manson's dick." The girls just sat there on the sidewalk and laughed, because they knew that oral-genital relations did not constitute a capital offense.

When we returned to their apartment, Sandy asked if I wanted to take a hot bath. I felt ambivalent. I knew that one of the attorneys in the case had participated in a *ménage à trois* with Squeaky and Sandy, but I had also been told by a reporter, "It certainly levels the high to worry about getting stabbed while fucking the Manson ladies in the bunkhouse at the Spahn Ranch — I've found that the only satisfactory position is sitting up, back to the wall, facing the door."

Visions of the famous shower scene in *Psycho* flashed through my mind, but despite the shrill self-righteousness that infected their true-believer syndrome, they had charmed me with their honesty, humor, and distorted sense of compassion. They sensed my hesitation, and Squeaky confronted me: "You're afraid of me, aren't you?" she asked.

"Not really. Should I be?"

Sandy tried to reassure me: "She's *beautiful*, Paul. Just look into her eyes. Isn't she beautiful?"

Squeaky and I stared silently at each other for a while — I recalled that Manson had written, "I never picked up anyone who had not already been discarded by society" — and my eyes began to tear. There were tears in Squeaky's eyes, too. She asked me to try on Charlie's vest. It felt like a perverted honor to participate in this ceremony. The corduroy vest was a solid inch thick with embroidery — snakes and dragons and devilish designs including human hair that had been woven into the multicolored patterns.

Sandy took her bath, but instead of my getting into the tub with her — assuming she had invited me — I sat fully dressed on the toilet, and we talked. I was thinking, *You have pert nipples*, but instead I said, "What's that scar on your back?" It was from a lung operation. Brenda asked for another tab of acid, to send to Manson in prison. She ground it into powder which she then glued to the paper with vegetable dye and the notation, *Words fly fast*, explaining that Charlie would know what it meant. She stayed up late that night, writing letters to several prisoners with the dedication of a polygamous war wife.

Squeaky visited me a few times in San Francisco. On the way to lunch one day, she lit a cigarette, and I told her about the series of advertisements by which women were originally conditioned into smoking: a woman standing next to a man who was smoking; then a woman saying to the man, "Blow some my way"; and finally, a woman smoking her own cigarette. Squeaky simply smiled, said "Okay," and dropped her cigarette onto the sidewalk, crushing it out with her shoe.

Another time, when I attempted to point out a certain fallacy in her logic, she responded, "Well, what do you expect from me? I'm crazy!" Once, she told me she had been beaten up by members of the Mel Lyman family from Boston because she wouldn't switch her allegiance to them, even though they'd had plans to break Manson out of jail, by means of a helicopter, while his trial was taking place. She said they were "well organized."

Squeaky mailed me her drawing in red ink of a woman's face with a pair of hands coming out of her mouth. Written in script was the song lyric: "Makes me wanna holler, throw up both my hands ..."

In 1975, she tried to shoot President Gerald Ford. She was wearing a Red Riding Hood outfit. I sent her a note in prison, teasing her about fading into the crowd. I never heard from Squeaky again.

However, I did receive an email in November 2017 from an old acquaintance, and here's his surprise greeting:

> We met in roughly 1975 when you were living in San Francisco. I took a
> series of photos of you and thought I had one of you standing in front of
> a sign saying "Stop When Flashing" that I thought would be memorable
> but haven't tracked it down.

In the spirit of your button [Come Clean], I wanted to tell you that at the time we met, I was an undercover investigator working for the Church of Scientology's Guardians' Office, who were going quite insane trying to figure out who wrote "The Awful Truth About Scientology" in *The Realist*. I failed to get that from you, but we did smoke a joint together, and that was happily the start of my gradual exit from the Church. Drove them crazy. Long story.

I've always admired your spirit and read your recent *AlterNet* piece on Manson with some fascination. Anyhow, embarrassed as I am about the circumstances of our meeting back then, I was able to leave that outfit in the nick of time. Running a medicinal cannabis lab now ... Long. Strange. Trip.

PAUL KRASSNER

Operation Chaos Lives

IF A PSYCHOLOGIST in a free association test said to you, "Vietnam War deserters," it's likely that you might reply "Canada." However, Matthew Sweet, the British author of *Operation Chaos: The Vietnam Deserters Who Fought the CIA, the Brainwashers, and Themselves*, would definitely respond "Stockholm," as proven by the comprehensive research he did for that nonfiction book.

By 1968, more than a thousand American deserters and draft resisters had escaped to Sweden. Many of them founded a group they named the American Deserters Committee. The ADC might just as well have been formed to be insane, inadvertent, satire. For example, a few of them held a woman in her apartment, night after night, "playing Beethoven in an attempt to reprogram her brain." Others bought into the conspiracy theories of Lyndon LaRouche, the leader of a growing cult, that Great Britain had started the Vietnam War, the Beatles were created to be "an instrument of psychological warfare," and Queen Elizabeth II had a secret genocidal plot to start World War III.

And now, Donald "Fire and Fury" Trump, himself a frequent promoter of conspiracy theories, has met, for whatever purpose, with the same Queen Elizabeth.

Sweet reported that in January 1974, LaRouche, using the alias "Lyn Marcus," addressed an audience of delegates from the National Caucus of Labor Committees (NCLC), journalists, activists, and others in a shabby New York ballroom and revealed "the greatest conspiracy of modern times" — the takeover of the United States by the CIA. LaRouche, who, even though he was the head of the NCLC, maintained his persona as "Marcus" as he began describing a psy-war operation, already into its second phase, that the CIA was conducting on its own people on four continents. The Agency, "Marcus" said, had turned some of its most trusted colleagues into killers — drugging and imprisoning them, reconditioning their minds, erasing their memories of the experience, and returning them to their friends "as unknowing vehicles of a murderous conspiracy."

Sweet described how "Marcus" claimed those activities had gotten their start at a secret facility near Stockholm. Brainwashing candidates were hypnotized, "subjected to electric shocks, forced to eat their own excrement and endure sexual humiliation, and tortured until they whined like puppies. Once they had been reduced to mental pulp, the programming began. A literal kind of programming, following the rules of the computer age. Numbers linked to functions. Infinite loops of coded instructions drilled into the subject by repetition, violence, the application of electrodes to bare skin. Finally, cyanide pills had been secreted inside their bodies in order to eliminate the killers once they had fulfilled their programs."

No wonder, Sweet mused:

> If I were to die without finishing this book, then someone out there would undoubtedly set up a web page claiming that I'd been bumped off, by either the CIA, the Swedish secret services, or the bizarre political group that had once counted many of my interviewees as its members — and would, by the time my research was concluded, come to regard me as an enemy infiltrator. And that was when I knew I'd been swallowed by my own story.
>
> Swallowed, but not brainwashed.

Sweet's book was published in 2018. He's still alive.

Back in New York in 1968, LaRouche was the leader of a faction of the Students for a Democratic Society (SDS) that would split off and morph into the NCLC. For better or worse, he was delivering a charismatic economics lecture to an enthusiastic SDS crowd. That summer, the SDS protested the Vietnam War at the Democratic National Convention in Chicago. The Yippies nominated a pig as a presidential candidate, and I started a rumor that we planned to drop LSD into the reservoir. And yes, Lyndon LaRouche decided to drop his alias into pure manure.

LaRouche was an unlovable conspiracy theorist who ran for the U.S. presidency eight times. He played himself as a cartoon character in a 1996 episode of *The Simpsons* in which aliens kidnapped presidential candidates Bill Clinton and Bob Dole, immersing them in tanks of bubbling pink liquid and assuming their forms. Homer shouted, "Oh my God! Lyndon LaRouche was right!" And *Saturday Night Live* featured "Lyndon LaRouche Theater," in which Randy Quaid played LaRouche, with a bald wig, bow-tie, and spectacles, narrating melodramatic twists, conspiracies, and confessing, "I am insane."

NOT MENTIONED IN SWEET'S BOOK, I delivered a keynote address at the Youth International Party convention in New York near the end of March 1981. (These were the latter-day Yippies, originally launched as the anti-Yippie "Zippies" during the 1972 Democratic and Republican conventions, which were both held in Miami.) To that Yippie audience, I posed a rhetorical question, "How would you like to be a Secret Service agent guarding Ronald Reagan, *knowing* that his vice president, George Bush, is the former head of the CIA?"

Once again, satire would be outdistanced by reality. Days later, on March 30, 1981, the new president was shot by John Hinckley who wanted to make a favorable impression on actress Jodie Foster so that he could take her bowling on a date. Ironically, Hinckley came out for gun control, and Reagan came out against it.

I was scheduled to perform stand-up at Budd Friedman's Improvisation Comedy Club in Hollywood the following month. Budd asked me to try and get some advance publicity. On April 2, the *Los Angeles Herald-Examiner* quoted a dispatch from the New Solidarity International Press Service (a LaRouche propaganda outlet) that quoted from its affiliated LaRouche house organ, *New Solidarity*:

> A group of terrorists and drug traffickers linked to *Playboy* magazine met in New York City's Greenwich Village area and publicly discussed an assassination of President Ronald Reagan and Vice-President George Bush. The meeting, convened by the Yippie organization, featured former *Playboy* editor Paul Krassner and numerous individuals associated with *High Times*

magazine, *Hustler* magazine, and the *Chicago Sun-Times*. In a statement this afternoon, National Democratic Policy Committee advisory board chairman Lyndon LaRouche urged that this information be made public at this time as a means of assisting government investigators pursuing the assassination attempt against President Reagan. *Playboy* magazine, as an international dossier released in the March 30, 1981, issue of *New Solidarity* indicates, is at the center of an international apparatus that has in the past been directly implicated in high-level political assassinations.

Playboy's response: "Absolute, unequivocal nonsense." And Budd Friedman told me, "Paul, that's not exactly what I meant by advance publicity."

My show went fine, but in July, *New Solidarity* escalated the attack and published a whole dossier on me:

In the early 1950s, Paul Krassner was recruited to the stable of pornographers and "social satirists" created and directed by the British Intelligence's chief brainwashing facility, the Tavistock Institute, to deride and destroy laws and institutions of morality and human decency. Among Krassner's circle of Tavistock iconoclasts, peddling smut in the name of humor and "creative expression," were Lenny Bruce ...

These people were taken seriously in certain quarters. LaRouche received enough campaign contributions to qualify him for matching funds from the government. And the newsletter of the U.S. Labor Party (another LaRouche vehicle), *Investigating Leads*, was subscribed to by police departments across the country.

In fact, when 2,000 demonstrators protested the construction of the Seabrook nuclear power plant in New Hampshire, LaRouche's private intelligence network briefed a state police lieutenant that the demonstration would be "nothing but a cover for terrorist activity" — the exact same phrase the governor would use to the media a few days before the rally.

Incidentally, I was never in England. Moreover, *Tavistock ... Tavistock ...* I just can't seem to remember anything about ever having been brainwashed at the Tavistock Institute. They must've deprogrammed it right out of my consciousness.

ALTHOUGH LAROUCHE AND I both taught at the Free University of New York in 1966, we didn't cross paths. One student said, "LaRouche presented the most credible, most articulate, and best-argued version of Marxist economics that I ever heard." My class was "Journalism and Satire and How to Tell the Difference." My friend Ed Sanders — leader of the Fugs and publisher of *Fuck You: A Magazine of the Arts* — taught "Revolutionary Egyptology." In 1967, he orchestrated the levitation of the Pentagon.

LaRouche and his followers spent the year 2016 snickering behind their hands at the Republican candidate for the U.S. presidency. The organization even recorded a satirical song suggesting that the candidate's core constituents were mentally ill. The singer trilled: "He's a festering pustule on Satan's rump! Don't you be a chump for Trump!"

But when Hillary conceded defeat, the tune changed. Suddenly, Trump was not, as had been previously thought, a maniac poised to legalize heroin and govern on behalf of Wall Street, but America's best chance to defeat the British Empire and forge a new alliance with Russia.

However, on February 12, 2019, when LaRouche died at the age of 96, there were increasing signs that the British coup against Trump was sputtering toward collapse.

Reportedly, LaRouche's wife, Helga Zepp-LaRouche, kept him "on a tight leash." Matthew Sweet described her:

> She is a German political activist and founder of the LaRouche movement's Schiller Institute, an international political and economic think tank, one of the primary organizations, with headquarters in Germany and the United States, and supporters in Australia, Canada, Denmark, Russia, and South America, among others.
>
> Helga believes that only with the support of the population will Trump be able to fulfill his campaign promises to the American people to restore Glass-Steagall and rebuild the country. The Glass-Steagall Act was signed by President Franklin D. Roosevelt in 1933 as the Banking Act, which prohibited commercial banks from participating in the investment banking business. Helga makes an appeal from abroad to the American people not to miss this great historic opportunity.

Dictator Trump has evolved from FDR's fireside chat to morning tweets. Feckless cunt, anyone?

PAUL KRASSNER

The Funny Side of 1968

The current FBI has swung a pendulum from 50 years ago, when the FBI was an enemy of progressive activists. An agent's poison-pen memo attempted to smear Tom Hayden with the worst possible label they could invoke with flyers — yep, an FBI informer. Others distributed a caricature depicting Black Panther leader Huey Newton "as a homosexual," and ran a fake "Pick the Fag" contest, referring to Dave McReynolds as "Chief White Fag of the lily-white War Resisters League" and "the usual Queer Cats — like Sweet Dave Dellinger and Fruity Rennie Davis." I was described as "a raving, unconfined nut." I thanked the FBI for that title of my autobiography.

Folksinger Phil Ochs observed, "A demonstration should turn you on, not turn you off." It was the credo of the Yippies (Youth International Party). We were in Chicago at the Democrats' convention, where a certain competitiveness developed between Yippie leaders Abbie Hoffman and Jerry Rubin. Abbie bought a pig to run as a presidential candidate, but Jerry thought Abbie's pig wasn't big enough, mean enough, or ugly enough, so Jerry went out and bought a bigger, meaner, uglier pig, which was released outside City Hall. In the elevator inside, a few cops were chanting, "Oink. Oink." On a quiz show, a contestant didn't know the name of that pig. However, a book, *Surveillance Valley*, states: "The generals wanted to be consumers of the latest hot information. During the Chicago riots of 1968, the Army had a unit called Mid-West News with Army agents in civilian clothes and they went around and interviewed all the antiwar protesters. They shipped the film footage to Washington every night on an airliner, so the generals could see movies of what was going on in Chicago when they got to work in the morning. That made them so happy. It was a complete waste of time. You could pick up the same thing on TV for far less, but they felt they needed their own film crew. The main thing they were going after was a pig named Pigasus, who was the Yippies' candidate for president. They were really excited about Pigasus."

Feminist Robin Morgan helped organize a protest of the Miss America Pageant in Atlantic City. A few hundred women were there on the boardwalk, holding a special ceremony. Icons of male oppression were being thrown into a trash barrel — cosmetics, a girdle, a copy of *Playboy*, high-heeled shoes, a pink brassiere — with the intent of setting the whole mix on fire. But there was an ordinance forbidding you to burn *anything* on the boardwalk, and the police were standing right there to enforce it. So there was no fire, but that didn't matter. The image of a burning bra has become inextricably associated with women's liberation. It's a metaphorical truth.

I was a guest on *The Joe Pyne Show* on KTTV in Los Angeles. He was a mean-spirited right-wing interviewer. His questions were vicious. "Well, Joe," I said, "if you're gonna ask questions like that, then let me ask *you*: Do you take off your wooden leg before you make love with your wife?" Pyne had lost his leg as a marine in World War II. Now his jaw literally dropped, the audience gasped, the producers averted their eyes, and the atmosphere became surrealistic as Pyne went through the motions of continuing the interview.

On another occasion, he asked Frank Zappa, "Your hair is so long. Are you a girl?" Zappa replied, "You have a wooden leg. Are you a table?"

Steve Post asked me to guest-host his nighttime radio program in New York while he was away. At the time, a mass student strike was going on at Columbia University, so with a couple of talented friends, Marshall Efron and Bridget Potter, we pretended that we were Columbia students who had taken over WBAI. We used code names — Rudi Dutschke, Emma Goldman, and Danny the Red. In nasal tones, I explained that we were all taking a course in alternative media, that our assignment was either to write a term paper or participate in an activity, and that we had decided to take over a radio station for credit. "The airwaves belong to the people," we chanted. We had planned to carry on this hoax for fifteen minutes, but it lasted four hours. KNBC in San Francisco and several other stations put us on the air live. New York listeners called the police, but when the police arrived, we told them it was a put-on. Then, after they left, I went on the air again, snickering as I told of the way we had fooled the cops. And they came again.

An excerpt from President Lyndon Johnson's remarks at the Annual Dinner of the White House Correspondents' Association: "A very funny thing happened to me tonight when I was on my way out of the White House [*laughter*] — I mean tonight. When I joined George Christian [his Special Assistant] to come over here, he said, 'Mr. President, I think you forgot something.' [LBJ indicated his White House identification pass.] So that is how I came to be wearing this. You may not like to wear your pass, but what do you think about me? I finally had to start using it after my announcement on March 31st [that he had decided not to run in the next election]. One day, as I was walking over to my nap, a guard stopped me in the hall and looked at me very carefully and said, 'Excuse me, buddy, but do you work here?' So, Frank [Cormier of the Associated Press] and Carroll [Kilpatrick of *The Washington Post*], I am so glad you all remembered me tonight. You do remember me, don't you, Hubert?"

["And how!" replied Vice President Hubert Humphrey.]

But Tricky Dick Nixon defeated both Humphrey *and* Pigasus.

PAUL KRASSNER

Alternative Facts

BETWEEN THE CHOICE of a one-man-one-vote (Supreme Court Justice Antonin Scalia) and fake news of Weapons of Mass Destruction, invasion of Iraq, and horror of ISIS, George Bush was elected president in the year 2000. It was due to the electoral college (a rigged system which was originally intended to prevent slaves from voting and evolved to gerrymandering), even though Bush's opponent, Al Gore, won the national popular vote.

Hillary Clinton was elected senator that year, and she announced that the first thing she would do was to get rid of the electoral college. A few years later, as a columnist for the *New York Press*, I sent her a letter asking about the status of that promise. She didn't reply.

On November 8, 2016, a crooked businessman, liar extraordinaire, bragging pussy-grabber, make-America-white-again, anti-choice, anti-Semite, false Christian, climate-change hoaxer, Nobamacare, homophobic, apprentice politician, fascist tweeter, and Vladimir Putin's "useful idiot" — namely, Donald Trump — was elected as an insanely narcissistic dictator by the electoral college, whereas his opponent, Hillary Clinton, won the national popular vote by almost three million.

Irony lives.

But an incredibly mean monster inadvertently awakened a sleeping population to counteract the essence of evil with love, laughs, and law, fueled by the aid of true news. Incidentally, Putin had 88 journalists murdered. No wonder Trump told him, "It's an honor to be with you." Now Putin wanted Obama's new sanctions on Russia to be reprieved.

National Security Adviser Michael Flynn had discussed it with the Russian ambassador a month before Trump took office. Although

General Flynn joined Trump's campaign and shared criminal secrets, he denied doing so to the FBI. It was a felony offense. The Justice Department warned Trump that Flynn had misled Vice President Mike Pence and that Flynn could be vulnerable to blackmail. Trump asked Flynn to resign, and yet he offered Flynn his job back when Flynn got out of prison. Why? Because Flynn was the scapegoat, taking the fall for the president and vice president. Flynn preferred a trial with immunity since they knew all. Pence said Flynn lied, and *that* was a lie.

If Trump and Pence had been kicked out of the White House prior to the 2018 election, the next in line would have been the then-Speaker of the House, Paul Ryan. Steve Bannon described Ryan as "a limp-dick motherfucker who was born in a petri dish at the Heritage Foundation." In turn, Trump's communicator Anthony Scaramucci boasted, "I'm not Steve Bannon. I'm not trying to suck my own cock." Ah, but Bannon said he wanted to *destroy* Ryan.

Hallelujah!

Trump once tried to trademark "You're fired." Professional hater Bannon resigned. Back to running his *Breitbart News*. He had taken over the original right-wing website, *Breitbart.com*, after the death of editor Andrew Breitbart, who, ironically, was adopted and raised as a proud Jew.

Orson Bean is my oldest living friend. He became a Christian libertarian conservative, and we've had an ongoing email dialogue about religion, but he's still a Christian, and I'm still an atheist. Not a militant atheist, as I used to be, though. I changed when I realized that Martin Luther King was a Christian, yet I was inspired by his actions, and George Lincoln Rockwell, head of the American Nazi Party, was an agnostic, yet I abhorred what he stood for. It no longer mattered to me what anybody's religious belief was, only how they treated others. Either kind or cruel. That simple.

I decided to email Orson: "If you can arrange for me to interview Andrew Breitbart" — his son-in-law — "I'll believe in God." Orson must've forwarded my email to Breitbart, because *he* sent me an email saying, "Apparently there is a God," with his own phone number. I called, we spoke, and he agreed to do an interview. My only ground rule would be that neither of us would interrupt the other. I contacted Steve Randall, my editor at *Playboy*, and I got the assignment. I immediately sent an email to Orson with the good news. The subject line was "Praise the fucking Lord."

And so it came to pass that Kellyanne Conway coined the oxymoronic phrase "alternative facts" on CNN. Anderson Cooper couldn't stop giggling for five solid minutes because her phrase made no sense. Hey, though, what about all those 2,000 religions practicing around the globe? But wait. They're not facts. They're beliefs.

Amen.

PAUL KRASSNER

I Played
Thomas Jefferson's Violin

AT A UNIQUE HEROES CONVENTION, I met Lindsay Wagner, star of *The Bionic Woman*. She was unaware that the CIA served as technical adviser to her series, but she spoke poignantly of the positive influence that her TV alter ego had on young amputees she visited in hospitals.

I also met Tom Laughlin, of *Billy Jack* movie fame. A couple of years later, he and his wife Delores Taylor invited me to a large dinner party.

They were Thomas Jefferson enthusiasts. In their home, there was Thomas Jefferson's furniture, Thomas Jefferson's silverware, Thomas Jefferson's recipes — we started with peanut soup — and even Thomas Jefferson's violin.

I mentioned playing the violin as a child, and Laughlin invited me to play this one. I hadn't held a violin for 25 years, not since I had used it as a prop when I started doing stand-up comedy, and four decades had passed since that concert in Carnegie Hall. It felt like a previous incarnation. But now Billy Jack himself was handing me Thomas Jefferson's violin. How could I resist?

"I'd like to dedicate this to Thomas Jefferson's slaves," I said.

And then I played the only thing I felt competent enough to perform — "Twinkle, Twinkle, Little Star." While I was playing, I stood and, as unobtrusively as possible, balancing on my left foot, I scratched my left leg with my right foot.

It was a private joke between me and the God of Absurdity.

ABOUT THE AUTHOR

Paul Krassner published *The Realist* (1958–2001), but when *People* magazine labeled him "father of the underground press," he immediately demanded a paternity test. And when *Life* magazine published a favorable article about him, the FBI sent a poison-pen letter to the editor calling Krassner "a raving, unconfined nut." George Carlin responded, "The FBI was right. This man is dangerous — and funny; and necessary."

While abortion was illegal, Krassner ran an underground referral service, and as an antiwar activist, he became a co-founder of the Yippies (Youth International Party). Krassner's one-person show won an award from the *LA Weekly*. He received an ACLU (Upton Sinclair) Award for dedication to freedom of expression. At the Cannabis Cup in Amsterdam, he was inducted into the Counterculture Hall of Fame — "my ambition," he claims, "since I was 3 years old."

He's won awards from *Playboy*, the Feminist Party Media Workshop, and, in 2010, the Oakland branch of the writers' organization PEN honored him with their Lifetime Achievement Award. "I'm very happy to receive this award," he concluded in his acceptance speech, "and even happier that it wasn't posthumous." — paulkrassner.com